EXPLORER'S GUIDES

Detroit & Ann Arbor

W. Grand Blvd

EXPLORER'S GUIDES

Detroit & Ann Arbor

A Great Destination

Jeff Counts

FIRST EDITION

The Countryman Press · Woodstock, Vermont

Explorer's Guide Detroit & Ann Arbor: A Great Destination
978-1-58157-141-7

Interior photographs by the author unless otherwise specified
Maps by Erin Greb Cartography, © The Countryman Press
Book design by Joanna Bodenweber
Composition by Eugenie S. Delaney

Published by The Countryman Press, P.O. Box 748, Woodstock, VT 05091
Distributed by W. W. Norton & Company, Inc., 500 Fifth Avenue, New York, NY 10110
Printed in the United States of America

10 9 8 7 6 5 4 3 2 1

For all those who care about Detroit.

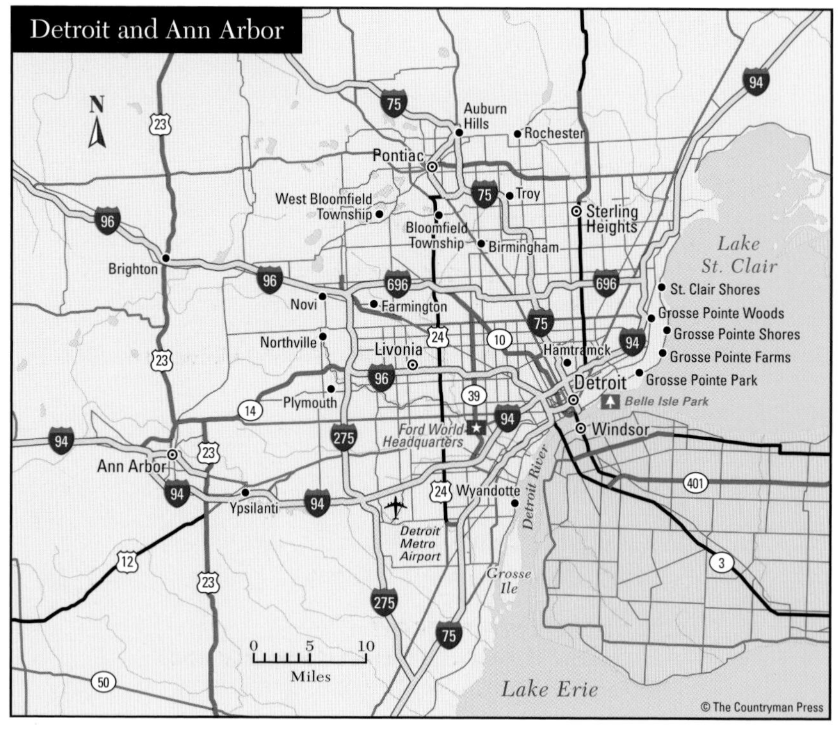
Detroit and Ann Arbor
N
Auburn Hills
Rochester
Pontiac
West Bloomfield Township
Troy
Sterling Heights
Bloomfield Township
Birmingham
Lake St. Clair
Brighton
St. Clair Shores
Novi
Farmington
Grosse Pointe Woods
Grosse Pointe Shores
Northville
Livonia
Hamtramck
Grosse Pointe Farms
Grosse Pointe Park
Detroit
Plymouth
Belle Isle Park
Windsor
Ford World Headquarters
Ann Arbor
Ypsilanti
Wyandotte
Detroit River
Detroit Metro Airport
Grosse Ile
0 5 10
Miles
Lake Erie
© The Countryman Press

Contents

Introduction

THE CHRYSLER CORPORATION and the rapper Eminem stole my thunder in a two-minute TV commercial that aired during the Super Bowl in 2011, giving an unflinching view of Detroit as a gritty town that's "been to hell and back" but is proud of its working-class heritage because "this is what we do."

They could have shined up Detroit, but they didn't, they filmed abandoned factories and idle smokestacks, and snow. They also acknowledged that Detroit isn't New York or Los Angeles, it's not the Windy City or the Emerald City—it's the Motor City. But as the commercial shows, this historic town is not without the "finer things in life," and visitors will find a lot of gems here.

After more than a century making steel and cars, Detroit is a city littered with decaying plants and neighborhoods, and tied to an industry that's been near collapse, but these days it's seeing an edgy revival as automakers are resurging and the city itself is finding new life.

Detroit may not be a big, sophisticated city, but it has a culture all its own. Sports are the common denominator, and you'll find all classes of people, and all races, cheering on the home teams.

As for style, it's pretty casual. Except for at a handful of restaurants, there's no dress code. And apart from some communities in the wealthy Oakland County and Grosse Pointe areas, you won't find people wearing the top fashions. And no matter what neighborhood you find yourself in, there's almost always a Coney Island restaurant nearby that serves a Detroit favorite—a hot dog covered with chili and onions—or a sports bar filled with big-screen TVs.

Detroit has never been a pretty town, but it is one that helped many achieve the American dream. People from all over the country and around the world came to the city when Henry Ford offered workers $5 a day beginning in 1914 so they could afford to buy the automobiles they were making, an act that helped create America's middle class.

The resulting immigration led to the development of vibrant ethnic communities, and Detroit's restaurants offer a range of cuisines, from Middle Eastern to American southern. And music? Detroit is where bouzouki meets bluegrass and the blues. During recent years, large numbers of Asian and German auto engineers have further enriched the culture.

The national media has done a number on Detroit by focusing on its problems: the Michigan Central Depot on Michigan Avenue, for example, has become a symbol of urban decay. As a native Detroiter, I'm tired of the bad press. Detroit has always been a city of neighborhoods, with very little high-rise-type housing. There are thriving communities with rich histories that tend not to get media coverage, places where the houses are well kept, the lawns mowed, and the streets free of trash.

This guide isn't just a listing of restaurants, hotels, and attractions. As a native Detroiter I've been part of this strange cultural stew since I was a child, and I've imbued this book with a sense of what it's like to have grown up and lived in Detroit. I'm a true product of Detroit, and like most Motor City residents, I've got an auto company name stamped on my birth certificate—in my case, it's Ford.

As for the cultural stew, I don't have to look any further than my family. My father moved north in the 1930s to work for Ford Motor Co., and my wife's family came to Detroit from Greece to run restaurants. My children are part southern and part Greek—quite a combination, but such blending is characteristic of Detroit. I've also done stints in Detroit factories, so I know that life.

Those trying to understand the dynamics of Detroit simply have to look at where the auto companies are located. While downtown Detroit has historically been the commercial hub, the real corporate power resides in the western suburb of Dearborn, where Ford headquarters is located, and in the northern suburbs, where Chrysler and General Motors have traditionally had a large presence. Workers tended to live near the plants where they worked, so the city has a long history of urban sprawl.

I've tried to reflect that in this guide by treating auto company headquarters as though they were the traditional American downtowns. This being the Motor City, the best way to get around Detroit is by car, and I've designed various driving routes, or "auto cruises," highlighting the city's main drags and attractions. For example, there's a chapter devoted to cruising Woodward Avenue. Each summer the Woodward Dream Cruise attracts car buffs who drive the strip in their restored vintage vehicles, many of them 1960s "muscle cars" designed and built right here. During the 1960s, baby boomers drove Woodward looking for drag races—myself included, in a 1968 red Mustang. The event now attracts thousands of spectators. Other auto cruises described here are Eight Mile Road, made famous by the 2002 Eminem movie *8 Mile*, and Michigan and East Jefferson Avenues.

There is more to the region than hot cars and factories. The auto industry has also helped develop budding artists who've worked in the design studios and at ad agencies. The city's thriving arts and design community is served by the Center for Creative Studies in Detroit, and Cranbrook, in Oakland County.

It's a major-league city when it comes to sports, with baseball, basketball, football, and hockey teams playing on the national level. The Red Wings, Tigers, Lions, and Pistons usually play for capacity crowds, no matter what their record. Apart from the Pistons, which play in Auburn Hills, the other teams have their stadiums and arenas in downtown Detroit.

Although it's not Las Vegas, there are three major casinos downtown, and along with the sports teams, the core city has seen revitalization in recent years, with the opening of bars and restaurants.

And then there's Ann Arbor. The quintessential college town, home to the University of Michigan, is only about 45 miles west of downtown Detroit but a world away from Detroit's urban vibe. Its tree-shaded campus near the Huron River is a hub of cultural activities, and on fall football Saturdays it's jammed with students and alumni watching their Big Ten team. Ann Arbor's cultural venues make it a regional destination, and there are many restaurants catering to people out for a night on the town.

It's a short drive to Ontario, Canada, across the Detroit River via either the Ambassador Bridge or the Detroit-Windsor Tunnel, both of which take you to Windsor, a city that resembles in some areas a small English town, with rose-covered brick homes facing the Detroit River. The many ethnic restaurants and specialty shops in Windsor make it a worthwhile destination for the American traveler.

In the tradition of The Countryman Press, this guide is intended to help you navigate Detroit's not-always-friendly urban landscape to find the best of what the city and surrounding regions have to offer.

The Way This Book Works

THIS BOOK IS DIVIDED into regions and cities within the Detroit metropolitan area, which has more than 3 million residents spread through four major counties (Wayne, Oakland, Macomb, and Washtenaw). There are separate chapters on Ann Arbor, home to the University of Michigan and a large entertainment district, and nearby Windsor, Ontario.

Sign at the Walter P. Chrysler Museum in Auburn Hills.

The guide begins with suggestions for where travelers might base themselves during a visit to the region. This is followed by a brief history of Detroit focusing on how it became the Motor City. Any city is a reflection of those who lived and worked in it, and in the "Industrial Pioneers" section and throughout this guide you'll find short profiles of people who made the town run, ranging from automaker Walter P. Chrysler to African American boxing champion Joe Louis. Detroit has a rich musical heritage, and a section pays tribute to the many artists who have started their careers in and around the city, including Kid

Rock, Eminem, White Stripes, and of course all of the Motown artists.

Getting to and around the Detroit metropolitan area is covered early on. This is the Motor City, and except for a light-rail system with limited service in the downtown area, visitors won't find any serious mass transit, as the bus system is dysfunctional and even getting a taxicab is iffy. Since driving is visitors' best option, the book has information about navigating the region's excellent freeway system and numerous surface roads, and helping visitors deal with the somewhat off-kilter road system in downtown Detroit.

Geographical coverage of the area begins with downtown, and the book's organization reflects the major corridors that run through the metro Detroit area: you'll find Woodward Avenue, Michigan and East Jefferson Avenues, and other of the city's noteworthy strips featured as "auto cruises" catering to the region's premier mode of transport. Since many travelers to Detroit come to do business with the automakers, in addition to a discussion of downtown Detroit, where General Motors has its headquarters, there are sections on Dearborn, where Ford Motor Co. is located (see chapter 3), and Oakland County's Auburn Hills, where the Chrysler Corporation has its offices (see chapter 5). The guide includes information about historic auto plants and related museums.

Cruising Woodward Avenue is a Detroit tradition.

Eight Mile Road marks the northern edge of Detroit and has long been known as the dividing line between city and suburbs, rich and poor. North of Eight Mile are the trendy communities of Royal Oak and Birmingham (see chapter 2), in which are located some of the region's finest restaurants and entertainment venues.

There's an entire chapter

devoted to Oakland County (chapter 5), one of the largest counties in the state, and its many suburbs, including Troy, Farmington Hills, the Bloomfield area, and Novi.

AUTO CRUISES

A car is essential to travel in the Motor City, and the auto cruises featured in this book will help you get the most from the ride. The Woodward Avenue Cruise (chapter 2) takes visitors for a drive on metro Detroit's main street and its surrounds, from the Detroit River to Pontiac; yep, the car took its name from the city. Many of the city's better downtown restaurants are along the Woodward corridor, along with its sports stadiums, cultural institutions, historic neighborhoods, auto plants, and its major university, Wayne State. The Michigan Avenue Cruise (chapter 3) takes drivers through the city's thriving Corktown and Mexicantown neighborhoods, and on to Dearborn, where Ford Motor Co. and the area's top tourist attraction, The Henry Ford, is located. From there it's on to Ypsilanti, where bombers were built during World War II and an ill-fated automobile, the Tucker, was developed.

The Motor City is made for cruising. Here, a red Mustang cruises the strip in Plymouth.

The Michigan Avenue Cruise takes drivers through Detroit's vibrant Mexicantown.

The East Jefferson Avenue Cruise (chapter 4), follows the Detroit River and Lake St. Clair and features Detroit's East Side and Grosse Pointe communities along the waterfront, which have long been home to some of the area's most affluent residents. The many mansions to see here include that of Edsel Ford, the only son of Henry

Fellowship - Mutual

go to mtg. online

Hello.

*Love your neig

- ar yourself —

attitude toward

- Hello my name is

Remembering very s

Some are seeker

Accept and Stay in the Gol

Ford. Other auto cruises you'll find in this guide include the storied Eight Mile (see sidebar, chapter 2).

LOCAL KNOWLEDGE

To introduce visitors to the real Detroit, I've included a chapter called "Where Detroiter's Eat and What They Drink," which takes note of the favorite restaurants of Motor City area residents, ranging from Coney Islands to local diners and burger bars. These types of places don't always make it into guidebooks, but are most definitely worth a look.

In the Information chapter that closes the book, readers will find important phone numbers, information on Detroit's weather and how to survive it, and a list of recommended reading.

Note that this guide uses price codes to convey a general understanding of what travelers to the area should expect to pay for accommodations, dining, and attractions. The codes are as follows:

Code	Lodging (per adult)	Restaurants (per entrée)
$	up to $75	up to $10
$$	$76–150	$11–25
$$$	$151–250	$26–40
$$$$	more than $250	more than $40

Finding Your Home Base in Metro Detroit

MANY VISITORS TO DETROIT are here on business with the auto industry or come for the North American International Auto Show in January, to gamble in the downtown casinos, attend sporting events, or to visit metro Detroit's top tourist attraction, The Henry Ford, in Dearborn. This book provides all the information you'll need about where to stay, where to eat, and what to do in this destination city.

Because of its location, with all the region's major freeways connecting there, downtown is a central place that's accessible to most points of interest. General Motors headquarters is located there, in the Renaissance Center, which has a major hotel. Ford Motor Company and The Henry Ford are about 30 minutes from downtown, via I-94 (the Edsel Ford Freeway), and the Chrysler Corporation is about 45 minutes north on I-75 (the Chrysler Freeway), in Auburn Hills.

Apart from the Detroit Pistons, the city's major sports franchises are located downtown, as are the casinos. The People Mover light-rail system in downtown Detroit connects many of the major areas of interest along its routes. Downtown also offers an entertainment district in the Greektown area, where there are numerous restaurants. The casinos—Motor City, Greektown, and the MGM Grand—offer top-flight lodging at affordable prices. They all have restaurants on site.

An alternative to staying in downtown Detroit is to find a room in Windsor, Ontario, across the Detroit River. A number of hotels have river views, and "Little Italy," along Erie Street, provides plenty of eateries. See the transportation section of this guide for detailed information about how to cross over the border into Canada using either the Ambassador Bridge or the Detroit-Windsor Tunnel.

If you're coming to do business with Ford Motor Co. or to visit the Henry Ford, there are several large hotels across the road from Ford World Headquarters at Michigan Avenue and the Southfield Freeway.

Oakland County lies just north of Detroit, and it's where Chrysler makes its home in Auburn Hills. Also nearby are the General Motors Tech Center and advertising agencies that do business with the automakers. Oakland County is a sprawling place of many suburbs and has numerous chain hotels located on business strips. Troy and Novi, for example, have many corporate office parks serving numerous auto-related firms, and there are a number of hotels and restaurants. The Somerset Collection is an upscale mall in Troy that offers accommodations and restaurants, and is a convenient place to stay if you're here to do business with Chrysler or the many other Fortune 500 firms that have offices and headquarters in Troy.

Ann Arbor is about 45 miles west of Detroit and is accessible via I-94 or M-14, both of which are freeways. Because it's a college town, it offers a variety of chain hotels on arteries surrounding the city, but there are few accommodation options on or near the University of Michigan campus. There are, however, a good selection of restaurants, bars, and shops nearby.

History of Detroit

BECOMING THE MOTOR CITY

DETROIT HAS BEEN MANY THINGS in its more than 300-year history: a Native American settlement, a river port, a French fur-trading village, an outpost of the British Empire, a station on the Underground Railroad, a 19th-century Victorian-style city, a factory town, the auto capital of the world, "the great arsenal of democracy" during World War II, and a Rust Belt town suffering from urban decay.

Located on the Detroit River, with a commanding view of that waterway and access to the Great Lakes, the area that we now know as Detroit was first coveted by Native Americans, and later by the French and British.

On July 24, 1701, French settlers led by Antoine de la Mothe Cadillac founded Port Pontchartrain du Détroit as a fur-trading post. Beaver hats were all the rage in Europe, and Native American and French Canadian trappers traveled the Great Lakes region in quest of the pelts, which they traded for manufactured items. A shopping area in Detroit's Greektown was once a fur-trading spot and is now called Trapper's Alley in tribute to that history.

The fort was ruled by the French until 1760, when the British took control of it during the French and Indian War, but even as English, Irish, and Scottish settlers started moving in, the region retained its French flavor, with area newspapers in the early 19th century being published in French and English. The French had also established strip farms that ran inland from the Detroit River, their owners giving their names to streets such as Gratiot.

The British ruled Fort Detroit during the Revolutionary War and did not surrender it until July 11, 1796. During the war, Britain used the fort as a supply depot to arm its troops and Native American

Henry Ford's first plant on Piquette Street in Detroit.

allies. The British retook the fort during the War of 1812 and held it for about a year before abandoning it to the Americans once more.

Continuing tensions with the British through the 1840s resulted in the construction of Fort Wayne, at the foot of Detroit's Livernois Avenue, as a defense of the U.S. border with Canada. It was active during the Civil War, and was manned until 1920 as a garrison post, then serving as an induction center for Michigan troops entering U.S. conflicts. Historic Fort Wayne now operates as a museum.

Detroit remained a frontier outpost until 1806, when it was incorporated as a city, but even with that formal title, it was hardly a populated place; by 1820 there were only 1,442 persons counted in the census. However, the groundwork for the city was put in place in 1805 by Augustus B. Woodward, who had been appointed the first chief justice of the Michigan Territory. When he arrived on June 30, he found the town in ashes from a fire that devastated most buildings. He and others put together a city plan that defined the development of Detroit and its suburbs.

They conceived a city with major arteries radiating out of downtown like spokes in a wheel, a suitable image for what would become the nation's auto capital. They modeled their plan on that devised by the architect Pierre Charles L'Enfant for Washington, DC. The spoke-like roads feed into downtown, and include Michigan Avenue,

Grand River, Woodward, Gratiot, Fort Street, and East and West Jefferson. Woodward Avenue, which runs north-south, became the city's main street.

The city's growth was limited due to the fact that it was nearly inaccessible from the East Coast, but the opening of the Erie Canal in 1825 changed that, and immigrants from upstate New York and New England streamed in. These new residents built towns and settlements having a New England look and feel.

By 1860, the eve of the Civil War, there were only 45,619 residents in the city. Soon the population would explode, as people poured in from around the country and the world to work for a man born in 1863 on his family farm in nearby Dearborn—Henry Ford.

Post–Civil War Detroit found itself well positioned for industrial development. The coming of the railroads and the port of Detroit made the city accessible to markets and raw materials. The city became the iron-stove-making center of the nation, since iron was mined in the Upper Great Lakes and easily shipped to Detroit via boat. It also became a center for the manufacture of railroad cars, wire, and paints and varnishes. Those industries needed mechanics, metalworkers, and other skilled trades people, and by 1890 the city had grown to 205,877.

Also aiding Detroit's expansion were the fertile farmlands surrounding the city, producing enough meat, dairy products, and produce to feed a large population. One agricultural firm founded in Detroit and still in business is Ferry Seeds, which had extensive farms in Greenfield Township. Now known as Ferry-Morse, the company sells seeds and gardening supplies.

IMMIGRATION

While Detroit never saw the number of European immigrants that Chicago or New York did in the late 19th and early 20th centuries, many made their way to the area starting in the 1840s, when Irish fleeing the Great Potato Famine found a home in the city's Corktown neighborhood.

Germans also came to Detroit, establishing businesses such as breweries, including Stroh's, which had a 150-year run in the city. Eastern Europeans, Greeks, Italians, and Jews started to arrive in the 1890s, the population swelling to 285,000 by 1910, the eve of the auto boom. In 1914 Henry Ford announced his $5-a-day wage for autoworkers, and that sparked even more immigration from Europe and the American South by both whites and African Americans. By the 1930s there were more than 1.5 million city residents.

PROHIBITION

While the city's factories were making automobile production the top industry during the 1920s, a group of gangsters operating out of Detroit were producing another product for American consumers, liquor, which was illegal in the nation after Prohibition went into effect in 1920. Called the Purple Gang by newspapers of the day (one theory holds that the name originated in the gangsters' use of purple dye in shaking down area dry-cleaning businesses), it was a loose alliance of individuals who had grown up in the poor neighborhood surrounding Hastings Street. Although not as organized as Al Capone's gang in Chicago, which was a prime customer for Detroit alcohol, the group trafficked so much liquor that by 1929 booze was estimated to be the city's second-largest industry, at $215 million each year.

Detroit, with its border with Canada, was perfect for the bootlegger. The Detroit River and nearby Lakes St. Clair and Erie provided distribution routes in both summer and winter. The Purple Gang, whose membership was primarily Jewish, was also known as the Jewish Navy, because it used boats to smuggle liquor from Canada to the Detroit area. During winter, cars made the trip over the ice.

Canada had its own version of Prohibition, but the province of Ontario allowed some breweries and distilleries to remain open. Their products were designated export-only, and it didn't matter to the Canadians if their offerings ended up on a boat headed for Detroit.

Downriver Detroit, and especially Grosse Ile, an island in the Detroit River, was a hotbed of bootlegging, partly because of the short distance to Canada. There are still many boathouses on the island and in the surrounding area that were once used by bootleggers. Old-time Detroiters often claim there were alcohol pipelines running under the river. There were police patrol boats on the river, but the expanse of the water region favored the bootleggers.

As in other parts of the country, Prohibition had the unintended consequence of making alcohol consumption even more attractive, and while there were 1,500 licensed taverns in Detroit before the ban went into effect, there were as many as 25,000 "blind pigs," as Detroiters called speakeasies, during the '20s. That seems like ancient history, but as late as the 1970s an old Detroit newspaperman I knew pointed out to me where the pigs were located as we surveyed the Downtown area from a historic building. There was one every few blocks, and most weren't the elegant nightclubs portrayed in the movies. They were just places where you could (easily) get a drink. As another newspaperman of the time, Malcolm Bingay, joked: "It was absolutely impossible to get a drink in Detroit unless you walked at least ten feet and told the busy bartender what you wanted in a voice loud enough for him to hear you above the uproar."

WORLD WAR II TO THE PRESENT

During World War II, Detroit boomed as its plants churned out planes, tanks, and other materiel, and workers from around the country came to the city to take the jobs. A housing shortage developed and some boarding houses rented beds in shifts for the workers.

But even during war and boom times the city's 200,000 African Americans were jammed into a small district along Hastings Street, unable to move to other areas. Tensions were high in the city during the war as a result of housing and job discrimination, and a race riot broke out on Belle Isle, a city park in the Detroit River, on June 20, 1943, when sailors from the nearby Naval Armory and black residents started fighting. A rumor had spread in the black community that a black woman and her baby had been thrown over the Belle Isle Bridge and into the Detroit River, and that prompted looting and attacks on whites. White mobs retaliated, attacking African Americans and black-owned businesses. Authorities called in 6,000 federal troops and peace was restored, but not before 25 African Americans and 9 white residents were killed.

After the war, Detroit thrived as veterans returned home and bought automobiles. The Big Three—General Motors, Ford, and Chrysler—started coming out with new models each year, and as sales exploded Detroit's population hit its highest point, in 1950, with 1.8 million residents. However, many returning veterans took advantage of GI housing benefits to move out of the city; the exodus to the suburbs started in the 1950s and accelerated in the following decades, as people relocated first to Redford, Dearborn Heights, Inkster, Livonia, and Hazel Park, and then farther to exurbia. In many cases it was autoworkers following their jobs, as manufacturers abandoned older, outmoded plants and built facilities elsewhere.

Smaller auto parts plants were spread thoughout western Wayne County, like this former plant in Northville.

Then came the 1967 riots in Detroit, a racial disturbance sparked by a police raid on an after-hours drinking establishment on 12th Street. The riot lasted for five days and left 43 people dead, including 33 African Americans, and 467 injured. The National Guard was eventually called in to quell the disturbance.

The '67 riots sparked more white flight from the city, and a controversial court-ordered school busing system aimed at integrating Detroit schools contributed to the city's population decline. In recent years, the black middle class has been leaving the city for the suburbs, and the city's population is now about 714,000—down from 950,000 in 2000.

In the first decade of the 21st century, urban decay marred Detroit's landscape, with abandoned homes dotting many neighborhoods and an estimated one-third of the city's nearly 140 square miles laying vacant. Plans are being proposed to turn many of those abandoned acres into urban farms. There's also talk of relocating residents into denser areas of the city, which is facing a budget crisis, in an effort to shrink the size of government services. These initiatives have been hampered by a complex corruption scandal that saw public officials, including the mayor, receive prison sentences in 2010.

But Downtown Detroit is not without its success stories. The long-vacant Book Cadillac Hotel underwent a $200 million renovation beginning in 2006, reopening in 2008 as a luxury accommodation with 453 rooms and 67 condos.

BLUE-COLLAR DETROIT

When you drive past one of Detroit's abandoned factories, it's hard to imagine that it was once a magnificent economic machine that allowed immigrant families to quickly gain a foothold in the middle class.

If you were lucky enough to get an auto job in the 1920s, you could buy a house, a car, and live relatively comfortably. For immigrants who had secured such work, the transformation to established citizen was quick, dependent more on brawn than on technical training. But while these good jobs were hailed at the time, they also sowed the seeds of Detroit's eventual decline.

For decades, boys with a few years of high school could easily get factory jobs that paid as much money or more than their fathers or even high school teachers made. I remember being in high school in the mid-1960s in Detroit and hearing the grousing of teachers about how a certain troublemaker in school would be making more money than they did in a few months.

That ability to quickly make a middle-class living didn't exactly create an atmosphere for learning in the city. When I was graduating from college in the early 1970s, students who had worked their way through school had to decide if they would teach school, become social workers, or try some other profession—all of which paid half of what factory workers made.

For much of the 20th century, Detroit was a middle-class workingman's town, with plenty of well-paying "dirty" jobs available. Unlike Chicago, where there was more of a commercial class, Detroit was a worker's town.

AFRICAN AMERICANS IN DETROIT

There were few African Americans in Detroit prior to the Great Migration of blacks fleeing discrimination and racial violence in the South during the early 20th century, but there was an active community that founded the city's first black church. The Second Baptist Church, at 441 Monroe Street, was formed in 1836 by 13 former slaves who left the white First Baptist Church because of discrimination. Because Detroit was a major stop on the Underground Railroad, the church quickly became an important institution, helping as many as 5,000 escaped slaves reach freedom in Canada. The current building was constructed in 1914 and is listed on the National Register of Historic Places.

There were only 5,741 African Americans living in Detroit in 1910, but during the Great Migration the promise of good jobs in the auto industry drew many to the city, and by 1920 there were 40,838 black residents. Most blacks were jammed into a neighborhood along

Hastings and St. Antoine Streets on Detroit's Near East Side. Ironically, the area had long been called Black Bottom, not for its ethnic makeup but because the land was composed of rich soils. The neighborhood had previously had a predominantly eastern European Jewish population; the bootlegging Purple Gang originated there.

Just to the north of Black Bottom was Paradise Valley, a business and entertainment district along Hastings Street that was home to many black-owned businesses, nightclubs, and bars. The top African American entertainers of the era often performed there, including Count Basie, Billy Eckstine, Pearl Bailey, Duke Ellington, and Ella Fitzgerald. Urban renewal efforts during the late 1950s and early '60s changed the face of the old neighborhood, replacing it with housing projects and some upscale development in Lafayette Park, and Hastings Street disappeared under the Chrysler Freeway.

HISTORIC DETROIT NEIGHBORHOODS

Apart from downtown and on the city's East Side along the riverfront, there are few high-rise apartment buildings in Detroit. That's because Detroit is a city of neighborhoods, many of which reflect the region's rich ethnic heritage. These neighborhoods were typically oriented toward the auto plants rather than downtown, and are worth visiting for their historic interest and architecture.

Indian Village. Located on the city's East Side and bounded by East Jefferson and Mack Avenues, the early-20th-century structures here were once home to Detroit's elite, including Edsel Ford. Many of the homes, some of which are larger than 12,000 square feet, have been restored. There's an annual home and garden tour in early June. The district is listed on the National Register of Historic Places, and the homes are located on Burns, Iroquois, and Seminole Streets.

Bush Park Historic District. From the 1850s to the 1880s, the 24-block park just north of downtown was home to the city's wealthiest residents, who built intricate Victorian homes in the district bounded by Woodward, Mack, and Beaubien Avenues. The neighborhood started to decline in the early 20th century, and by the time of the Great Depression in the 1930s many of the homes had been turned into apartments. During the 1990s restoration efforts got under way, and now there are about 150 homes remaining. One was recently put on the market for more than $2 million.

East Ferry Avenue Historic District. This two-block district is on the National Register of Historic Places and is home to the Inn on Ferry Street, a bed & breakfast. It's located in the midtown area, near Wayne State University and the city's medical center, and was founded in the 1880s by D. M. Ferry, owner of the Ferry Seed Co. The area was developed as a less expensive alternative to the pricier Woodward Avenue, and has survived as a residential district, while Woodward became a commercial avenue.

The Inn on Ferry Street.

Woodbridge Historic District. Dating back to the 1870s, this district somehow escaped the urban renewal craze that hit Detroit during the late 1950s and early '60s, and has been left nearly intact. The Victorian-era homes were lived in by upper-middle-class Detroiters. During the 1950s I had a chance to work on one of the homes. My father was a painting contractor in Detroit, and was redoing the house, lived in by two elderly sisters. I was intrigued by the residence and the stories told by the women, whose father had been an officer in the Union army during the Civil War. The district is just east of the intersection of Grand River Avenue and Trumbull Street, and is bound by Calumet, West Warne, and Wabash Streets.

Arden Park–East Boston Historic District. The 92-home district near Woodward Avenue and East Boston Boulevard was developed in the early 20th century, coincident with the rise of the auto industry. Many of its early residents were automotive executives or other business leaders in Detroit. It's on the National Register of Historic Places.

West Canfield Historic District. Occupying West Canfield near Wayne State University, this area was developed during the 1870s by the daughter of Lewis Cass, an early governor of Michigan. Construction of the Queen Anne–style homes took place through the 1880s, and these residences were occupied by professors until the district's decline in the 1930s. Beginning in the 1960s preservation efforts saved many of the homes.

Virginia Park. Virginia Park was one of the first suburban neighborhoods in Detroit that was home to professionals and businesspeople, who first purchased the bungalows, Tudor, and arts and crafts homes built between 1893 and 1915 in an area just west of Woodward, just north of Grand Boulevard, which was then on the outskirts of the city. Virginia Park Avenue runs from Woodward to the John Lodge Freeway.

Palmer Woods. There are about 290 homes in this National Register of Historic Places neighborhood, which is on the Woodward Corridor near Seven Mile. The Colonial Revival and Tudor homes, mostly on Strathcona Drive, were built between 1917 and 1929. The district was named in honor of Thomas Palmer, a U.S. senator, whose estate was located on both sides of Woodward in the district. He donated land to the city for the establishment of Palmer Park.

One of Detroit's historic mansions.

Sherwood Forest. Most of the 435 homes in the neighborhood were built during the 1920s and 1930s. The area is bounded by Seven Mile, Livernois, Pembroke, and Parkside.

University District The neighborhood of nearly 1,200 mostly Tudor homes was developed during the 1920s and '30s, during which time the University of Detroit was established here. The area is about a mile west of Woodward and is bounded by Six and Seven Mile Roads.

Corktown. With at least one house dating from the 1840s, Corktown is the oldest neighborhood in Detroit. So many people from Ireland's County Cork arrived here during the Great Potato Famine of the 1840s that the district derived its name from their homeland. Here visitors can see how working-class people lived during the 19th and early 20th centuries. The neighborhood is filled with workmen's cottages, mostly simple wood-frame homes with a bit of Victorian trim work. Corktown is bordered by the Lodge Freeway and Bagley and Porter Streets. Tiger Stadium, Detroit's longtime baseball venue, was located near Corktown at Trumbull and Michigan Avenues until it was demolished in 1999. Corktown residents have been particularly active in the district's resurgence and in city affairs in general in recent years.

Rosedale Park neighborhood.

Rosedale Park There are 1,533 homes in this historic district at Grand River Avenue and the Southfield Freeway. The mostly brick-residence neighborhood in northwest Detroit is home to many city officials and Detroit leaders, and was developed starting in about 1917 through the '40s. It's on the National Register of Historic Places. The homes are more modest than in some of the other upscale city neighborhoods, but Rosedale has retained a strong identity and has been immune to the urban blight that has hit other districts.

East English Village The East Side neighborhood of about 2,000 homes is similar to Rosedale Park, with mostly brick homes built from the 1920s to the 1940s in the area bounded by Outer Drive, Cadieux and Harper Roads, and Mack Avenue.

Industrial Pioneers

THE MOVERS AND SHAKERS

THE INDIVIDUALS WHO MADE DETROIT the Motor City were a colorful bunch of characters who left a lasting imprint on Detroit.

HENRY FORD

Detroit was largely shaped by Henry Ford (1863–1947), who revolutionized the way automobiles were made with his moving assembly line, and helped create the middle class by raising his workers' pay to $5 a day in 1914—an unheard-of wage for factory workers at the time. But Ford had many critics: some capitalists claimed he was ruining the working class by paying laborers too much, and the labor movement charged that his production line dehumanized workers, and that Ford's monitoring of employee behavior violated their privacy.

He was a study in contradictions, and his name can still evoke passion in shot-and-a-beer workers' bars in and around Detroit. Ford was firmly rooted in 19th-century values of family, religion, and agrarian living. He loved square dancing, and as a young man would travel miles by horse and buggy to indulge that passion. He created The Henry Ford museum and village to preserve the rural past, at a time when his automobiles were enabling unprecedented freedom of movement for people and prompting many social changes. Though automobiles made it easier for young people to eventually leave the family farm, they also increased the standard of living for those who had access to them. Farmers could more easily get their crops to town, and those in company towns could get to the next town, where goods might be cheaper than at the company store.

Ford's practice of monitoring employee behavior off the job

A statue of Henry Ford at the Henry Ford Centennial Library in Dearborn.

through a designated Ford Motor Co. department was controversial. The conservative Ford did not smoke or drink, and for a time he linked employee advancement and profit sharing with clean living. He later renounced paternalism in business.

Ford was also criticized because his $5-a-day wage didn't extend to African Americans, who were assigned to the worst jobs or to work in the hot foundries. However, Ford employed more African Americans in his plants than did any other industry in the nation at the time, and he was known to consult with black ministers in recruiting workers.

Ford was also accused of anti-Semitism, charges that stemmed from his sponsorship during the 1920s of a newspaper, the *Dearborn Independent,* that espoused anti-Semitic views. But Ford relied almost exclusively on the prominent Detroit architect Albert Kahn, the son of a rabbi, to design his industrial buildings as well as The Dearborn Inn.

Henry Ford was born on the family farm in Dearborn, but his father described him as a tinkerer, not a farmer. Although the younger Ford stuck to farming until he was married, an interest in mechanics lured him to Detroit, where he worked in an Edison Electric power plant. Ford had a sixth-grade education, and although he attended a business college for a short while, it was at his job that he learned his trade and eventually started building cars.

While living on Bagley Street in Detroit, Ford started work on his first automobile in a brick garage behind his house. He fitted a gas engine on a carriage-like vehicle, and put bicycle tires on it. When it came time to take the vehicle for a drive, the garage door was too small to accommodate it, so a sledgehammer was used to enlarge the opening. For viewers of the TV show *Home Improvement,* it sounds like something Tim "The Toolman" Taylor (played by Birmingham, Michigan, native Tim Allen) would get himself into.

Some people think Ford invented the automobile. He didn't. What he did do was perfect an assembly line that sped up production, bringing the cost of autos down so that average folks could buy one. Until then, autos were too expensive for most Americans.

Affordable automobiles and the wages Ford was paying his employees greatly contributed to the establishment of a middle-class consumer culture, and also changed the American landscape by prompting the paving of roads and, in turn, the establishment of roadside businesses. Ford is credited with putting the first "auto tourists" on the road. Ford Motor Company lured many workers to Detroit, helping to nearly double the city's population between 1910 and 1920, from 465,766 to 993,687.

Ford was very much anti-union, and hired Harry Bennett, a former prizefighter and ex-Navy man, to head an internal security department at Ford Motor Company. By most accounts, Bennett had caught Ford's eye during a business trip to New York, but some old-time Ford workers swear he was a former mobster. Whatever his history, Bennett was a feared man at Ford, and had so many enemies that he lived in a house surrounded by a moat and equipped with an escape tunnel. When Ford died in 1947, Bennett was fired by Henry Ford II, a grandson of the founder. The firing was done in person by the younger Ford, who reportedly was wary enough of Bennett to bring a pistol with him.

During the Roaring Twenties, Ford established the Rouge Complex in Dearborn, the largest industrial complex in the world, with 93 buildings, its own docks on the Rouge River, and 100 miles of railroad track. The Albert Kahn–designed complex made use of natural light for workers. Basically, the raw materials for autos, such as iron, wood, and coal, arrived at the complex, and Fords came out the other end. There was a foundry, glassworks, and supporting shops. The complex started out making Model Ts and Model As and built Mustangs for more than 40 years. Today it's where the popular Ford 150 pickup truck is built.

But the Rouge land didn't start out as a factory site. Ford, who was an angler and hunter, and his wife had become birdwatchers, and he bought about 2,000 acres on the Rouge River with the idea of turning it into a bird sanctuary. During World War I he was persuaded by future President Franklin Roosevelt, who was then secretary of the Navy, to produce antisubmarine ships at the site. Ford was a pacifist, but knew a good business opportunity when he saw one, and started producing the ships. At one point Ford tried to stop World War I by chartering a peace ship and sailing to Europe. His view was that mankind could be better served by making things people needed rather than by making war.

By the 1930s, the Depression hit Detroit hard, with people cutting back on the purchase of new cars, and the auto factories, including Ford, were forced to lay off workers in droves. Workers were trying to organize what would become one of the most powerful unions in America, the United Auto Workers, and those activists, including communists, staged a hunger strike on March 7, 1932, and marched on the Ford Rouge plant. When it was over, four workers had been killed by Dearborn police and Ford security men, and another 60 were injured.

Labor troubles continued through the '30s and culminated in what's been called the Battle of the Overpass, near the Ford Rouge complex. It started when a newspaper photographer asked two union leaders, Walter Reuther and Richard Frankensteen, to pose for a picture on Miller Road near the plant, to publicize a drive to have the UAW recognized and to increase wages. When the two labor leaders were attacked and beaten by men from Ford's security department, the incident was well documented by a photographer from the *Detroit News,* James Kilpatrick. While the other auto companies came to terms with the UAW and accepted collective bargaining contracts, Ford held out until one day in April 1941 when a sit-down strike closed the Rouge. Ford talked of breaking up the company, but his wife, Clara, would have none of it because she wanted her son and grandchild to take over the business. Ford listened to his wife, and the UAW had a contract with Ford by June.

JOHN AND HORACE DODGE

The Dodge brothers were part of the first generation of auto pioneers who honed their skills in machine shops, not graduate schools. John Dodge (1864–1920) and brother Horace (1868–1920) were inseparable as children, and died the same year, during the Spanish flu epidemic that spread through the world.

The brothers were born in Niles, Michigan, and later moved to Detroit, where they both went to work in a boilermaker plant and were later machinists in nearby Windsor at a typographic firm. Like Henry Ford, Horace was a tinkerer. He invented and patented a dirt-proof ball bearing and started a machine shop in Detroit. In 1902 he began making transmissions for the auto industry, and eventually built engines for the Ford Motor Co. At one point the brothers owned a significant amount of Ford stock, but Henry Ford bought the shares back for $25 in 1919.

By 1910 the brothers were well enough established to build what would become the Dodge Main Plant in Hamtramck, which employed as many as 30,000 workers and built Dodges for 70 years until it was demolished in 1981 to make way for General Motor's Poletown plant.

After the brothers' death in 1920, their widows eventually sold the business, and it ended up in the hands of Walter P. Chrysler, the founder of the Chrysler Corporation.

WALTER P. CHRYSLER

Chrysler (1875–1940), like many other auto pioneers, started out as a machinist and railroad mechanic before helping to found the Chrysler Corporation in the mid-1920s. He was born in Kansas, and worked as a mechanic for various railroads in Texas and Iowa before ending up in Pittsburgh, where he became the works manager of the American Locomotive Co.

Chrysler shifted gears in 1911, going to work for General Motors as the production chief at Buick, in Flint, Michigan. He came up with ways to reduce costs, but by 1916 he had a falling out with William Durant, who had founded General Motors in 1908. He eventually stayed with GM, but by 1919 he left the corporation and was hired by a group of bankers to oversee Willys-Overland Motor Co., in Toledo, for which he received a salary of $1 million annually. He left Willys after an unsuccessful attempt to take control of the firm from its founder, John Willys.

The formation of Chrysler Corporation came out of Chrysler's acquisition of a controlling interest in Maxwell Motor Co. in the mid-1920s. He phased out the Maxwell and added the Plymouth and DeSoto nameplates, and bought out the widows of the Dodge brothers, which helped form the foundation of the corporation.

The Walter P. Chrysler Museum is located at the Chrysler Corporation headquarters in Auburn Hills. The three-story museum houses more than 54 antique, custom, and concept cars, along with interactive displays and historical exhibits that tell the story of the automaker.

WILLIAM A. DURANT

Durant (1861–1947) did not follow the traditional career path of a modern-day auto executive. He started out as a cigar salesman and ended his career managing a bowling alley in Flint, Michigan. In between he founded what began as a horse-drawn carriage company, Chevrolet, and ran General Motors several times.

He was born in Boston but moved to Michigan, where he worked in the lumberyard of his grandfather, Henry H. Crapo, and eventually sold cigars and then helped found the Coldwater Cart Co., which made horse-drawn wagons. In 1904 he became the manager of Buick, in Flint, and with his sales background he helped establish the modern automobile franchise system. He was eventually named president of Buick and helped form the General Motors Corporation.

Durant saw the possibilities of creating various market segments for automobiles, unlike Ford, who produced one type of car, and Durant merged with Cadillac, which even then was a high-end automaker. But by 1910, Durant lost control of GM to banking interests. Undeterred, he went on to form the Chevrolet brand with Louis Chevrolet. With the money from Chevrolet, he was able to buy enough shares of GM to regain control of the corporation, into which he merged Chevrolet during his tenure as head of the firm from 1916 to 1920. By then he was out of GM, and he founded Durant Motors, which produced various automobiles during the 1920s, many of them aimed at the luxury market dominated by Cadillac and Packard.

During the 1920s Durant became heavily involved in Wall Street but was hit hard by the stock market crash, and by the mid-1930s he was bankrupt. He eventually lived on a small pension from GM and managed a bowling alley in Flint.

LOUIS CHEVROLET

In photos, Louis Chevrolet (1878–1941) looks like a bit of a wild man, and he was, an auto racer who also got into the car-building business, and although he gave his name to one of the most popular cars in America, he ended up working as a line mechanic in a Chevrolet factory and died nearly broke in Detroit.

He was born in Switzerland, but his family moved to France, where he worked as a mechanic before immigrating to Quebec and ending up in New York. He started racing cars for Fiat in 1905 and eventually raced for Buick and became a friend of Billy Durant's, the founder of General Motors. In 1911 Chevrolet partnered briefly with Durant to found Chevrolet Motor Car Co., but had differences with Durant and eventually returned to auto racing. He competed in the Indianapolis 500 four times. The 1929 stock market crash wiped out his savings, and he ended his days as a mechanic.

ALBERT KAHN

Visitors to southeastern Michigan will hear his name many times, if they're interested in public and private buildings in the region. Kahn was everywhere, and designed office buildings in Detroit and other Michigan cities, homes, educational buildings, and even factories, including the mammoth Ford Rouge plant. Kahn was born in Germany in 1869 and died in Detroit in 1942. He came to Detroit with his parents in about 1880 and as a teenager went to work for an architectural firm, but later studied abroad, and eventually founded his own firm, Albert Kahn Associates, in 1895. The firm is still in business in Detroit.

He was in the right place at the right time, as Detroit was emerging as a manufacturing powerhouse, and his construction style of using steel and concrete instead of wood, appealed to the emerging auto industry. He designed the Packard Motor Car Co. factory, which was built in 1907, and then went on to draft Henry Ford's first Model T plant in Highland Park.

Over the years I have worked in several Kahn-designed buildings, and was impressed by the large amount of natural light built into the design. They were more than plain, utilitarian structures, and featured delightful architectural details.

The diversity of the buildings is also impressive. Kahn designed a home for a Canadian whiskey baron in nearby Windsor, the headquarters of the Detroit police, which is still being used, and Detroit's art deco Fisher Building on West Grand Boulevard, also still in use.

In total, Kahn came up with the designs for 60 buildings listed on the National Register of Historic Places.
Here's a sampling of Albert Kahn's buildings that can be viewed in southeastern Michigan.

• The Dearborn Inn, 20301 Oakwood Blvd., Dearborn, which is still a functioning hotel and restaurant. (See Dearborn, chapter 3.)

• The Edsel and Eleanor Ford House (fordhouse.org), Grosse Pointe. The home of Henry Ford's son, Edsel, has an English cottage look, with sandstone walls. Tours are available and various events are held at the estate, which is on Lake St. Clair. (See Grosse Pointe, chapter 4.)

• The Fisher Building in the New Center area of Detroit on West Grand Boulevard. The 30-story skyscraper, built in an art deco style, opened in 1928 and contains offices and the 2,000-plus-seat Fisher Theatre. Detroiters have long called it the "golden tower" because it is lighted at night, and possibly because the oldest building tenant is WJR, a long-popular Detroit radio station (760 AM) whose announcers habitually state that they are broadcasting from "the golden tower of the Fisher Building."

• The Packard Plant in Detroit on East Grand Boulevard.

• The Bonstelle Theatre, 3424 Woodward Ave., Detroit, was built in 1902 as Temple Beth-El and was later turned into a theater.

• The General Motors Building on West Grand Boulevard, between Cass and Second, was built in 1919 and was the largest office building of that era. It's now called Cadillac Place and is used as office space for the State of Michigan.

Detroit's Music

FROM MOTOWN TO EMINEM

IF THERE'S ANYTHING that expresses Detroit's gritty nature best, it's our music. No matter the artist—John Lee Hooker, Diana Ross and the Supremes, Bob Seger, the MC5, Madonna, Eminem, the White Stripes, or Kid Rock—there's always some commonality, some Detroit attitude. Detroit's a tough town and its music reflects that.

While the upper middle class long had its symphonies and operas, working-class Detroit has its own sound track, with the Irish bringing their distinctive laments, the Germans, Polish, and other eastern Europeans dancing to polka tunes, and white and black southern Americans adding their own blues, jazz, R&B, country and western, and bluegrass sounds to the mix.

The African American community has long been a hotbed of Detroit music. From the time of the Great Migration, beginning in the 1910s and continuing through the 1950s, Paradise Valley along Hastings Street on Detroit's Near East Side was the center of that, with talents like Count Basie, Billie Holiday, and Billy Eckstine performing in nightclubs there.

If it was still around today, Hastings Street would be an entertainment district, but by the early 1960s the heart of the African American business district became the target for urban renewal, which some have since called "urban removal."

Motown Records was the full flowering of African American music in Detroit, starting in the late 1950s when Berry Gordy began producing hit after hit from a small house, formerly a photographic studio, on West Grand Boulevard. Motown recorded such groups and performers as the Temptations, the Four Tops, Martha Reeves and the Vandellas, Diana Ross and the Supremes, Stevie Wonder, Marvin

Gaye, the Jackson Five, and Smokey Robinson and the Miracles.

Gordy, by all accounts, was a tough taskmaster, whose background was in the auto industry. Accordingly, he set up a music assembly line, with a group called the Funk Brothers serving as studio musicians and working a shift, giving new meaning to the term "Motown."

But Motown wasn't the only place where talented musicians gravitated; Fortune Records was a family-operated recording studio housed in a cinder block building. There, some of the best rhythm and blues sounds were produced. The Fortune label was home to a mysterious singer, Nathaniel Mayer, who disappeared suddenly in the late 1960s and reappeared more than 20 years later. One of his early hits was "Village of Love," which was popular in Detroit but not elsewhere. Mayer blended doo-wop with rhythm and blues. His raw sound is reminiscent of the garage bands of the late 1960s and early 1990s, when grunge emerged.

Another such group was Nolan Strong and the Diablos, which in 1962 issued "Mind Over Matter," again a mix of doo-wop music and R&B, a premonition of garage bands that would come later. Another song of theirs, "Jump and Shout," moves from the early 1950s swing sound to the R&B era.

John Lee Hooker (1917–2001) was born in Mississippi but had a long relationship with Detroit. The legendary blues singer ended up in Detroit in the late 1940s. He worked for the Ford Motor Co., and also performed in various clubs in Paradise Valley, the African American entertainment district of that time. Hooker eventually made his way in music, and was able to quit his factory job.

If Detroit first revolutionized the world by putting cars in most garages, we kept it up by starting bands in those same spaces. If you want the brief, rock-centric history of local music, listen to the first few lines from original shock-rocker and newly inducted Rock and Roll Hall of Famer Alice Cooper's song "Detroit City," from 2003's *The Eyes of Alice Cooper*. In it he refers to Iggy Pop, the MC5, Ted Nugent, and Bob Seger, who all came up with homegrown Cooper in and around the Motor City way before Kid Rock, Slim Shady (aka Eminem), and the Insane Clown Posse got started.

The 1960s produced some popular Detroit rock artists, probably none better known than Bob Seger, who played many of Detroit's bars during that era and went on to have a national career. His raspy voice and hard-edged lyrics appealed to working-class Detroiters, and he has been particularly popular among bikers. Seger uses many Detroit and Michigan references in his songs. "Roll Me Away," from his 1982 release *The Distance,* conveys the feelings of many Detroit office and factory workers who would love to cut loose and take a long-distance motorcycle trip.

Mitch Ryder is another Detroit rock musician who made it out of the local bar circuit and became a national act, with his band the Detroit Wheels. His raw sound was influenced by Little Richard, and one of his best songs is "Devil with a Blue Dress On." Ryder sometimes played shows at the Grande Ballroom, a concert hall that operated from 1966 to 1973 and hosted many local and major rock, blues, and jazz acts. Pronounced GRAND-ee, the short-lived but historic auditorium is located at 8952 Grand River Avenue and has since fallen into disrepair, but is fondly remembered as the location of a lot of searing shows. The psychedelic handbills that were printed to announce performances are highly collectable now. Punk rock Ann Arbor natives Iggy Pop and the Stooges got their start at the Grande, and counterculture noise makers the MC5—that's the Motor City 5—recorded their first album, *Kick Out the Jams,* at the Grande. If you know the lyrics, you know why we're not quoting them in this family-friendly guide. Locals Alice Cooper, Grand Funk Railroad, and the self-proclaimed "Motor City Madman" Ted Nugent played there too.

Important Detroit techno pioneers include Derrick May, Juan Atkins, and Kevin Saunderson. All three began DJing at parties and clubs in the 1980s and continue to perform around the world, having started their own genre of electronic music and inspired subsequent generations of DJs. The Detroit Electronic Music Festival (DEMF) began in 2000. Renamed Movement, but still known by both names, it's an annual showcase for electronic-music performers. Held each year in late spring/early summer, after some early financial and contractual complications, the festival is still a huge draw as technoheads come from all over the world to attend.

The current crop of Detroit musicians includes Kid Rock (Robert Ritchie), who started in the bar and club scene in Detroit like some of his local rock forefathers and has since brought his blend of rock, rap, and country music to a national audience. He has been loyal to his Michigan and Detroit roots; one of his more recent music videos was filmed in Michigan's Pictured Rocks National Lakeshore in the Upper Peninsula. One of his most popular singles is 2008's "All Summer Long," a naughty/nostalgic track about teens spending a summer in northern Michigan, learning about love and life. It's become a sort of good-times anthem for Detroiters lucky enough to relate to spending vacation time "up North."

Rapper Eminem (Marshall Mathers III) is another Detroiter who didn't forget his roots. An edgy two-minute Chrysler commercial featuring Eminem aired during the 2011 Super Bowl and has helped renew a national interest in Detroit. The commercial stands out because it acknowledges Detroit's problems, even saying the city "has been to hell and back." Eminem starred in the movie *8 Mile,* as a dynamic young white rapper honing his rhymes while growing up poor in the city. The movie put Eight Mile Road into the national consciousness. The road itself is the dividing line between Detroit and its more affluent suburbs to the north, and for many years it represented a racial divide between blacks and whites.

White Stripes was an alternative-rock duo that formed in the Detroit area as part of the garage-rock revival of the early 2000s. Influenced by the blues and country along with classic rock, many of the band's early tracks feature only a guitar and drums, but White Stripes was known for its big sound. The duo, Jack and Meg White, were married early on but continued to record and tour for years after their divorce before announcing the breakup of the band in early 2011. Their first hit song, "Hotel Yorba," from the 2001 release *White Blood Cells,* was recorded in the Detroit hotel of the same name.

The Insane Clown Posse (also known by the initials ICP) is a Detroit hardcore hip-hop duo that formed in the late 1980s. Made up as clowns, ICP puts on elaborate stage shows and frequently makes reference to a Detroit-made soft drink brand, Faygo. Their fans are known as Juggalos, and don't seem to mind getting doused with Faygo at live shows.

Madonna (born Madonna Ciccone) is another metro Detroit native who made it big in the rock and pop school of music. She was born in Bay City, Michigan, and grew up in suburban Detroit. Madonna briefly studied at the University of Michigan on a dance scholarship but left for New York in 1977, and has minimal public connection with the region now.

Transportation

IT'S CALLED MOTOWN FOR A REASON

SITUATED ON THE DETROIT RIVER, with access to the Great Lakes, Detroit was first visited by boat. First the Native Americans came in canoes, and then the French in larger canoes built for the then-flourishing fur trade. Later, ships brought new immigrants to Michigan, many of them from New England and upstate New York, especially after the opening of the Erie Canal in the 1820s.

The city's location made it critical to control of the Northwest and the Great Lakes, and was coveted by the British and later by the Americans. The French established Fort Pontchartrain and later the Americans built Fort Wayne. The city has a commanding view of the river and boat traffic on it.

River travel was the most efficient during the 19th century, and the city grew from a few hundred residents in 1805 to more than 200,000 by 1900. Railroads came in the 1830s, establishing links with the East and West.

At one time, Detroit had an extensive trolley car system that shuttled workers and shoppers to their destinations, but that has devolved into an undependable bus system, with hardly any way to get from the city to the suburbs.

The main mode of transportation is the auto, so unless you're driving your own, plan on renting one when you get here. There are plenty of rentals available at Metro Airport.

There is AMTRAK service to the metro area from Chicago, but the service has a reputation for being late, very late. A train trip to Chicago from Detroit took me more than seven hours, instead of the five or so that it should have. A recent addition, the Megabus, has gained popularity with those traveling on the cheap, and service has expanded over the past few years. From Detroit you can travel to Chicago and reach other American and Canadian cities.

GETTING TO DETROIT

Detroit is intersected by I-94 and I-75, and there are numerous beltways around the city. One plus about the freeways is that the traffic is mostly local. Detroit is located in Michigan's Lower Peninsula, which has the shape of a mitten: the city is tucked away in the lower right corner of the mitten, below the "thumb," so there's little east-west or north-south interstate traffic passing through. The city is about four and a half hours east of Chicago, and about one hour north of Toledo, Ohio.

By Bus

Greyhound (313-961-8011; greyhound.com; 1001 Howard St.) The terminal downtown is the major one in Detroit, and offers connections nationwide. Open daily.

There is bus service in the Metro Detroit area.

Megabus (us.megabus.com) There are connections to Chicago, which serves as a hub for its other routes. There are no stations; visit the website for information on fares and schedules and to obtain tickets.

SMART (www.smartbus.org) offers bus service through the metro Detroit area, but it is very limited, and travelers to the area shouldn't rely on it as a way to get around. Many suburban communities have no bus service.

By Plane

Detroit Metro Airport is the 13th-busiest airport in the nation. It is a major hub for Delta Airlines and has national and international flights to Europe and Asia. Located in the suburb of Romulus, it is about 20 miles from downtown Detroit. The airport was modernized and expanded in the 1990s and has new access roads to the nearby I-94 freeway. Apart from holidays, there's rarely a wait to pick up or drop off passengers. Special cell phone lines facilitate traffic waiting to pick up arriving passengers.

Airlines Serving Detroit

Air Canada
Air France
AirTran Airways
American Airlines
American Eagle
Continental Airlines
Continental Express
Delta Air Lines
Frontier Airlines
KLM
Lufthansa
Republic Airlines
Royal Jordanian
Southwest Airlines
Spirit Airlines
United Ailines
United Express
US Airways

Bishop Airport, just south of Flint, is lesser known than Detroit Metro Airport, but it's conveniently located near the intersection of two major freeways, I-75 and US 23, which makes it a good option for travelers heading to northern Oakland County. It's less crowded than the Detroit airport, and it just may be closer to your ultimate destination.

Airlines Serving Bishop

AirTran Airways
American Airlines
Continental Connection
Delta Air Lines
Frontier Airlines

By Train

There are AMTRAK (www.amtrak) stations in Detroit, Ann Arbor, Dearborn, and Pontiac, all with enclosed waiting areas and offices. If you arrive by train, don't expect to find much ground transportation at the stations. Rarely are there waiting cabs nearby, so plan on having somebody pick you up, or

The Amtrak station in Ann Arbor.

call for a cab. The Detroit station is located near Woodward Avenue in the Midtown District, and bus service is available. The Detroit station is at 11 West Baltimore; Ann Arbor, 325 Depot St.; Royal Oak, 202 South Sherman St. There are connecting trains to Chicago and Toledo. VIA Rail Canada (viarail.ca) in nearby Windsor, Ont., offers service to Toronto, Montreal, and Quebec on VIA Rail. The station is at 298 Walker Rd., Windsor.

GETTING AROUND METRO DETROIT

By Vehicle

Except for Oakland County, just north of Detroit, there's an extensive freeway system, along with surface roads. Downtown Detroit is served by the Chrysler (I-75), Edsel Ford (I-94), and John Lodge Freeways, traffic on which tends to flow pretty smoothly, even during rush hour. Most of the businesses the freeways were intended to serve have fled to the suburbs. I-94 and I-75, both of which carry out-of-state traffic into the city, are the busiest. But perhaps the most used are the beltway freeways, such as I-275 and I-696, which run through the heavily populated suburbs and carry commuter traffic. The Ambassador Bridge to Canada is served by I-96.

One thing to remember about southeastern Michigan and the rest of the state is that it's fairly isolated from the remainder of the nation, being surrounded by the Great Lakes. One benefit is that apart from river crossings to Canada, there's little east-west or north-south traffic through the city.

A few words of caution: Watch out on those freeways. Driving is a blood sport in Detroit. Pay special heed on entrance ramps; freeway drivers may not let you merge easily. Also, the speed limit on the freeway is 65 miles an hour, but for most drivers that's only a suggestion. Speeds can hit up to 80 or more.

In the late winter and early spring there can be massive potholes in roads and freeways. Southern Michigan winter weather, with its freeze-thaw cycle, causes concrete to break up on older roads. Potholes can cause accidents as well as damage to vehicles.

Give trucks a wide berth: the ones around Detroit are often hauling heavy loads of steel or auto parts destined for the region's various auto plants.

East Side, West Side, Downriver

For generations, metro Detroit has been separated into three distinct areas, whether you're in the suburbs or the city: East Side, West Side, and Downriver. In conversations to this day, you'll hear people being described as an East Sider, West Sider, or Downriver resident. There are several reasons for that, the first of which is that when Detroit first developed, it was difficult to travel from the East to West Sides, and getting downriver was even more difficult. Detroit's original city plan created spokelike roads going in various directions from the center of the city off Woodward Avenue downtown. Those became the major streetcar arteries and later roadways, so to get from the West Side to the East Side, a traveler pretty much had to go downtown and catch another street car. This holds true into the 21st century. To this day, only I-94 and Eight Mile connect east and west. Generations of families tended to settle along certain corridors, partly because of a reliance on public transportation.

Winter Driving

The metro area receives an average of 45 inches of snow during the winter, in addition to its share of freezing rain and ice. The winter season can arrive in late November and last through March, and sometimes into early April, so be prepared. Take your driving cues from the locals; they're accustomed to maneuvering in the stuff. The best advice is to simply slow down, especially on ice. Because of the region's cold temperatures, the metro area avoids many ice storms, and receives snow instead, which is easier to drive in, as there's more traction. If you're renting a vehicle during winter, it may be a good idea to pick one with four-wheel drive. Also, make sure there's an ice scraper in the vehicle, and ample windshield-wiper fluid. In treating roadways, metro crews use a lot of salt, which can leaves a film on windshields, making it difficult to see. If you do get stuck, or your vehicle is disabled, it's best to call for roadside assistance. Police will often stop to help disabled vehicles on the freeways.

Routes to Canada

By Bridge

The Ambassador Bridge (313-963-1410; www.ambassadorbridge.com; 2744 W. Fort Street) The bridge is easily accessible from I-96 in Detroit, and has two lanes going each way. The bridge is privately owned, but the state of Michigan and the Canadian government are

The Ambassador Bridge.

looking to build a second span. Until that happens, the bridge, opened in 1929, is the only span over the river. It's the busiest international border crossing in North America, and carries many trucks, and there are often long backups. The daily traffic count is 10,000 trucks and 4,000 vehicles. A good alternative for travelers is the Detroit-Windsor Tunnel (see below). The bridge is an attractive structure with art deco elements. In the aftermath of 9/11, waits to cross it have been longer, and Americans are required to have either a passport or enhanced driver's license. There is a duty-free store at the bridge's service plaza that sells alcohol and tobacco products fairly cheaply, but there are restrictions on what can be brought back to the United States. Check with the U.S. Department of Homeland Security (cbp.gov). The toll is $4 U.S. and $4.75 Canadian for vehicles.

By Tunnel

Detroit-Windsor Tunnel (313-567-4422; dwtunnel.com; 100 E. Jefferson Ave.) Your other option across the river to Canada is tricky to find; located off Jefferson, just west of the Renaissance Center, the Detroit-Windsor tunnel is not well marked, but it's worth the effort because there are often fewer delays in crossing than via the Ambassador Bridge. The tunnel is the second-busiest crossing between the United States and Canada, after the bridge. The tunnel opened in 1930 and is owned jointly by the cities of Detroit and Windsor. The toll is $4.50 U.S. and $4.75 Canadian. A passport or enhanced Michigan driver's license is required. For information about what items can be taken across the border, check the website of the U.S. Department of Homeland Security (cbp.gov).

Freeways

I-75

The freeway, which stretches from southern Florida to Michigan's Upper Peninsula, is a major artery running to Detroit and carries a lot of truck traffic. Many are hauling steel for the auto industry and are quite heavy. From the south, the freeway splits into two, with I-275 running north through the area's western suburbs before connecting to I-96 in Farmington. It also crosses other freeways and major surface streets, including I-94, Michigan Avenue Ford Road, and M-14. The I-75 portion goes to downtown Detroit before turning north and heading through the city and into Oakland County, which is home to the booming business district of Troy and to Auburn Hills, where Chrysler Corporation is headquartered.

I-94

In Detroit it's called the Edsel Ford Freeway. I-94 links Detroit with other southern Michigan cities and is the major interstate to Chicago. It runs east-west, but makes a bend in Detroit and heads north to Port Huron. Detroit Metro Airport is located in Romulus on the I-94 corridor, and the freeway connects with both Detroit and Ann Arbor. In the metro area it has interchanges with US 23, I-275, Telegraph Road, the Southfield Freeway, I-96, the John C. Lodge Freeway, Woodward Avenue, and I-75 (the Chrysler Freeway in Detroit).

I-96

This freeway connects Detroit to Lansing, the state capital, but it takes a circuitous route. It's called the Jeffries Freeway in Detroit, but is also marked with I-96 signs. It runs northwesterly from the Ambassador Bridge to Canada, but merges with I-275 in the suburb of Livonia, and heads north for several miles until an exit, when it again becomes I-96. The freeway takes drivers through the older suburbs of Redford and Livonia and then into the newer, booming communities of Northville, Farmington, and Novi.

I-696 (Walter Reuther)

The freeway runs east-west and connects the Oakland County suburbs with the East Side, intersecting with I-96, I-275, I-75, and I-94.

Freeway Names

If Detroit's freeways have a familiar ring to them, it's because they're named after historic figures in the American auto industry.

The Walter P. Reuther Freeway, I-696, is named for a well-known labor leader; Reuther (b. 1907) was the president of the UAW from 1946 until his death in a plane crash in 1970. He was a socialist who supported the Democratic Party, and started in the auto industry as a tool and die worker, a skilled trade, at Ford Motor Co. in the 1920s. He was laid off, and contended that his union activities contributed to his firing. He went to the Soviet Union and briefly worked in a factory there, but returned and got a job at a General Motors plant. He was involved in what became known as the Battle of the Overpass in 1937, a confrontation between union organizers and Ford Motor Co. security forces.

Interestingly enough, the Reuther doesn't intersect with the Edsel Ford Freeway, I-94. Edsel Ford (1893–1943) was the only son of Henry Ford, the company's founder, and served as the company president from 1919 until his death in 1943 from a stomach ailment. The freeway, which connects Detroit's East and West Sides, has survived much longer than the Ford vehicle named after him, the Edsel. Ford made the Edsel from 1958 to 1960, and it never sold well, even though it had a distinctive grille and advanced styling. It's often cited as the poster child for a marketing failure.

The Ford Freeway does cross paths with another automaker, Walter P. Chrysler (1875–1940). The Chrysler is the segment of I-75 that runs north from the city, and crosses the Ford Freeway near the Midtown area. Chrysler was first a railroad mechanic who traveled the West during the 19th century, eventually ending up as a railroad executive. From there he entered the auto business and was the founder of the Chrysler Corporation.

Ford Road (M-153), in the city's western suburbs, isn't named for the automobile magnate but for his father, William Ford, who was a farmer in the area.

It and I-94 are the only freeways that connect the West and East Sides in the metro Detroit area. During the morning and evening commutes, traffic can be bumper to bumper.

M-10 (John C. Lodge)

Detroiters simply call it "the Lodge," and it runs from downtown Detroit to the northwestern suburbs. It can be crowded during rush hour.

I-275

Running north-south from near Monroe to Farmington in metro Detroit, I-275 is part of the beltway system circling the area. It connects with three other freeways, I-94, I-96/M-14, and I-96, and is one of the busiest in the region. Speeds on it regularly hit 80 miles an hour and higher. (The limit is 65.)

M-8 (Davidson Freeway)

The Davidson is a short stretch of freeway running through Highland Park in Detroit, and it has the distinction of being the first stretch of sunken expressway built in the nation. It was quickly constructed during World War II to help workers get to their jobs at defense plants, and the 1.3-mile freeway opened in 1942. It has since added two more miles. Over the years, its importance has dwindled, as manufacturing plants have moved out of Highland Park.

M-14

Really an extension of I-96, the Jeffries Freeway in Detroit and its western suburbs, M-14 is a major artery to Ann Arbor. It eventually connects with I-94 just west of Ann Arbor.

The Southfield Freeway

The freeway carries the state designation of M-39, but locals know it mostly as Southfield, which was the name of the road it was built on. The freeway dates to the early 1960s and is narrower than most, with a very narrow shoulder. It's an in-ground freeway for most of its 14 miles, and runs through Detroit and Dearborn for most of its life as a freeway. In Dearborn, from Ford Road to I-94, the Ford Motor Co. World Headquarters is located on it, at the junction with Michigan Avenue, along with The Henry Ford and Greenfield Village. There isn't a freeway exit for the museums, but getting off at the Michigan Avenue exit is a good option. Drivers can also exit at Ford Road.

Telegraph Road (US 24)

While not a freeway, it's an important north-south artery that runs from the Downriver area to Pontiac in Oakland County. The divided highway has multiple lanes going in each direction, and while there are traffic lights about every mile, traffic proceeds at a fairly fast clip. If you can time the lights right, it's a smooth drive. If you're coming from Detroit Metro Airport and are headed to Oakland County, this is the route to take, and it will save you the time of taking I -94 to downtown Detroit and then getting on I-75. Oakland County is more difficult to get around in, partly because of the large number of inland lakes in its western portion that have impeded road construction.

Car Rental

Detroit Metro Airport offers a full range of vehicle rentals, with companies grouped together in the airport complex. If you're coming here on business (especially auto company business), make sure to rent an American-made vehicle. Detroiters take note of the makes of automobiles people drive. During winter months, consider a four-wheel-drive vehicle to contend with the ice and snow. There are shuttle buses to the rental area, as well as to parking lots and nearby hotels. You won't find too many taxicabs, but there are limo services at the airport, and it's best to arrange ground transportation prior to arrival.

Airport Rental Car Center

Company	Toll-Free
Alamo	800-327-9633
Avis	800-331-1212
Budget	800-527-0700
Dollar	800-421-6878
Enterprise	800-325-8007
Hertz	800-654-3131
National	800-277-7368
Thrifty	800-367-2277

Bicycling

While there are many bike paths in the suburbs, Detroit is not known as a cycling-friendly city. There are a few dedicated bike lanes, and a few hardcore city cyclists, but because of the crime rate, I wouldn't recommend that visitors use the city's paths. There are numerous bike trails in the suburbs. Hines Drive in western Wayne County offers a 17-mile trail that follows the Rouge River from Dearborn to Northville (see Hines Drive Cruise, chapter 6). Ann Arbor is a great place to bicycle.

MGM
GRAND
Third

Downtown Detroit

RIVERFRONT, FINANCIAL DISTRICT, CAMPUS MARTIUS PARK, GREEKTOWN

DETROIT'S FORMAL DOWNTOWN AREA is roughly bounded by three freeways that cut it off from surrounding neighborhoods: the John C. Lodge (M-10) to the west, the Fisher Freeway (I-75) to the north, and the Chrysler Freeway (I-375) to the east. For first-time visitors, the street system can be a bit confusing, with some streets at angles, laid out under the city's first plan, in 1805, and others on a more traditional grid.

There's also the problem of the city not being on a true north-south or east-west axis, because the Detroit River bends near downtown. It's a geographical oddity that Windsor, Detroit's Canadian neighbor, is actually *southeast* of Detroit.

Much of the focus over the centuries has been on the Detroit River, first because of Great Lakes shipping and the industries that sprang up along the waterway, and later for its scenery and recreational opportunities.

Downtown Detroit is actually fairly small, about 1.1 square miles in size, and includes the Riverfront, the Financial District, Campus Martius Park, and Greektown, a restaurant and entertainment area. The downtown area is also the location of several casinos.

LEFT: The MGM Grand Casino in downtown Detroit.

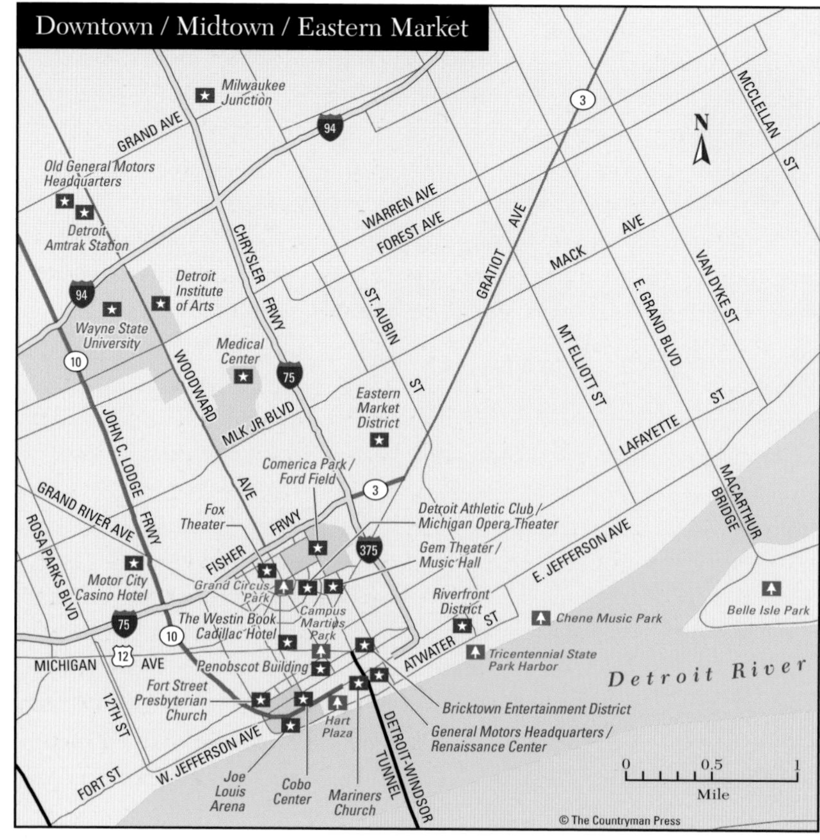

A bit farther afield of the downtown area is the Rivertown-Warehouse District, an entertainment district just to the east (see sidebar, p. 68), and the popular Eastern Market just to the north (see p. 66).

RIVERFRONT

The Renaissance Center is the heart of downtown in Detroit's Riverfront area, and its image often accompanies news stories about General Motors, which has its world headquarters in the seven-tower complex. But while it's owned by GM, a Ford helped build the complex in the early 1970s: Henry Ford II, the grandson of the auto-company founder, conceived the idea, and the Ford Motor Co. contributed to and helped gain financing for the center. Detroit at that time was still suffering the aftereffects of a 1967 civil disturbance, the five-day Detroit Riot, and the name "Renaissance" was intended to signify a rebirth. The lofty goal at the time was to rebuild the city's waterfront from "bridge to bridge," from the Ambassador Bridge to the MacArthur Bridge, which connects the city with Belle Isle, an island in the Detroit River. While the Renaissance Center opened in 1976, work on revitalizing the Riverfront has been spotty.

The RenCen, as Detroiters call it, has four 39-story office towers surrounding a 73-story hotel, the Detroit Marriott at the Renaissance Center, and also has many shops, restaurants, and a movie theater. The RenCen is served by the People Mover elevated light-rail system, which encircles the downtown area. Some of the center's shops have struggled over the years to stay open, partly because of poor pedestrian access to the complex, and partly because of the center's design. For many years, Detroiters have complained that finding their way around it is difficult, with endless rampways running through the buildings. Though it's difficult to enter the complex from street level, there is ample attached parking that is fairly easily accessed. (If you're planning a visit, consult the RenCen's website, gmrencen.com, for directions and a map of the complex's interior.)

General Motors headquarters in downtown Detroit.

Just west of the RenCen is the Philip A. Hart Plaza. Named for a longtime U.S. senator from Michigan, it is located at the foot of Woodward Avenue, at an intersection with Jefferson, near where Antoine de la Mothe Cadillac landed in 1701 and founded Fort Pontchartrain du Détroit. Hart Plaza is a major gathering place for Detroiters and hosts various events throughout the year, including July 4th fireworks and an annual country-music festival held in May. The Horace E. Dodge Fountain is located in the center of the plaza. It was a gift to the city from Anna Thompson Dodge, the widow of Horace E. Dodge, who along with his brother founded the Dodge car company, which eventually merged with the Chrysler Corporation. Anna Dodge (1871–1970) outlived her husband by about 50 years, and was thought to be one of the richest women in the world during her lifetime. She was born in Dundee, Scotland, and married Dodge in 1896. Upon the death of her husband, she inherited part of Dodge Brothers Co., which was sold in 1926 for a reported $146 million. She lived in a home in Grosse Pointe until her death. The large, abstract-design fountain has two stainless steel legs supporting a 30-foot-high ring with a black granite pool below. Its complex system of 300 water jets and 300 lights creates a variety of displays for onlookers.

Riverboat Cruise

A good way to see Detroit's riverfront is on a cruise aboard the Detroit Princess Riverboat (877-338-2628; detroitprincess.com), a 222-foot craft built in 1993. The boat offers cruises to both the general public and private groups. There's a restaurant onboard, and dinner cruises are an option.

The Detroit RiverWalk is a 5.5-mile paved trail that runs through downtown along the river from the Ambassador Bridge to Belle Isle, and ties various destinations together, including Hart Plaza, the Renaissance Center, William G. Milliken State Park, Stroh River Place, Chene Park, and Gabriel Richard Park. Chene and Richard Parks are small green spaces offering views of the Detroit River and are nice stopping places for walkers and bicyclists. (See East Jefferson Avenue Cruise, chapter 4, for information on Milliken State Park and Stroh River Place.)

Just to the west of Hart Plaza is Cobo Center (313-877-8111; cobocenter.com; 1 Washington Blvd.), where the annual North American International Auto Show (naias.com) is held during January. Most Detroiter's still call it Cobo Hall, even though there are actually two facilities here, a sports arena and performance venue and the adjacent convention and exposition hall. The Joe Louis Arena, where Detroit's hockey team, the Red Wings, play, is nearby. The hall and arena opened in 1960 and were expanded in 1989, and the hall now has 2.4 million square feet of space. There has long been talk of further expanding Cobo, and in 2009 a five-member board of city and suburban representatives was appointed to oversee prospective development. Apart from the auto show, Cobo hosts conventions and other events. Cobo Arena is a popular venue for concerts (local rocker Bob Seger recorded *Live Bullet*, and Detroiter Kid Rock recorded *Live Trucker*, here).

The intersection of Jefferson and Woodward Avenues is the center of Detroit; it's where the city hall is located, along with several other landmarks. Within a few blocks of it are many of the art deco buildings that arose during the 1920s, when the city was feeling a new financial power that came with the emergence of the auto industry.

Located in the middle of the Woodward Avenue median is a sculpture known to Detroiters simply as The Fist. It's a memorial to Joe Louis, the world heavyweight boxing champion of the 1930s and '40s. Created by sculptor Robert Graham, the 24-foot bronze arm, extended horizontally and ending in a clenched fist, is suspended by 24-foot-tall support beams. The work was commissioned by *Sports Illustrated* and presented to the city in 1987. The sculpture was controversial when it was unveiled; some were threatened by its evocation of the symbol of black power. Others wanted to know why a tribute to a boxer didn't include boxing gloves.

The Fist at Jefferson and Woodward Avenues is a memorial to Detroit boxer Joe Louis.

Not far across Woodward Avenue from the Joe Louis Fist monument is another of Detroit's best-known pieces of outdoor sculpture, the *Spirit of Detroit*. The 26-foot bronze statue is located in front of the Coleman A. Young Municipal Center (formerly the City-County Building), and depicts a seated figure holding a gilt bronze sphere symbolizing God in one hand, and a family

Joe Louis

Joe Louis (1914–1981) was an African American boxer who held the world heavyweight title from 1937 to 1949, during what some consider the golden age of boxing. Louis, who was called the Brown Bomber, was born in Alabama, but his family moved to Detroit, where his brother got a job at the Ford Rouge plant. Joe worked there for a short time too. Louis attended a vocational school, but eventually got interested in boxing at the Brewster Recreation Center, and worked his way up from a Golden Gloves amateur to professional status.

At the time, an unofficial color barrier discouraged black boxers from vying for the heavyweight championship, so when Louis won the title in 1937, he became a hero to African Americans in Detroit and elsewhere. He also played a part in the escalating tensions between the United States and Germany prior to World War II, especially when he defended his title against German boxer Max Schmeling in 1938. Before the event, Louis was invited to visit the White House, where he received encouragement from President Roosevelt. Louis won the bout in two minutes and four seconds.

group symbolizing all human relationships in the other. It was made and donated to the city by Birmingham-based sculptor Marshall Fredericks (1908–1998), whose distinctively heroic, stylized figures are found in many public sculpture gardens around metro Detroit. Unveiled in 1958, the figure has often been decorated by Detroit sports fans with their team's colors when they win championships. Some locals call the figure the Jolly Green Giant because of its Statue of Liberty green cast.

Across Woodward is another well-loved piece of outdoor sculpture, of a nude ballet dancer standing with her hands lifted over her head. The 11-foot bronze sculpture ***Passo di Danza*** (Step of the Dance) is in front of the skyscraper known as **One Woodward Avenue**, formerly the MichCon Building, and was unveiled in 1961. In the 1960s, a group of wags painted giant footsteps from the *Spirit of Detroit* sculpture over to the dancer statue, implying that the Spirit had paid the nude beauty a nocturnal visit.

The *Spirit of Detroit* statue at Woodward and Jefferson Avenues.

FINANCIAL DISTRICT

Detroit's Financial District is listed on the U.S. Register of Historic Places. Many of downtown Detroit's buildings were constructed in the 1920s, when art deco was in fashion, and there are some must-sees for architecture buffs. They are located just off Woodward Avenue, mostly on Larned between Shelby and Griswold Streets. One Detroit favorite is the Penobscot Building, 645 Griswold, which was opened in 1928. At 45 stories, it was the city's tallest building until the construction of the Renaissance Center in 1977. A distinctive red ball at the top of its spire makes it a good landmark for negotiating the downtown area. Named for Maine's Penobscot Indians, the building has many Native American motifs in its decorative elements.

The Buhl Building was constructed in 1925 and is across Congress Street from the Penobscot Building. It was done in the neo-Gothic style, with Romanesque accents. The architectural sculpture is by Corrado Parducci, and the building's designer was Wirt C. Rowland, a Detroit architect who worked at several different firms. Rowland was also the architect for the Penobscot Building and the nearby Guardian Building. He also designed the Kirk in the Hills Presbyterian Church in Bloomfield Hills.

Detroit's Financial District is known for its art deco buildings.

The Guardian Building, 500 Griswold, was opened in 1929 as the Union Trust Building, and the art deco–style structure was named a National Historic Landmark in 1989. It now houses the offices of Wayne County government. Step inside and check out the ornate, impressive lobby, with its cathedral-like ceiling and murals that detail Detroit's past. The Guardian is decorated with Pewabic Pottery tiles, the product of a Detroit firm (see Pewabic Pottery, chapter 4, p. 161). There are also Native American themes on the outside walls.

CAMPUS MARTIUS PARK

Located at Michigan and Woodward Avenues, Campus Martius was a main gathering spot for Detroiters in the 19th century, but with the coming of the automobile, city fathers chipped away at its size to enlarge roads and accommodate traffic. Hart Plaza was designed to replace the park, but the plaza is a paved surface that lacks an intimate feel and park-like atmosphere. Located in Campus Martius is the Soldiers and Sailors Monument memorializing Civil War veterans, which for years was simply circled by traffic, allowing the public little contact with it. The new park, dedicated in 2004, has an ice-skating rink, stages, public sculptures, and open spaces. It's home to the annual Motown Winter Blast festival (winterblast.com) and to a

Downtown Transportation: The People Mover

Downtown is the one area of Detroit in which you can get around using public transportation. **The People Mover** (313-224-2160; peoplemover.com) is an elevated light-rail system with 13 stops in the downtown area, including the Renaissance Center. The system circles downtown and is a boon during the city's harsh winters. The operating hours are Monday–Thursday, 6:30 AM–midnight; Friday and Saturday, 6:30 AM–2 AM; Sunday, noon–midnight. Fares are 50 cents. Be sure to check that the system is in operation before planning to use it, as there have been breakdowns.

The People Mover provides light-rail service to downtown Detroit districts.

Many Red Wings fans park in Greektown to take advantage of the restaurants and bars in the area, then take the People Mover to the Joe Louis Arena for the game.

The People Mover makes the following stops:

- **Times Square,** the home base for the People Mover.
- **Grand Circus Park,** close to restaurants, entertainment venues like the Fox Theatre and Comerica Park (the Tigers' home field).
- **Broadway,** an arts and entertainment district.
- **Cadillac Center,** serves Campus Martius and Compuware headquarters.
- **Greektown,** home to restaurants and the Greektown Casino.
- **Bricktown,** with access to pubs, restaurants, and music clubs.
- **Renaissance Center,** home to General Motors as well as shops, restaurants, and the RenCen's Marriott.
- **Millender Center,** location of a Courtyard by Marriott hotel and shopping.
- **Financial District,** location of the Guardian, Buhl, Ford, and Penobscott buildings.
- **Joe Louis Arena,** home of the Detroit Red Wings hockey team.
- **Cobo Center,** exhibition center hosting the North American International Auto Show and a major concert venue.
- **Fort/Cass,** serves local media outlets, including the Detroit Free Press.

Downtown Art Galleries

G. R. N'Namdi Gallery (313-831-8700; grnnamdi.com; 52 E. Forest) The gallery has been around since 1981 and has an extensive collection of abstract art.

Du Mouchelles (313-963-6255; dumouchelle.com; 409 E. Jefferson Ave.) is a fine arts auctioneer and estate appraiser with a Detroit history dating to 1927. Six to eight auctions are held monthly, with items such as weaponry, books, costumes, decorative objects, fine arts, furniture, jewelry, lighting fixtures, rugs and tapestries, and sports items. You don't have to buy anything to watch the auction. Check the website for dates and times.

yearly Christmas-tree-lighting ceremony. The redevelopment of the park, and the construction of the nearby Compuware Building, has been the centerpiece of the downtown's revival.

The Compuware Building, located at 1 Campus Martius, is the world headquarters of Compuware and was one of the first office buildings constructed in downtown Detroit in many years. One of the company's founders, Peter Karmanos Jr., lives in the Detroit area and is very active in the community. The building is in the late modernist style, constructed from glass, granite, and limestone; it has a dramatic entryway and its atrium features an indoor waterfall.

GREEKTOWN

Detroit wasn't a major destination for the large number of immigrants who came to America from the 1890s to 1920, but those who did come here often settled what was then called the Near East Side, just off Woodward. These included Jews, Greeks, Italians, Poles, and African Americans. The Poles headed slightly north to Poletown, and eventually to Hamtramck; African Americans settled along Hastings Street.

The only true ethnic section of the Near East Side to survive has been Greektown, along Monroe Street, which for many years was the heart and soul of the Greek community in Detroit. Up until the 1970s the Greek flavor was strong, with many of the storefronts taken up by coffee shops, barbershops, and bakers patronized by Greeks, but as

Greektown is a major entertainment district in the downtown area.

The Laikon Café is known for authentic Greek cuisine.

residents moved to the suburbs, their influence waned. My wife is Greek American, and she tells stories about taking her grandfather to a Greek barber in the district. She'd drop him off and pick him up later at one of the coffee shops, which were at that time men-only: no women allowed. During the urban-renewal efforts of the late 1950s and early '60s, the district lost some of its territory, with part of Monroe Street becoming the Chrysler Freeway.

The Greektown entertainment district centers on two blocks of Monroe Street, with some spreading to surrounding blocks. All is not Greek in Greektown, though: one of the area's mainstays is the Old Shillelagh, at Monroe Street and Brush. The Irish tavern is packed on St. Patrick's Day. If you're looking for the real deal as far as Greek food goes, try the Laikon Café on Monroe. My wife says it offers the most authentic cuisine in the district, the kind of fare you'll find served in Greek homes. Other restaurants serving Greek food are the New Parthenon, Cyprus Tavern, and Pegasus Taverna. Sunday afternoon is a good time to visit a Greek restaurant, as that's when Greek families tend to patronize these establishments. If traditional Greek lamb dishes aren't your thing, try Fishbones Rhythm Kitchen on Monroe, which serves Cajun fare (see Restaurants, Greektown, for complete listings).

Greektown is home to Saint Andrews Hall (313-961-6358; 431 E. Congress St.), with a one-thousand-capacity event space. Saint Andrews is a live-music venue favored by hip concert-goers. National touring acts stop at the venerable institution, which used to be a meeting place for the Saint Andrew's Society. Expect rock, punk, indie, rap, hip-hop, or techno, depending on who is coming through town. DJs spin on club nights. Many local and smaller touring bands play at the Shelter, located in the lower level of the hall. Eminem got his start there.

St. Mary Roman Catholic Church in Greektown.

Also worth a look is St. Mary Roman Catholic Church (646 Monroe St.), one of the oldest Catholic churches in Detroit, dating back to the 1840s when the parish was first organized to serve a large German population. The school building was constructed in 1868 and was in operation until 1966. The current church dates to 1885. Another historic institution, Annunciation Greek Orthodox Cathedral (707 E. Lafayette), was founded in 1910 to serve the Greek community along Monroe Street.

The Downtown Sports Scene

Teams and Arenas

Detroit sports fans are known to support their teams no matter how well they perform on the field, and three of its teams play their home games in downtown Detroit facilities. The fans also help support numerous bars and restaurants.

The most successful local sports franchise is the Detroit Red Wings hockey team, one of the original six teams of the National Hockey League and often in the playoffs for the Stanley Cup. The team has won 11 Stanley Cup championships, six conference championships, and 18 division championships in its history. One of the more bizarre Red Wings traditions is the throwing of an octopus on the ice during the playoffs. It started during the 1950s, when the owner of a fish market tossed one on the ice. According to local legend, the octopus's eight legs symbolize the number of wins needed for a Stanley Cup.

The Wings play at Joe Louis Arena (313-396-7444; olympia entertainment.com; 600 Civic Center Dr.; west of Woodward Avenue, near the Cobo Center) Detroiters call it "the Joe," and it's named for legendary Detroit boxer Joe Louis, who held the heavyweight world championship during the 1930s and '40s. Tickets to the hockey game are coveted in Detroit.

The Detroit Tigers baseball team has a pedigree similar to that of the Red Wings, but the Tigers don't have a record to match. The Tigers have been playing in Detroit since 1894, and were one of the American League's eight charter franchises. The team has won the World Series four times, and the American League Pennant ten times. But that doesn't keep the fans from coming to the games, and Opening Day in April is nearly a holiday in the city. The team played in Corktown at the corner of Michigan and Trumbull from 1912 until 1999, when it moved to new digs. That move angered many traditional Detroit baseball fans, who saw the corner where the team played for many years as hallowed ground and fought the demolition of the old Tiger Stadium. It was eventually demolished.

The team now plays at Comerica Park (detroit.tigers.mlb.com/det/ballpark/index.jsp; 2100 Woodward), which is a brick open-air stadium nestled between the Greektown entertainment district and the Woodward Avenue corridor. The Tigers play their home games here, and since it opened in 2000, it has won the hearts of many Detroiters for its design and almost neighborhood feel. Because it's located near Greektown and a casino, there is enough parking for most games, and fans often patronize the nearby restaurants and taverns. When the Tigers made the move from their Corktown neighborhood, many thought it would be the end of several venerable sports bars and restaurants along Michigan Avenue near the old stadium, but Detroit

PuppetART

Detroit Puppet Theater

(313-961-777; www.puppetart.org; 25 Grand River) The 70-seat theater in the heart of downtown offers eight different productions annually for children and adults. Many of the puppeteers were trained in the former Soviet Union. There is also a puppet museum, and various workshops are held. Located near the Broadway stop on the People Mover.

The Detroit Tigers home field is Comerica Park off Woodward.

fans have stayed loyal to their hangouts, and the baseball hot spots now offer shuttle buses to Comerica Park, Ford Field, and Joe Louis Arena on game days (see Sports Bars).

The Detroit Lions football team hasn't been a top performer in years, but it's a longtime fixture, having joined the National Football League in 1934. The team is owned by William Clay Ford Sr., a member of the Ford Motor Co. family.

The Lions play at Ford Field (313-262-2011; detroitlions.com/ford-field/index.html), a covered stadium that can seat up to 70,000 fans and opened in 2002. Concerts and other events also take place at the facility.

Eastern Market

Just northeast of the downtown area is the 430-acre Eastern Market, bounded by Gratiot Avenue, Mack Avenue, St. Aubin Street, and the Chrysler Freeway. More than just a place where farmers bring their produce to sell, it's an entertainment district ringed by restaurants and specialty food purveyors.

Detroit had a farmer's market in 1841 at Cadillac Square and it was moved several times before finding its current home in 1891. There are hundreds of stalls in the six-block-long market. Seasonally

The DAC

Close to Ford Field and visible from Comerica Park is the exclusive **Detroit Athletic Club** (313-963-9200; www.thedac.com; 241 Madison Ave.). Built in 1915, the neo-Renaissance-style building was designed by the well-known early-20th-century architect Albert Kahn, who worked on many noteworthy Detroit buildings and the Ford Rouge Complex. It is a private club with a restaurant and athletic facilities, but has agreements with other such clubs that allow visitors to use the facilities.

on Saturdays and Sundays it attracts a diverse group of as many as 40,000 customers, ranging from city folk looking for bargains to well-heeled suburbanites. Apart from fresh produce, the market also offers wholesale meats and garden plants.

Restaurants in the Market

Restaurants ring the market area, and include some Detroit favorites.

Farmers' Restaurant (313-831-1800; 2542 Market St.) This is the place where the real farmers eat. The breakfasts are large, and for lunch, the specialty is corned beef. The décor is nothing special, just basic tables and chairs. It's open at 5 AM most days. $

Louie's Ham and Corned Beef (313-831-1800; louieseastern market.com; 3570 Riopelle) This newer restaurant is a great place for breakfast or lunch before a walk in the market. Portions are large. Egg dishes and sandwiches, along with Coney Island hotdogs, burgers, salads, and stir-fry. $

Louisiana Creole Gumbo (313-446-9639; 2051 Gratiot) The family-style place is small but friendly and offers an interesting mix of Creole-style cooking and soul food. $

Roma Café (313-831-5940; romacafe.com; 3401 Riopelle St.) The restaurant has strong ties to the market. The building dates to 1888; by 1890 the Marazza family had opened a boardinghouse catering to the farmers who needed a place to stay when they brought their products to town. Mrs. Marazza started cooking for them, and opened a café that same year. It has been run by members of the Sossi family since about 1918, and these days the waitstaff is clad in tuxedoes and the patrons are less likely to wear overalls. The menu

Just East of Downtown

Rivertown-Warehouse District

An entertainment district started to develop along Atwater Street in the 1980s, but its emergence as a full-fledged enclave was thwarted by the City of Detroit, which wanted to redevelop the area by putting a gambling casino there and went so far as to buy property. That put other plans in limbo, and some bars and restaurants closed. The casino never came. There are a few places still thriving, and if you like that warehouse feel it's a good area to see. It's located just east of the Chrysler Freeway (I-75), and along the river. The hot spots here include:

Atwater Block Brewery (313-877-9205; atwaterbeer.com; 237 Joseph Campau) The brewery produces beer that's served at its facility and available in stores in various states. $

Studio 51 (313-393-0051; 1995 Woodbridge St.) Located in a historic restored building near the river, the club prides itself on its martinis and party atmosphere. Dancing takes place on the third floor. There's also a sports bar with large-screen TVs. There's a cover charge on weekends. $$

includes many pasta and seafood dishes, with such favorites as calamari, frog legs, lake perch, surf and turf, and lobster. There are also many Italian-style veal dishes. There's an extensive wine list. $$$

Roma Café at Detroit's Eastern Market is a longtime favorite.

Russell Street Deli (313-567-2900; russellstreetdeli.com; 2465 Russell) Corned beef sandwiches are the specialty, and they come in various versions. Turkey and pastrami are also on the menu. Breakfast is served on Saturdays. $

Sala Thai Restaurant (313-831-1302; www.salathai.us; 3400 Russell) The Asian restaurant is located in a historic Detroit firehouse dating from 1888 and has wood paneling and a high ceiling. There's a sushi bar, and traditional Thai fare is offered. Entrées include Pad

Vivio's is a popular Eastern Market restaurant.

Thai with chicken, beef, pork, or seafood, as well as fish and duck dishes. $$

Vivio's Food & Spirits (313-393-1711; viviosbloodymary.com; 2460 Market St.) The place has a party atmosphere, but its menu is a step up from pub food, with offerings such as steamed mussels, a house specialty. Burgers are a mainstay, but there's also chicken and fish sandwiches, and barbecue ribs. $$

Specialty Foods

While many of the businesses located around the market are wholesale food–type places, there are some retail outlets open to the public.

Al's Fish, Seafood & Chicken (313-393-1722; 2925 Russell) A good source for fresh meats and fish.

Butcher & Packer (800-521-3188; butcher-packer.com; 1468 Gratiot Ave.) The specialty store has all the gear for those who want to make sausage and other meat products at home, including hardware, seasonings, knives, sausage makers, and equipment for smoking meats.

Capital Poultry (313-567-8200; 2456 Riopelle) As fresh as chickens can get.

Detroit Cheese Company (313-877-7674; randys-sausage.com/Detroit_Cheese_Co.html; 1429 Gratiot) The store is adjacent to Randy's Sausage Shop, and offers more than 100 types of cheese, including Cotswold, blue Stilton, and smoked English cheddar.

Germack Pistachio Co. (313-566-0062; germack.com; 2140 Wilkins) The Germack family started operating in Detroit in the 1920s, importing nuts and other food products from the Mediterranean. The warehouse-style store offers pistachios and other nuts.

Rocky Peanut Company (313-567-6871; rockypeanut.com; 2489 Russell) Rocky Russo took over his father's business and along with a brother, Dominic, started selling roasted peanuts at Detroit Tigers games in 1969. Since then the business has expanded. The store is a good source of peanuts at near-wholesale prices.

Checking In

Best places to stay in and around Downtown Detroit.

Atheneum Suite Hotel (313-962-2323; atheneumsuites.com; 1000 Brush Ave.) The luxury hotel is a find in Detroit, and its location in the heart of Greektown gives guests easy access to the major sports stadiums, the Greektown casino, and the district's best restaurants. The modern entranceway is very inviting, and the rooms are sleekly designed, with complimentary wireless Internet and other in-room conveniences. $$$

Detroit Marriott at the Renaissance Center (313-568-8000; www.marriott.com) is the centerpiece of the Renaissance Center complex; its chrome and glass feel creates an appropriate atmosphere for those in the auto business. If you're in town to do business with GM, it's the best place to stay. Those attending the North American International Auto Show will find it convenient to Cobo Center, with a short ride on the People Mover. There are some shops in the hotel, including Pure Detroit (313-259-5100; www.puredetroit.com; Tower 400, Level 1),which offers boutique items along with Detroit-themed apparel, books, photographs, and gifts; and Calumet Market & Spirits (313-259-1122, Tower 300, Level 1), the place to go in the RenCen for beer, wine, liquor, and health and beauty products. $$$

Hilton Garden Inn (313-967-0900; hiltongardeninn.com; 351 Gratiot Ave.) Located in Harmonie Park, a small park and entertainment area, it is close to Greektown and not far from Comerica Park and Ford Field. The rooms are clean and modern and have high-speed Internet service, cable TV, and coffee makers. There is a special work area in the rooms, and there's a fitness center in the hotel. Valet parking is available. $$$

Milner Hotel (313-963-3950; milner-hotels.com; 1526 Centre St.) Centrally located in a 1917 flatiron-type building that has continuously operated as a hotel, this is a great choice for

The historic Milner Hotel.

visitors looking for a moderately priced hotel with charm. The rooms have been refurbished and have a clean, contemporary design. There are some suites with kitchens available. The lobby has retained its early-19th-century look and feel, with high ceilings and ornate light fixtures, along with a tile floor. $$

Westin Book Cadillac Hotel (313-442-1600; westinbookcadillac.com; 1114 Washington Blvd.) The historic hotel, long a downtown landmark, was brought back from the dead with a $200 million renovation in 2008. The neo-Renaissance building was opened in 1923, replacing an earlier Cadillac Hotel that once stood at the northeast corner of Michigan Avenue and Washington Boulevard. The hotel for many years was considered the top place to stay downtown, but in the late 1970s occupancy rates began to fall and by the mid-1980s the property was closed and abandoned. In 2003 the city was able to acquire the building and find a developer to restore it. The hotel once had more than 1,000 rooms, but the renovation work cut that down to 550 by expanding their size to accommodate modern tastes. While the architecture outside is old school, the rooms are updated and large, averaging 475 square feet, with all the modern amenities of a big-city hotel. There's a business center and a retail shop, along with a lobby bar. Valet parking is available. $$$

Casinos

Go out on the town.

It's not Las Vegas, but Detroit does have a casino scene, with three major gambling resorts in the downtown area. There's also a casino across the river in Windsor. The casinos are fairly self-contained, with free parking as well as accommodations and dining options. Typically they offer midrange buffets, bars with pub food, and one high-end restaurant. Even if you're not a gambler, the array of restaurants can be a draw.

Greektown Casino (greektowncasino.com; 888-771-4386; 555 E. Lafayette Blvd.) offers slot machines and card games and free parking in an adjacent structure. There's also a 30-story hotel featuring 400 rooms and suites in a modern building. There are several restaurants in the complex: Bistro 555 and International Buffet; the seafood buffet is a popular draw. Shotz Sports Bar & Grill has walls of TVs tuned in to sporting events, and basic pub food and drinks. The resort's Eclipz Lounge offers entertainment on the weekend and pizza and bar food. $$

MGM Grand (mgmgranddetroit.com; 877-888-2121; 1777 Third St.) The Grand offers lodging and restaurants in addition to casino gambling. The Palette Dining Studio is the place for upscale dining, including prime rib, steaks, seafood, and chicken. The Breeze Dining Court is a less expensive option, serving chicken, wings, burgers, and pizza. The hotel features modern rooms and suites. In the casino, entertainment includes DJs and live acts. $$

Motor City (motorcitycasino.com; 866-782-9622; 2901 Grand River Ave.) The 400-room hotel is one of the few AAA Four Diamond hotels in the Detroit area, and boasts modern rooms, most with a view of the downtown area. Although much of the casino is new construction, the complex includes a historic building, the Wagner Baking Co., built in 1915. The restaurant atop the hotel tower, Iridescence (313-237-6732), requires reservations. The focus there is on American food, but there are plenty of options, including three- and five-course prix fixe dinners. Entrées range from steaks to chicken and seafood. $$$ The Assembly Line Buffet offers more-moderate-priced fare, including a seafood station. $$ The Pit Stop offers burgers and sandwiches. $

Local Flavors

Taste of the town—restaurants, cafés, bars, bistros, etc.

Andiamo Detroit Riverfront (313-567-6700; andiamoitalia.com/detroit; 400 Renaissance Center, Suite A-403). Andiamo is a Detroit chain with nine restaurants serving upscale Italian food in elegant settings, often with entertainment. Entrées include pasta dishes, chicken, steak, and fish and seafood offerings, all with an Italian twist. The baked lasagna with meat sauce topping is a good bet. There's a large selection of wines. $$$

Angelina Italian Bistro (313-962-1355; www.angelinadetroit.com; 1563 Broadway) The inviting bar/restaurant near many of the city's cultural venues is a good place to stop before or after an event. There are small tasting plates that include calamari strips, bruschetta, crab cakes, and Italian sausage. As for entrées, the wild mushroom risotto is a good choice for a light appetite, and there is a seafood risotto and a Sicilian chicken. $$$

Bourbon Steak (313-465-1644; www.mgmgranddetroit.com; 1777 Third St., located in the MGM Grand casino) You don't have to be a gambler to enjoy a meal here, and chances are good that the bar/restaurant will appeal to your American tastes. The menu focuses on hearty midwestern foods, such as fried chicken, venison, beef short ribs, and steaks cooked over a wood grill. Side dishes include whipped potatoes, broccoli and cheddar, and grilled asparagus. $$$

Caucus Club Restaurant (313-965-4970; caucusclubdetroit.com; 150 W. Congress) The old-school, clubby restaurant opened in 1952 in the Penobscot Building and has been serving lunch and dinner to judges, lawyers, bankers, and stockbrokers ever since. Barbra Streisand performed here in 1961 and it was one of her first paying jobs. The menu has been updated a bit, but it still focuses on ribs, steak, burgers, and fish. Open Monday–Saturday (no lunch served Saturday). $$$

Cliff Bell's (313-961-2543; cliffbells.com; 2030 Park Ave.) is a jazz venue and restaurant that offers the flavor of old Detroit. While the city is known for its musical heritage, there wasn't always a place to listen to jazz until Bell's reopened in 2005

Cliff Beels off Grand Circus Park in downtown Detroit offers jazz.

after a renovation. The original bar/restaurant opened in 1935 and was owned and operated by Cliff Bell, who had spent the Prohibition years running speakeasies, or blind pigs, as many Detroiters called them. Bell was the son of an Irish saloonkeeper who was also a socialist labor agitator, and the younger Bell followed his father into the tavern trade. He ran the establishment from its opening until his retirement in 1958. The menu ranges from pork to steak and lake perch, and there are some creative meals such as pork bellies braised with pork and beans and Faygo brand root beer, from the local soft drink maker. $$$

Detroit Seafood Market (313-962-4180; thedetroitseafoodmarket.com; 1435 Randolph St.) Located on the first floor of an attractive brick building, the restaurant offers a vast array of seafood, with a few meat dishes tossed in for good measure. A top choice is the steamer bucket, which includes lobster, clams, crab, and mussels. $$$

Forty-two degrees north (313-568-8699; Marriott Hotel at the Renaissance Center) The restaurant, part of the Marriott, offers breakfast, lunch, and dinner and has a bar with a good view. Entrées include burgers, meatloaf, steak, and salmon. There are lunch buffets that include southern, Italian, and Mediterranean foods. $$$

Opus One (313-961-7766; opus-one.com; 565 E. Larned St.) Opus One is a destination for many metro Detroiters, serving French and American dishes and offering a large wine list. It has an elegant dining room, and a cozy, casual bar that has its own menu. The dining room menu covers all the bases, with beef, lamb, pork, and seafood, and it's easy to understand, free of the pretensions often encountered in expensive restaurants. Entrées include pan-seared Chilean sea bass, lake perch, and a rack of lamb done Greek style. $$$

24Grille (313-964-3821; 204 Michigan Ave.) This place exemplifies the resurgence of down-

The 24Grille in the Westin Book Cadillac Hotel.

town Detroit. It's located in the Westin Book Cadillac Hotel, which opened in 1924 but fell on hard times and was closed in the 1980s until a $200 million renovation enabled it to reopen in 2008. The hotel was long a bastion of high style during its heyday, hosting conventions and weddings for Detroit's upper-middle-class brides and grooms. The menu focuses on steaks and seafood. Entrées are $136 per couple. $$$

Greektown

Fishbone's Rhythm Kitchen Café (313-965-4600; fishbone susa.com; 400 Monroe) All isn't Greek in Greektown. Fishbone's is a favorite of Detroiters with a taste for New Orleans–style food and music. Locals stop by here on a regular basis for the seafood, steaks, and even sushi. Try the farm-raised fried catfish or the shrimp Creole. There's also chicken, ribs, and pasta. For lunch, the seafood gumbo is a good choice. Bands perform often on Saturdays. $$

Golden Fleece (313-962-7093; 525 Monroe) This place has seen better days and could use some cleaning up, but the gyros sandwiches—lamb on flat bread—are so large you can barely finish them. It's a good place for lunch. $

The Laikon Café (313-963-7058; 569 Monroe) is where you'll find many of Detroit's Greek Americans enjoying a traditional meal of lamb and rice, especially on Sunday afternoons. It's not as fancy as other places in the district, but it does serve some of the most authentic Greek fare. For starters, try the potent mix of mashed potatoes and garlic. Traditional dishes include spinach pie. Another good bet is the garlic lamb. Family-style service is an option. $$

The New Parthenon (313-963-8888; 547 Monroe St.) is a great blend of the old and new. Diners will find traditional Greek food in a contemporary setting. On a recent stop with a large party, we took the waiter's suggestion to go with a family-style dinner, and let him order for us, much to my delight. We were served appetizers of Greek sausage, and saganaki, a flaming goat cheese. There was plenty of bread, and Greek salad with beets and Greek cheese. Then there were platters of lamb chops, rice, peas, and spinach pie. We also ordered several bottles of retsina, a white wine with a taste of pine resin. My wife doesn't much care for it, but I've taken to it over the years and think it goes well with lamb. $$

Pegasus Taverna (313-964-6800; pegasustavernas.com; 558

Pegasus Taverna in Greektown.

Monroe) is newer and trendier than its neighbors, and usually more crowded. While traditional Greek lamb dishes are offered, the menu is expansive. $$

Red Smoke Barbecue (313-962-2100; redsmokebarbeque.com; 573 Monroe) Southern-style smoked pork, beef, and chicken takes center stage at this casual restaurant. There's also a bar. $$

Sports Bars

Cheli's Chili Bar (313-961-1700; chelischilibar.com; 47 E. Adams Ave.) Owned by former Red Wing Chris Chelios, the place is dominated by a hockey theme and attracts fans before and after games. The menu is a step up from standard burgers and includes ribs, calamari, pulled pork, beef brisket, soups, and, of course, chili. There's a second location in Dearborn (see entry in Dearborn chapter). $

Coach's Corner (313-963-4000; coachescornerdetroit.com; 1465 Centre St.) is a short walk from both Ford Field and Comerica Park, and offers big-screen TVs for fans, and a rowdy atmosphere for watching a game or having a burger and a beer after an event. Pub food prevails, but there are also some Mexican offerings and a few Greek sandwiches. $

Elwood Bar and Grill (313-962-BEER; elwoodgrill.com; 300 Adams Ave.), is perfectly located near both Comerica Park and Ford Field, attracting football and baseball fans to the art deco structure. The 1937 building was previously located at the corner of Woodward and Elizabeth, and its turret and sleek-looking tile exterior of blue and white was long a fixture on the Woodward corridor. However, by the late 1990s it was in the way of plans to build Ford Field and Comerica Park. Instead of tearing it down, developers moved it to its current location at the corner of Adams and Brush. $

Hockeytown Café (313-965-9500; hockeytowncafe.com; 2301 Woodward Ave.) The food is nothing special, but it's the place to be before or after a Detroit Red Wings hockey game or when the Tigers are playing in town at nearby Comerica Park. Hockeytown is plastered with giant TV sets tuned in to sports events. The fare is mostly burgers and beer. When the home team wins, it's difficult to get inside. $$

Post Bar (313-962-1293; postbar.com/detroit; 408 W. Congress St.) Another great spot for hockey fans. It's near the Joe Louis Arena, and attracts those going to the games. It's a burger-and-beer type place that's popular with the young and single set. $

Watering Holes

Anchor Bar (313-964-9127; 450 W. Fort St.) The bar has been in various locations over the past 40

The dive bar vibe is alive and well in the downtown area.

years, and it was once the hangout of hard-drinking newspaper reporters and editors who toiled away at the Detroit Free Press and Detroit News. These days it's more of a sports bar, with large-screen TVs. Burgers are a mainstay on the menu. $

Beaubien Street Saloon (313-961-5766; 641 Beaubien St.) The drinks are cheap, there's an old pool table, and there is beer on tap or in the bottle. There's some pub food on offer, but the real draw is the dive-bar feel of the place.

Checker Bar & Grill (313-961-9249; 124 Cadillac Square) It's a favorite burger bar of some Detroiters, but they also serve fresh perch and cabbage rolls. The décor is eclectic and hasn't changed much over the years. $

Detroiter Bar (313-963-3355; 655 Beaubien St.) Burgers and other pub food are on the menu at this traditional-style Detroit shot-and-a-beer tavern. $

Detroit Beer Co. (313-962-1529; detroitbeerco.com; 1529 Broadway St.) This brewpub occupies the first two floors of the Hartz Building, which has been recently restored. Among its most popular beers are Detroit Dwarf and the People Mover Porter. The menu includes pizza, pasta, and sandwiches. $

Jacoby's German Biergarten (313-962-7067; www.jacobysbar.com; 624 Brush St.) The old redbrick tavern is one of the few reminders that the neighborhood in which it sits was once a German enclave. The historic establishment has been around since the late 19th century, called Jake's Tavern when it was owned by the Voight Brewing Company. In 1904 a personable bartender from Luxembourg, Albert Jacoby, took over management, and the place was run by several generations of the family until it was sold in the 1990s. Its German heritage is reflected in its menu, which includes potato pancakes, sausages, German sausage soup, and spaetzle, along with standard pub food. There are a large number of German beers. The second floor hosts bands on occasion. $$

Sweet Water Tavern (313-962-2210; 400 E. Congress St.) It's located in a historic late-19th-century building, and is a favorite lunch and after-work pub for workers in the downtown area. The fare is mostly pub-style burgers and such. $

1001

2

Woodward Avenue Cruise

GRAND CIRCUS PARK, MIDTOWN, HAMTRAMCK, HIGHLAND PARK, FERNDALE, ROYAL OAK, BIRMINGHAM, PONTIAC

THERE'S NO BETTER WAY to see metro Detroit than to take a drive on Woodward, which has long been the region's main street and has the distinction of having the road designation M-1.

Detroit's founding fathers laid out the city in a way that resembles spokes in a wheel, more than 100 years before the advent of automobiles. Woodward Avenue was named for Augustus B. Woodward (1774–1827), who served as the first chief justice of the Michigan Territory. After being appointed to the job by President Thomas Jefferson, he arrived in Detroit on June 30, 1805, and found the territorial capital in ruins from a fire.

Using French-born planner Pierre Charles L'Enfant's layout for Washington, DC, Woodward and several other officials came up with a rebuilding plan for Detroit that gave it the spokes-in-a-wheel design; this included Woodward, which then ran from the Detroit River to Grand Circus Park. Ever since, Woodward has been the city's main street.

The Woodward corridor is home to many of the city's cultural institutions, government buildings, department stores, downtown

LEFT: Woodward Avenue is the city's main street.

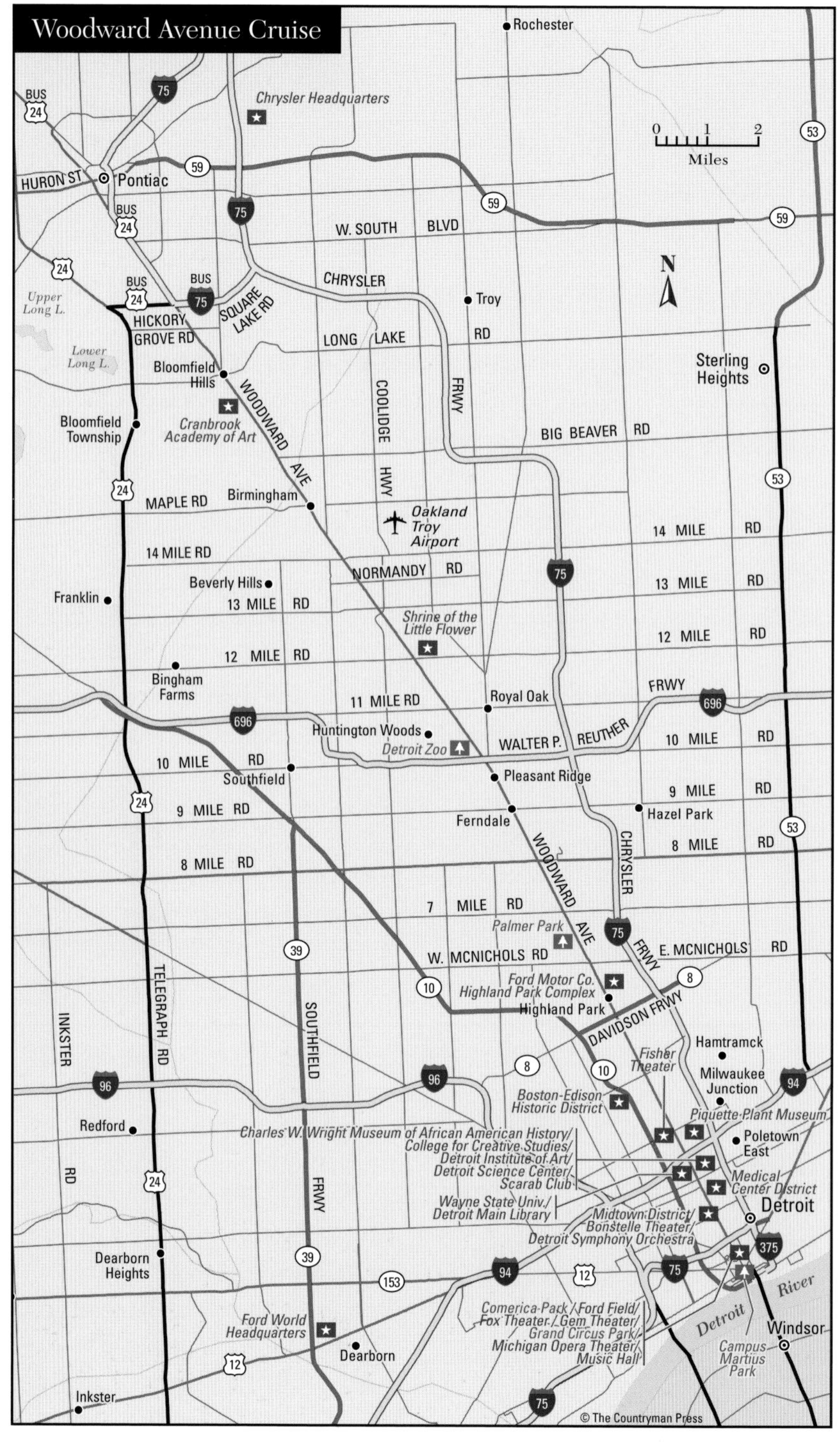
Woodward Avenue Cruise
Rochester
Chrysler Headquarters
Pontiac
HURON ST
W. SOUTH BLVD
CHRYSLER
Troy
Upper Long L.
Lower Long L.
HICKORY GROVE RD
SQUARE LAKE RD
LONG LAKE RD
Sterling Heights
Bloomfield Hills
Bloomfield Township
Cranbrook Academy of Art
WOODWARD AVE
COOLIDGE HWY
FRWY
BIG BEAVER RD
MAPLE RD
Birmingham
Oakland Troy Airport
14 MILE RD
NORMANDY RD
Beverly Hills
Franklin
13 MILE RD
Shrine of the Little Flower
12 MILE RD
Bingham Farms
11 MILE RD
Royal Oak
FRWY
Huntington Woods
Detroit Zoo
WALTER P. REUTHER
10 MILE RD
Southfield
Pleasant Ridge
9 MILE RD
Hazel Park
Ferndale
8 MILE RD
CHRYSLER
7 MILE RD
Palmer Park
W. MCNICHOLS RD
E. MCNICHOLS RD
Ford Motor Co. Highland Park Complex
Highland Park
DAVIDSON FRWY
INKSTER RD
TELEGRAPH RD
SOUTHFIELD FRWY
Hamtramck
Fisher Theater
Milwaukee Junction
Boston-Edison Historic District
Piquette Plant Museum
Redford
Charles W. Wright Museum of African American History/
College for Creative Studies/
Detroit Institute of Art/
Detroit Science Center/
Scarab Club
Poletown East
Medical Center District
Wayne State Univ./
Detroit Main Library
Detroit
Midtown District/
Bonstelle Theater/
Detroit Symphony Orchestra
Dearborn Heights
Comerica Park / Ford Field/
Fox Theater / Gem Theater/
Grand Circus Park/
Michigan Opera Theater/
Music Hall
Detroit River
Ford World Headquarters
Dearborn
Windsor
Campus Martius Park
Inkster
Miles
N
© The Countryman Press

entertainment districts, historic churches, and sports stadiums. Henry Ford's first factory is here, as is Wayne State University, the city's medical center, and historic mansions of the well-to-do. Some structures are still in use and others have long been boarded up. Farther out, in Oakland County, Woodward traverses through many of the region's pricy suburbs such as Birmingham and Bloomfield Hills and ends in Pontiac.

Woodward was the first street in the world to have a mile of concrete paving, which was done between Six and Seven Mile Roads in 1909.

Although downtown Detroit was the historical center of finance, law, and culture, Detroit is different from other industrial northern cities in that significant hubs are located outside downtown: the headquarters of Ford Motor Co. and the Chrysler Corporation have become city centers in and of themselves.

Riverfront to Grand Circus Park

Woodward in downtown Detroit was once where the upper middle class shopped, worked, attended church, and went to the theater or movies. In the 19th century it was served by streetcars, and these days there's talk of putting a light-rail line along the corridor.

The First Congregational Church on Woodward is one of many historic churches lining the avenue.

An appropriate starting point downtown is the Renaissance Center, General Motors Headquarters (see chapter 1). The glimmering complex is on Jefferson, just east of where Woodward begins, near the river. The structure, built in the 1970s, was to be a symbol of a resurging Detroit. It towers over other downtown buildings from an earlier era, ironically attesting to the fact that the city has made only stumbling steps toward resurgence.

Downtown Detroit along Woodward Avenue.

Downtown Detroit is an uneven place, with many vacant buildings, many of them art deco gems that have outlived their usefulness, but there have been great strides made in recent years to revive and find new uses for them. While they once housed the offices of doctors and dentists, and served as retailing space, they have been transformed into condos, entertainment venues, and bars and restaurants.

GRAND CIRCUS PARK

The park is a short drive north on Woodward from Jefferson Avenue, and was part of the city's rebuilding plan after a fire destroyed much of Detroit in 1805. Grand Circus was once the city's outer limits. The park was established in 1850 and is a five-acre refuge of greenery in the midst of concrete and buildings. It was the site of a speech by General George Armstrong Custer, a Michigan native, to Detroiters gathered to mourn the death of President Lincoln in 1865. Named for an influential Michigan politician and industrialist, the Russell Alger Memorial Fountain is in the middle of the park, which is bisected by Woodward Avenue. There are also statues of William Cotter Maybury and Hazen Pingree, early city leaders. The park is encircled by historic buildings including the David Broderick Tower, the David Whitney Building, the Kales Building, and the Central United Methodist Church. Although some of the buildings are empty, renovation efforts are planned.

The Grand Circus Park area was a hub of first-run movie theaters from the 1920s to the 1960s, and it's still an entertainment district, with restaurants and cultural attractions and sports venues nearby. The area has long been home to the performing arts, and most of the city's major performance venues are located near it, including the Music Hall Center for the Performing Arts (313-887-8500; music hall.org; 350 Madison), just east of Grand Circus Park on Madison. This music venue opened in 1928 with much help from Matilda Dodge Wilson (1883–1967), the widow of the founder of Dodge Motor Co., who commissioned an architect to design the hall and paid for its construction. Since then the 1,700-seat theater has been home to classical, jazz, and pop performances. It now offers pop, big band, and other productions on the main stage, and smaller jazz concerts in its jazz café.

Nearby the park on Broadway is the Detroit Opera House (313-

A statue of Hazen Pingree, mayor of Detroit in the 1890s and then governor of Michigan, overlooks Grand Circus Park off Woodward.

961-3500; motopera.org; 1526 Broadway). The building dates to 1922, when it opened as the Capitol Theatre. It has undergone several reincarnations over the years, eventually opening in 1996 as the Detroit Opera House. The opera season runs from the fall through the spring and usually includes standard productions. Historic tours of the building are offered.

The Detroit Opera House is a major cultural venue in downtown Detroit.

Several blocks north of Grand Circus Park on Woodward is one of Detroit's restored gems, The Fox Theatre (313-965-3099; olympiaentertainment.com; 2211 Woodward), which was built during the city's heyday in the 1920s when art deco was at its zenith. The theater opened in 1928 as part of the Fox movie empire and was one in a chain of ornate theaters throughout the nation. The Fox seated more than 5,000 people when it opened, and for decades it was the top movie palace in downtown Detroit, but by the late 1970s the theater had fallen on hard times. It was saved by Mike Ilitch, owner of the Little Caesars Pizza chain as well as the Detroit Red Wings hockey team and the Tigers baseball team, who spent about $12 million to renovate the building during the 1980s, a low point for Detroit, and moved his pizza-chain headquarters into the office space there. The grandness of the building, with its distinctive marquee, bedecked with winged lions in neon lights, was a signal to observers that the city had a future. The interior is a bizarre but opulent blend of Chinese, Middle Eastern, and Asian design. The theater now hosts Broadway shows and music acts.

Grand Circus Park to Midtown

The drive from downtown to midtown is only a couple of miles, but it's clear that you've entered an uneven neighborhood. There are some true gems here, but also a fair share of empty lots and abandoned buildings. Detroit boomed during the 1920s when the art deco style of building was at its zenith, and the midtown area is a draw to architecture buffs.

Along Woodward, drivers will find the Bonstelle Theatre (313-577-0852; bonstelle.com; 3424 Woodward). The theater is on the National Register of Historic Places, and was built in 1902 as the Temple Beth-El. The beaux-arts structure was converted into a theater in 1922 and it's now owned by Wayne State University, which uses it for student productions. The season runs from the fall through late spring.

You can't miss The Whitney (313-832-5700; thewhitney.com, 4421 Woodward Ave.), billed as "Detroit's most iconic mansion," a remnant of an era during the late 19th and early 20th centuries when Woodward was a desirable address for upper-middle-class Detroit families. Since 1986 the 52-room Whitney house has been an upscale restaurant patronized by concert and event goers in the downtown and midtown areas (see Restaurants, Midtown). The 21,000-square-foot residence was built between 1890 and 1894 by David Whitney Jr., a wealthy lumber baron. The structure is made of South Dakota Jasper, a pink granite stone. It was listed on the National Register of Historic Places in 1972.

The Bonstelle Theatre stages Wayne State student productions.

The historic Whitney mansion is now an elegant midtown restaurant.

Farther along on Woodward is The Max M. Fisher Music Center (313-576-5111; detroit symphony.com; 3711 Woodward Ave.). Known to Detroiters as "the Max," the midtown venue features the restored Orchestra

Wayne State University

Wayne State is the largest state school in Detroit, with an enrollment of about 31,000 students. Most of the midtown campus is on Cass Avenue, but there are facilities along the Woodward corridor. Wayne State's medical school has supplied health professionals to several major hospitals in the area, including the nearby Detroit Medical Center district. Along with the Bonstelle, Wayne operates the **Hilberry Theatre** (313-577-2972; hilberry.com; 4743 Cass Ave.), which stages student productions and other events.

In recent years Wayne State has constructed student housing and helped rehabilitate older apartment buildings in parts of the Cass corridor that had been on the decline for decades, creating a vibrant scene that has lured young people back to the city. The university is considered one of the major players in the redevelopment of Detroit.

Old Main, 4841 Cass, an academic building on Wayne's campus, has been renovated and is worth seeing, especially its clock tower. The red brick structure was constructed in 1896 as a high school, but eventually became the first major building used by Wayne State. It has served the school in many capacities over the years, but is now home to Wayne's College of Liberal Arts and Sciences.

Also on the campus is the **Walter P. Reuther Library** (313-577-4024; reuther.wayne.edu, 5401 Cass Ave.), which is named for the labor leader and United Auto Workers president. The library's collection focuses on labor and urban affairs, and is the official repository for 12 national labor unions.

Hall, where Detroit Symphony Orchestra performances are held. The season runs from fall through spring. The venue also hosts other musical events.

Just north of Mack Avenue and about a block east of Woodward is the Detroit Medical Center, which includes the Wayne State University School of Medicine, Children's Hospital of Michigan, Detroit Receiving Hospital, Harper University Hospital, the John D. Dingell VA Medical Hospital, and the Karmanos Cancer Institute.

The medical center has spurred economic growth in the corridor, and the many high-rise apartment buildings here attest to the revitalization of this once-ailing area.

The Detroit Institute of Arts.

MIDTOWN

The midtown area is home to some of Detroit's most important museums and institutions, perhaps the most visited of which is the Detroit Institute of Arts (313-833-7900; www.dia.org; 5200 Woodward). The DIA, which is owned by the city, has an art collection valued at more than $1 billion; there are 100 galleries in its block-long historic beaux-arts-style building, which opened in 1927. The museum was founded in the 1880s and opened its first building in 1888 in a building on East Jefferson at Hastings Street.

Over the years the museum has received endowments from auto barons, wealthy industrialists, and newspaper owners. The building is close to Wayne State University and the main branch of the Detroit Public Library. It also contains the Detroit Film Theatre, a 1,200-seat venue that screens foreign and art films. The DIA's collection contains works by well-known artists including John James Audubon, Alexander Calder, John Singleton Copley, Winslow Homer, Georgia O'Keeffe, Frederic Remington, John Singer Sargent, Andrew Wyeth, and James Whistler. There are also ancient Egyptian artifacts, armor from the Middle Ages, and tapestries.

The biggest controversy to hit the Detroit Institute of Arts was the painting, in the early 1930s, of a set of murals for the museum by the Mexican artist Diego Rivera (1886–1957). Rivera was a Marxist whose *Detroit Industry* murals depict factory workers in auto plants.

Observers on the left felt that the works didn't go far enough in

The Cass Corridor

For decades **Cass Avenue between downtown and W. Grand Boulevard** represented the best and worst of Detroit, with many of the city's most important institutions located along it, but mixed in were blocks of decaying buildings where prostitution and drug dealing thrived.

General Motors long had its headquarters in the north side of the corridor at Cass and W. Grand Boulevard, before its move downtown to the Renaissance Center, and along Cass lay Wayne State University, the Detroit Masonic Temple, and, farther downtown, numerous office buildings. Many historic Victorian homes in the **Brush Park Historic District** are also in the corridor. Cass Technical High School, one of the city's best schools dating back decades, is nearby as well.

The district has long been associated with the 1960s counterculture, when activists of all sorts set up shop along Cass. Wayne State's student newspaper, the *South End,* was named during that era. Although the reference is now dated, the title was intended to convey that it was south of the General Motors headquarters, and on the other side of the issues from that of the giant automaker.

The district has also had a long relationship with rock 'n' roll. The now-defunct rock magazine *Cream* was first published in the corridor, and eventually became a national publication that stayed true to its industrial midwestern roots by poking fun at headliner rock bands of the area, while helping the careers of such Detroit bands as Bob Seger, Mitch Ryder, Alice Cooper, the MC5, and Iggy Pop.

describing the harsh conditions in the factories; those on the right thought that the murals were too harsh on factory management. Ironically, it was one of the auto barons, Edsel Ford, the son of Henry Ford, who came to the rescue when one faction wanted to have the murals painted over. He was able to persuade critics that Rivera's works should be judged on their artistic merits. The images are dramatic, and speak to anyone who has spent any time working in one of the city's factories. Men are toiling at their tasks, clad in overalls and work clothing, while members of management walk around watching, wearing white shirts and ties. There is a distinct separation between

The Masonic of Detroit.

Another institution on Cass is the **Old Miami** bar (313-831-3830; 3930 Cass Ave.), which for many years served as the unofficial hangout for returning Vietnam veterans who didn't feel comfortable at American Legion halls.

The **Detroit Masonic Temple** (313-832-7100; themasonic.com; 500 Temple St.) is thought to be the world's largest Masonic temple, and is also home to a theater that musicians have praised for its excellent acoustics. The neo-Gothic temple was dedicated and opened for use in 1926, and over the years it has been the center of Masonic activity in the Detroit area. The 14-floor building has 1,037 rooms and is on the National Register of Historic Places. The theater seats more than 4,000 people and has hosted rock concerts, classical music performances, comedians, and other acts.

the classes.

Other museums, institutions, and art galleries have sprung up near the DIA over the years, including the College for Creative Studies (collegeforcreativestudies.edu; 201 East Kirby). The center's automotive-design program places a number of its graduates in jobs with Detroit automakers. The school traces its roots back to 1906 when the Society of Arts and Crafts was formed, and by the 1920s it was offering an arts education program, but the school did not formally become a college until 1962. The private school offers degrees in various arts areas, including animation, digital media, arts education, crafts, fine arts, and graphic design.

The Museum of Contemporary Art Detroit (313-8312-6622; mocadetroit.org; 4454 Woodward Ave.) is housed in a 22,000-square-foot building that offers a large exhibition space for contemporary artists. There are also lectures, musical performances, films, and literary readings. Admission is free.

The Scarab Club (313-831-1250; scarabclub.org; 217 Farnsworth St.) was founded in 1907 and has evolved over the years to encompass a gallery and studio, which also hosts musical performances. It was called the Hopkin Club after its founder, Robert Hopkin, a marine painter, but was renamed the Scarab Club in 1913, and its current building was opened in 1928. There are many examples of Pewabic Pottery tiles (see Pewabic Pottery entry, chapter 4), which were inspired by the arts and crafts movement of the early 20th century. The club has hosted many social events over the years. The building is an example of Northern Italian Renaissance–style architecture. There are two contemporary galleries, and eight exhibitions a year, which are open to the public and are free. The second-floor lounge is for members only and is lined with chestnut walls, a stone fireplace, and art deco decorations. Many of the original founders were involved in the auto industry and included designers, advertising illustrators, graphic artists, photographers, architects, and business owners.

Not far from the DIA is the Detroit Artists Market (313-832-8540; detroitartistsmarket.org; 4719 Woodward Ave.). Founded in 1932, the market, promotes the works of local artists with exhibits and sales. Open Tuesday to Saturday.

The Detroit Artists Market in the midtown area showcases the works of local artists.

Across the street from the DIA on Woodward is the main branch of the Detroit Public Library (313-833-1490; detroit.lib.mi.us; 5201 Woodward Ave.) Detroit's first library dates to 1865, when a public reading room opened at a high school then located at State and Gris-

The main branch of the Detroit Public Library is on Woodward in midtown.

wold Streets, but it wasn't until 1921 that the main library opened at its current location on Woodward. The library houses the Burton Historical Collection of documents, maps, and pictures of the city's history. The collection was put together by Clarence M. Burton (1853–1932), who started the Detroit Historical Society. Over 40 years Burton collected and organized original documents and the personal papers of prominent Michigan residents. By 1914 the collection contained 30,000 volumes, 40,000 pamphlets, and 500,000 papers. The collection was moved to the main library in 1921.

Other Midtown Museums

Detroit Historical Museum (313-833-1805; detroithistorical.org; 5401 Woodward Ave.) The museum, which chronicles Detroit's history from a fur-trading outpost to the auto capital of the world, attracts about 250,000 visitors annually, many of them students. The museum was founded by the Detroit Historical Society, which was started by

Where Motown Was Born

Motown Historical Museum (313-875-2264; motownmuseum.com; 2648 W. Grand Blvd.) Visitors can see where Berry Gordy and his cohorts created the Motown sound in the early 1960s. The house-turned-music-studio and offices-turned-museum west of Woodward is where talented Motown artists such as Diana Ross and the Supremes, Stevie Wonder, Smokey Robinson, the Temptations, the Four Tops, the Contours, Marvin Gaye, Funk Brothers, Jackson 5, Rare Earth, and Martha and the Vandellas got their starts. The record company eventually turned into a giant, and moved to Los Angeles in 1972.

Clarence M. Burton, a Detroit lawyer and historian, and it was housed in various buildings until the present one was constructed and dedicated in 1951. A top attraction is some old cobblestones from Detroit streets and replicas of buildings from the 19th century. More recently the museum added an exhibit that traces the history of the auto assembly line and includes equipment from the General Motors Clark Street Cadillac plant. Admission is $6 for adults, $4 for seniors and children and students.

Detroit Science Center (313-734-3623; detroitsciencecenter.org; 5020 John R St.) The center is home to the Chrysler IMAX Dome Theatre, the Dassault Systèmes Planetarium, DTE Energy Sparks Theatre, the Chrysler Science Stage, and a Science Hall for traveling exhibits. Children enjoy hands-on displays. Basic admission, including one IMAX show, is $13.95 for adults, $11.95 for seniors and kids 2–12. Additional charge may apply for special exhibits.

Charles H. Wright Museum of African American History (313-494-5800; chwmuseum.org; 315 E. Warren Ave.) The museum is thought to be the largest permanent exhibit of African America culture and is housed in a 12,000-square-foot building. A major ongoing exhibit is "And Still We Rise: Our Journey through African American History and Culture," which covers the horrors of the slave trade and the experience of African American slaves, the Underground Railroad, emancipation, and the civil rights movement. Admission is $8 for adults and $5 for children 3–12.

The midtown area has its share of noteworthy shops. Some highlights are listed here.

Bureau of Urban Living (313-833-9336; bureauliving.com; 460 W. Canfield St.) Popular with in-the-know city shoppers for its selection of home goods, stationery, and chic and pretty stuff.

City Bird (313-831-9146; ilovecitybird.com; 460 W. Canfield St.) A lovingly curated, Michigan-centric shop featuring gifts and useful items made by the Detroit-loving brother-sister owners and other local artists and crafters.

Peoples Records & Collectibles (313-831-0864; peoplesdetroit.com; 3161 Woodward Ave.) Relocated after a 2008 fire, the shop stocks used LPs, 45s and 78s, in a wide variety of genres. The goods are decently organized for browsing, and Peoples has a friendly and knowledgeable staff if you're looking for something specific or just want to talk wax.

Midtown to Grand Boulevard

For many years this was called the New Center area; it was considered Detroit's "second downtown" anchored by General Motors headquarters, the Fisher Building, and Henry Ford Hospital as well as dozens of thriving restaurants, bars, and related businesses. The area was hard hit when General Motors moved from W. Grand Boulevard to the Renaissance Center on the Detroit River, but it has stabilized in recent years.

Detroiters in the 19th century thought that Grand Boulevard would be the ultimate city limits; the idea for such a thoroughfare was based on a similar plan for Paris. While "the Boulevard," as Detroiters call it, is a commercial district in the Woodward corridor, it is residential through much of the 12-mile path that takes it in a U shape around the central city, ending on both its east and west portions at the Detroit River. Grand Boulevard was built in the early 1890s during horse-and-buggy days, and palatial homes quickly sprang up on what was then seen as a pleasing, park-like corridor. Its planners didn't foresee the rapid growth of the city when it became the center for auto production in the early 20th century.

The former General Motors headquarters is at W. Grand Boulevard between Cass and Second, and is now called Cadillac Place. General Motors built the 15-story, block-long structure to serve as its

The Fisher Theatre in Midtown.

headquarters and used it from 1923 to 2001, when it moved to the Renaissance Center. It was designed by Henry Ford's favored architect, Albert Kahn. The neoclassical structure is on the National Historic Landmark list. The building is now used by the State of Michigan for its workers, and houses the Michigan Court of Appeals.

The Fisher Building is a 30-story art-deco-style office building at Second and W. Grand Boulevard that opened in 1928 and housed the offices of many medical practitioners for decades. It's also home to the 2,000-seat Fisher Theatre, which has hosted many Broadway shows and musical performances. Its ornate Aztec interior unfortunately fell victim to an interior renovation, and it now has a midcentury modern look. It's also home to one of the city's most popular radio stations, WJR (760 AM), which has been a tenant since the building opened. The Detroit Public Schools has its offices in the building.

Also in the area is the Henry Ford Hospital (313-916-2600; henryfordhealth.com; 2799 W. Grand Blvd.) The hospital was built by Henry Ford and opened in 1915, and has since expanded into a modern medical center and a health system with other hospitals and medical facilities scattered throughout the metro Detroit area. The Detroit facility is still the main branch of the health system and operates an 805-bed hospital and an emergency room.

Grand Boulevard to Eight Mile

This part of the Woodward corridor was the Silicon Valley of the auto industry in the early 20th century and the home to Ford, General Motors, and Chrysler plants and offices, as well as the personal residences of many of the auto pioneers.

It's a strange mix of industrial, residential, and commercial areas that were once the hub of activity for factory owners, management, and workers alike. Along the corridor Ford built his first two factories; General Motors had and still has extensive operations; and Chrysler headquartered in Highland Park until moving to Auburn Hills. Apart from the General Motors Poletown plant, the old factories lie vacant and unused. Even some of their names sound unfamiliar, such as the Packard Plant.

Along the corridor are two cities within the city of Detroit, Hamtramck and Highland Park. Highland Park has suffered the same urban decay as Detroit, but Hamtramck, with an enclave of Polish Americans, has remained vibrant and is home to many restaurants and bars. Its population also includes newcomers intent on living an urban experience and, in recent years, many Muslims.

The corridor has its roots in industry that developed at a place called Milwaukee Junction, which is located in an area bounded by E. Grand Boulevard, St. Aubin Street, Hamtramck Drive, and the Chrysler Freeway. It was the junction of the Detroit and Milwaukee and Grand Trunk Western Railroads, which gave early automakers easy access to transportation.

Henry Ford was one of the first to take advantage of the junction and established the Piquette Plant, which built some of the first Model Ts. The plant is now a small museum.

Other automakers followed Ford to Milwaukee Junction. Some are no longer around, like Hupmobile, Anderson Electric Car Company, Brush Motor Car Co., Packard, Oakland, and Studebaker, and others are still in business, such as Cadillac and Dodge (Chrysler Corp.). The area was also home to Fisher Body, which grew from being a maker of wooden carriages to building the metal frames of automobiles. The importance of the area faded in the late 1920s when Ford built his Ford Rouge Complex in Dearborn and General Motors and Chrysler started opening plants in other areas of the city.

Auto barons and industry executives took up residence along the Woodward corridor when the industry started to boom in the 1910s and early 1920s. The Boston-Edison Historic District is located west

Ford's First Plant

The **Ford Piquette Plant** at 411 Piquette Street, east of Woodward, now houses the **Model T Automotive Heritage Complex** (313-872-8759; tplex.org). Henry Ford actually lived in a duplex within walking distance of the plant, which was built in 1904 and was his first large facility. These days, it looks much like it would have appeared when Ford operated there. The redbrick, mill-style building backs up to the railroad tracks, and there are old photos of workers putting Model Ts on railroad cars to be shipped. It was in the plant that Ford and a team of engineers developed the Model T, which went into production in 1908. The first one sold was shipped to a medical professional in Chicago, but business wasn't brisk at first, with only 11 cars sold the first month. At the time, most cars were hand built and were significantly more expensive than Fords, thus the company was able to build vehicles for a market that previously saw cars as being beyond their economic reach. When business picked up, Ford outgrew the Piquette Avenue plant, and by 1910 production was moved north up the Woodward corridor to a new plant in Highland Park.

Model T buffs, many of whom belong to the Model T Ford Club of America, are avid fans of the Automotive Heritage Complex, the only example of an early Detroit auto factory that's open to the public. Ford wasn't part of corporate America when the plant went into production, and there's a focus on some of the colorful characters in the company's early history. The third floor of the plant has not been painted since Ford left in 1910, and it gives visitors the feeling of what it would have been like to work there. The original "Positively No Smoking" signs are still visible, probably put there at the request of Henry, who was an antismoking advocate long before that attitude became prevalent.

The exhibits focus on the stationary assembly process, which was used before the development of the moving assembly line. The museum is open from early April to late November, Wednesday through Sunday. Admission is $10.

of Woodward on four streets, West Boston Boulevard, Chicago Boulevard, Edison Avenue, and Longfellow Avenue, and stretches to Linwood Avenue. Many of the 900 homes here were built in the Colonial Revival style, although other styles were also used. Henry

Virginia Park.

Ford built an Italian Renaissance home at the corner of Edison and Second at a cost of nearly $500,000 in 1907 and lived there until moving to his Fair Lane estate in Dearborn.

Another historic neighborhood in the area is Virginia Park. Located near Henry Ford Hospital and Cadillac Place (the former General Motors headquarters), the neighborhood on both sides of Woodward Avenue just north of Grand Boulevard was favored by medical professionals and GM white-collar workers. It was developed between 1893 and 1915, and the architectural styles include Tudor, neo-Georgian, bungalow, and arts and crafts. The homes are still mostly well kept. There is a strong neighborhood association.

HAMTRAMCK

Located just east of the Woodward corridor and nestled between the Chrysler and Edsel Ford Freeways, the city of Hamtramck has long been a working-class Polish enclave, and is a cultural draw for Detroiters with Polish roots. There are clubs and bars here favored by young urban professionals (see Watering Holes, Hamtramck), and numerous Polish restaurants (see Restaurants, Hamtramck).

Many metro Detroiters wrongly assume "Hamtramck" is a Polish name, but it's actually French. It was named for a French Canadian soldier, Jean-François Hamtramck, who was the first commander of Fort Shelby in Detroit.

St. Florian Roman Catholic Church has long served the Polish American community in Hamtramck.

The Polish started to arrive in 1914 when a Dodge plant opened in the area, and the population grew from 3,559 in 1910 to 48,615 in 1920. The city hit its peak in 1940, with about 50,000 residents, and it has declined to about 21,000. The Polish influence has waned in recent years. The population was 90 percent Polish in 1970 and it's now about 23 percent. People of Middle Eastern and Albanian descent now make up a significant portion of the population.

One center of Polish culture in the city is St. Florian Church, 2626 Poland St., which was favored by Polish immigrants who came to work at the Dodge plant. The first Polish Catholic church in Detroit was St. Albertus, dating from 1872, and then came St. Florian, which was founded in 1907; the church building was dedicated in 1928. It was visited in 1969 by Karol Wojtyla, then an archbishop in Poland, who would later become Pope John Paul II. The church also operated parochial schools that were attended by many Polish Americans.

Polish Art Center in Hamtramck.

Also in Hamtramck is the Polish Art Center (888-619-9771; polartcenter.com; 9539 Joseph Campau St.) The center displays Polish cultural artifacts

Backyard Art

Hamtramck Disneyland, in an alley between Klinger and Sobleski Streets, is the folk-art project of a neighborhood guy; it's been compared to the Heidelberg Project on the East Side (see sidebar, chapter 4). It's relatively low budget and cheerful in its use of recycled materials, but people come from all over the world to see it. (To learn more go to www2.metrotimes.com/editorial/story.asp?id=4478 or www.yelp.com/biz/hamtramck-disneyland-hamtramck.)

at various events, and sells folk art, books, traditional Polish dress items, jewelry, and seeds from Poland and books on genealogy. Founded in 1958 it is run by Raymond and Joan Bittner, who are involved in metro Detroit ethnic festivals and give demonstrations at schools.

HIGHLAND PARK

Originally a rural farm community, Highland Park started to boom after 1910, shortly after Henry Ford built a plant along the Woodward corridor. The population surged from about 4,000 in 1910 to more than 46,000 ten years later. It hit its peak in 1940 with a population of slightly more than 50,000, and has declined in recent years to a little more than 13,000. The area has been hard hit by economic woes and crime, and the State of Michigan has been involved with governing it since 1990. The police force was disbanded, and the Wayne County Sheriff's Department now provides police protection.

The city's decline started in the 1950s when Ford closed its Highland Park plant, and worsened when Chrysler Corp. moved its headquarters there to a new complex 25 miles north in Auburn Hills.

Driving along stretches of Woodward Avenue here can be a dismal experience. The avenue was once a bustling business district that catered to autoworkers and their families, but there are now many abandoned stores and businesses.

Despite the decline, there are well-kept homes and neighborhoods straddling Woodward, many of them Craftsman-style structures built for the autoworkers who lived in the community during the early part of the 20th century.

Paczki Day

Pronounced "POONCH-key," Paczki Day is Detroit's Fat Tuesday, the day before Ash Wednesday, similar to New Orleans' Mardi Gras. Traditional paczkis are a calorie-laden pastry, basically jelly- or cream-filled doughnuts fried in lard. Paczki-making cleans out the cupboards of indulgent ingredients like sweets and fats on the day before Catholics start fasting for Lent.

Paczki was a mostly Polish tradition until the 1980s, when the media picked up on the story, and since then metro Detroiters of all ethnic backgrounds have become paczki devotees. A number of events have sprung up around the tradition in Hamtramck, including paczki-eating contests, pub crawls, and Polish music and dancing. The place to buy paczkis is in Hamtramck; a few of the best places are: **New Deluxe Polish Bakery** (313-892-8165; 11920 Conant); **New Martha Washington Bakery** (313-872-1988; 10335 Joseph Campau); **New Place Bakery** (313-872-1988; 9833 Joseph Campau); and **New Polka Bakery** (313-873-7959; 9834 Conant).

The Highland Park Ford Plant is at 91 Manchester Avenue, at Woodward Avenue. The building was part of a larger complex that opened in 1910 and included offices, factories, a power plant, and foundry. It was Ford's first moving assembly line and produced Model Ts and later models. Ford moved most of its operations to its larger Ford Rouge Complex in Dearborn by the late 1920s, but the Highland Park plant continued in operation making automotive trim and tractors until the 1950s, when much of it was demolished. What remains was named a National Historic Landmark in 1978.

Eight Mile to Pontiac

At Eight Mile, you cross the divide between Detroit and Wayne County into Oakland County, one of the wealthiest in the nation, and the scenery changes from urban decay to suburban affluence. If you're a fan of the rap star Eminem and have seen the movie *8 Mile,* you know the story: Eight Mile Road is the border between rich and poor. The route takes drivers through one of the most exclusive and affluent communities in the nation, the Bloomfield area (see chapter 5, Oakland County).

But while that's the poetic side of it, the reality is a bit different. Not all Oakland County suburbs are wealthy. The first you'll pass through is Ferndale, which is definitely working-class, but which has been catching up to its neighbor to the north, Royal Oak, in terms of being an entertainment district. At the end of the line is the poor urban community of Pontiac.

The route also passes through Birmingham, which has a nice, walkable downtown, and other upscale Oakland County locales like Bloomfield Hills (see chapter 5, Oakland County).

This stretch of Woodward Avenue is made for cruising, and is the home to the annual Woodward Dream Cruise (see sidebar) that

Where the Wild Things Are

The Detroit Zoo (248-399-7001; www.detroitzoo.org; 8450 W. Ten Mile Rd., Huntington Woods; located just off Woodward) Just north of Ferndale in Huntington Woods, The Detroit Zoo offers animal viewing, attractions, and some rides. The most traditional way to start off a visit is with a ride on the Tauber Family Railroad, added in 1931; this miniature railroad takes visitors for a relaxing ride through the zoo. There's also the Wild Adventure 3-D/4-D Theater, and the Giraffe Encounter, a chance for kids to feed the animals. The Arctic Ring of Life is one of the newest exhibits, opened in 2001. It houses polar bears and other cold-weather creatures, and visitors enjoy looking up to watch seals swim from the unique vantage point of a see-through underwater tunnel. Other favorite exhibits include the Free Flight Aviary, a building in which birds fly freely; the Penguinarium; Amphibiville, for frog and toad watching; the River Otter exhibit; a swan pond; the large Great Apes of Harambee exhibit with chimps and gorillas; bears; an African animal area with lions, zebras, and giraffes; the Australian Outback Adventure; a farm animal exhibit; and a pair of wolverines, one of the only places you'll spot such animals in-state even though Michigan is known as the Wolverine State. A food court is located at the center of the zoo and snack shacks open seasonally. There is plenty of parking available on Ten Mile. Admission is: $12 for adults and those over 15 years old; $8 for children 2–14; and $10 for seniors 62 and over. Parking is $5 per vehicle.

attracts more than a million drivers and spectators each year to admire classic cars. Woodward's four to six lanes going each way are separated by a landscaped median strip. The avenue is lined with businesses, familiar chains, and independent establishments, some of them restaurants with '50s and '60s car and rock 'n' roll themes catering to the Dream Cruise.

But there's more to be seen along this stretch of Woodward than cars and bars.

FERNDALE

Ferndale is primarily working-class residential, but it does have a small commercial district where Woodward intersects with Nine Mile Road (see listings under Restaurants and Watering Holes, Ferndale). One big draw on the entertainment front here is The Magic Bag Theater (248-544-3030; 22920 Woodward Ave.), which hosts concerts by national touring acts as well as local groups. Comedy acts are also booked here, and on some nights it screens older movies.

Just north of Ferndale is Huntington Woods, a small suburb of about 6,000 residents, with some lovely homes dating to the 1920s, when executives from Detroit firms started building English-influenced homes. It's worth it to turn onto one of the side streets off Woodward to do some sightseeing. Adjoining Huntington Woods is the even smaller community of Pleasant Ridge, which shares similar housing styles with its neighbor.

ROYAL OAK

The area along the Woodward Avenue corridor north of the Detroit Zoo isn't just another suburban bedroom community. A city since 1921, Royal Oak has become one of the hippest places to live in the metro Detroit area, partly because of its large number of entertainment venues, restaurants, and bars.

Much of the city's housing is older, but there was a resurgence in building during the 1990s and early 2000s because of the demand for condominiums and lofts in the downtown area. The city has a hip veneer, but the neighborhoods are packed with family homes, many of which were built during the 1920s and '30s.

The atmosphere is fairly liberal these days—an S&M supply shop, Noir Leather, is a standout among the antiques and kitsch shops and watering holes—but Royal Oak wasn't always that way. During the 1930s it was home to Father Charles Coughlin (1891–1979), a controversial Catholic priest at the National Shrine of the Little Flower at 12 Mile and Woodward Avenue. During the 1930s he was a precursor to the talk-radio hosts who hold forth these days, and used broadcasts of his sermons to spread his views on politics and economics. At first Coughlin was supportive of President Roosevelt and the New Deal, but he grew increasingly critical of the president's monetary policies and eventually was castigated for being anti-Semitic and anticapitalist, even going so far as to express sympathy for Hitler's fascist policies. By the late '30s, as World War II loomed, Coughlin was essentially banned from the airwaves. He remained a priest at the Shrine of the Little Flower until his retirement in 1966.

The church itself is still in use and worth a look. The art deco building's attention-getting tower features a nearly 30-foot-tall bas-relief sculpture of Christ on the cross that watches over Woodward Avenue traffic.

Most of Royal Oak's entertainment and shopping district is stretched along S. Main Street, which runs parallel to Woodward a few blocks to the east, and is bolstered by a campus of Oakland Community College located nearby.

The Royal Oak Music Theatre (248-399-2980; royaloakmusictheatre.com; 318 W. 4th St.) hosts live music and comedy performances in an opulent art deco–style venue that opened in 1928 as a movie house. By the late '70s it started staging live music, and sometimes comedy acts, fashion shows, and other events. Performers have included Bright Eyes, the Pogues, Motorhead, and Scissor Sisters.

Also in Royal Oak is Mark Ridley's Comedy Castle (248-542-9900; comedycastle.com; 310 S. Troy St.), which attracts top-notch comedians. Since its founding in 1979, such well-known performers as Michigan actor Tim Allen have been onstage here, as well as Jerry Seinfeld, Ellen DeGeneres, Jim Carrey, and Jay Leno. The venue also offers new comics a chance to hone their skills.

Mark Ridley's Comedy Castle in Royal Oak.

Dream Cruise

No other event in metro Detroit sums up what living in the region is all about like this one does. It's based on a time-honored tradition of teenagers cruising Woodward Avenue in their hot cars during the 1950s and '60s.

The Woodward Dream Cruise (woodwarddreamcruise.com) takes place on the third Saturday of August and attracts about 1.5 million people, many of whom bring lawn chairs and line Woodward. Technically a one-day event, though many cruisers can't wait and begin showing off their rides earlier in the week, it attracts as many as 40,000 cars. Many drivers park along Woodward before and after the cruise, which runs roughly **from Eight Mile to Pontiac.** The first cruise was held in 1995 and some clubs designate special meeting spots along the way.

It's a major economic event, bringing in more than $56 million to metro Detroit, particularly benefiting the communities along the route: Ferndale, Pleasant Ridge, Royal Oak, Huntington Woods, Birmingham, Bloomfield Hills, and Pontiac. The restaurants and bars along the Woodward corridor are packed during the cruise weekend.

While the cruisers are well behaved these days—mostly well-to-do aging baby boomers who can afford to restore and maintain the vintage hot rods and muscle cars they dreamed about as kids—things weren't also so peaceful. Cruising Woodward in the '50s and '60s was really about drag racing. And Woodward with its large median strip (cops on the other side of couldn't easily catch racers) and frequent traffic lights was the perfect place. The races took place from stoplight to stoplight. It was an era when teenage boys knew how to work on cars and would often spend months patching together a hot rod out of various parts.

Some of the cars back then looked the part, with special metallic colors, especially candy apple red, while others only had souped-up V-8 engines. Detroit's automakers took note of what teens were doing to cars, and started designing products that rolled off the

Royal Oak Shopping

More and more chains have appeared on Royal Oak's Main Street in the last couple of decades, but it's still a fun strip to explore on foot. Sports bars battle with record stores and club wear and trinket shops, assembly lines ready to race on the streets. By the mid-1960s car companies were producing the Mustang, Pontiac GTO, Dodge Charger, Chevy 409, and other muscle cars.

While Woodward was often the destination for racers, so were other streets, including Telegraph on Detroit's West Side, and also other roads where teens thought they could escape the eyes of police. Woodward was a prime road for drag racing, partly because of the keen competition. Many auto executives lived in the more pricy suburbs along the Woodward Avenue corridor, and in those days they could bring home cars for road testing. Many of those hot cars ended up in the hands of lucky teenagers who headed to Woodward.

There was a bit of class warfare in all this. Blue-collar kids who built their own cars took great joy in beating another driver at the wheel of a new car that his auto executive father had brought home for a test drive. Some blue-collar kids would intentionally use the body of a car that didn't look great or fast, and turn it into a racing machine.

The strip was also home to many drive-in restaurants where the drag racers could pull in for a burger and a pop, possibly waiting for the police cars to leave the area. One of the best-known drive-ins was Ted's on Woodward Avenue near Square Lake Road in Bloomfield Hills. Its location informally marked the end of the Woodward drag strip. The restaurant opened in 1954, just in time to cater to all those teens who had seen James Dean racing cars in the movie *Rebel without a Cause,* which was released in 1955.

The Totem Pole opened in the same year as Ted's and had a 16-foot totem pole carved by a Native American from Michigan. The restaurant was on Woodward in Royal Oak, and was long a landmark.

While patrons of those drive-ins may have been using them to dodge the cops, these days the cruise is a mainstream and generally slow-moving event attracting a variety of corporate sponsors.

and it's a good stretch whether you want to pick up a squeaking nun toy, an antique lamp, or someone to share a pitcher of Budweiser with.

Incognito (248-548-2980; www.goincognito.com; 323 S. Main St.)
A funky clothier with edgy men's and women's clothing. Fun shoes and accessories abound. Not for the subdued dresser.

Treasure Hunting in Royal Oak

A fun time for antiques and "junque" shoppers is the annual **Antique and Garage Sale** (royaloakchamber.com/antique_garage.htm), which fills a city parking structure one weekend each summer. Admission is $2 for adults.

Noir Leather (248-541-3979; noirleather.com; 124 W. Fourth St.) Fetish and club wear and gear since 1983. The shop occasionally hosts fetish nights at local clubs and dresses some of the folks who make warm-weather Royal Oak such a great place to people watch. This is also a place to score merchandise from the Detroit Derby Girls, the local Roller Derby association.

Royal Oak Farmers Market and Flea Market (248-246-3276; 316 East 11 Mile Rd.) Two blocks east of Main Street, the Farmers Market in the Civic Center building is open Fridays May–Christmas and Saturdays all year round. The Flea Market, popular with antiquers, is open on Sundays.

BIRMINGHAM

While Birmingham is now an exclusive suburb of Detroit, it's one of several towns surrounding metro Detroit that was once a rural town. Now it has its own identity and a downtown that is still thriving. For many years it has served as the downtown for surrounding Oakland County communities.

Birmingham serves as a downtown for surrounding Oakland County communities.

Early settlements in what was to become Birmingham thrived on the travelers between Detroit and Pontiac on Woodward Avenue, with various inns and taverns operated by a handful of early settlers. One of those settlers,

Shopping is a major attraction in Birmingham.

Roswell Merrill, ran a foundry and named the town Birmingham after Birmingham, England, hoping it would become an industrial town. Instead, it became one of the most sought-after addresses of upper-middle-class metro Detroit, a reputation that still holds true.

With the coming of the automobile in the 1920s it became easier to commute to Detroit via Woodward Avenue and also by railroad, and rural Birmingham started to boom, with new homes being built. The city and nearby Bloomfield Hills and Bloomfield Township (see chapter 5) are now home to some of the most exclusive housing in metro Detroit. The median income for a family is slightly more than $110,000.

The Birmingham Theater.

Birmingham's downtown astride Woodward Avenue and Maple has long been home to trendy shops, restaurants (see Restaurants, Birmingham), galleries, markets, and small boutiques. For many years, the community had the reputation of being a bit stuffy, and folks still head south on Woodward to nearby Royal Oak for music and entertainment, but in recent years a few notable spots aimed at a younger crowd have livened things up (see Watering Holes, Birmingham).

Some draws in terms of nightlife are Birmingham's Landmark Main Art Theatre (248-263-2111; landmarktheatres.com; 118 N. Main St.), part of a nationwide chain of theaters that shows foreign, independent, and 3-D movies, and the Birmingham Theater, aka the Birmingham 8 (248-644-3456; uptown entertainment.com; 211 S. Old Woodward Ave.), which opened in 1927 with one screen, but was restored in the 1990s, when seven new screens were added. The outside façade is reminiscent of the movie houses of the 1920s.

Birmingham Art Galleries

Birmingham has an active arts community, partly because of its close proximity to Cranbrook Educational Community (see sidebar), and there are many art galleries.

Hill Gallery (248-540-9288; hillgallery.com; 407 W. Brown St.) The gallery has been around since 1981 and has featured works by Milton Avery, Michael Heizer, Alfred Leslie, Mark di Suvero, and Tony Smith. The gallery also has many examples of American folk art.

Robert Kidd Gallery (248-642-3900; robertkiddgallery.com; 107 Townsend St.) The gallery was founded in 1976 by Robert Louis Kidd and Ray Frost Fleming, both graduates of the nearby Cranbrook Academy of Art. The space houses paintings, sculptures, and photography by established and emerging artists. Some big names include Larry Rivers, Helen Frankenthaler, Carl Milles, and Marshall Fredericks. The gallery has 5,000 feet of exhibition space and is located on two levels.

PONTIAC

The city that gave its name to the General Motors car, and even named one of its streets, Wide Track Drive, is the county seat of Oakland County, but it is also an aging community that has experienced severe decline, even though it borders some of the wealthiest places in the nation. It has long been home to General Motors plants, and was particularly dependent on the Pontiac brand.

Eight Mile Cruise

Eminem's Turf

8 Mile is more than just the name of a movie by rap star Eminem, it's a real road in Detroit that's the border not only between Detroit and its northern suburbs, but between Wayne County, which is traditionally more working class, and Oakland County, the location of many large homes and estates. Eight Mile is one of the mile roads that run east-west, the numbers of which denote the number of miles from downtown Detroit.

Although Eight Mile's formal state number designation is M-102, you'll never hear a Detroiter refer to it that way. You might hear it called Baseline Road, which is used in a few communities through which it runs. That designation comes from the area's use as a baseline for surveying the Northwest Territories in the early 19th century. In the Grosse Pointe area, one of the region's most exclusive places, Eight Mile is known as Vernier Road.

The Eight Mile strip isn't the most desirable route to take in the Detroit area, due to the many sleazy bars and strip clubs that dot the corridor.

But for those looking to experience Detroit at its grittiest, try a cruise from Woodward Avenue either east or west on Eight Mile Road. You'll pass a fair amount of strip clubs, interspersed with bars that you probably don't want to go into, but there are still plenty of mainline businesses that thrive along the route.

Intersection of Eight Mile and Woodward.

On the strip is **Northland Center** (21500 Northwestern Highway, Southfield), which was one of the first suburban malls to open in the United States, in the mid-1950s. The anchor stores are Macy's and Target, and there are about 100 other retail outlets that serve the predominantly middle- and upper-middle-class African American community of Southfield.

Cranbrook

The 174-acre **Cranbrook Educational Community** (248-645-3000; cranbrook.edu; 39221 Woodward Ave.) includes schools, an art academy, a museum, an institute of science, and the home and gardens of its founder, George Booth, a Michigan newspaper baron. Art, architecture, and garden buffs could easily spend a whole day or more exploring the campus.

The Cranbrook buildings are known for a fusion of arts and crafts and art deco–style architecture. Many of them were designed by two prominent area architects, Detroiter Albert Kahn and Finnish immigrant Eliel Saarinen, who taught at and was president of Cranbrook's Academy of Art. The art deco digs where Saarinen lived with his artist wife, Loja, known simply as **The Saarinen House,** is seasonally open to tours. Saarinen's son, the architect Eero Saarinen, studied for a time at Cranbrook and designed the sprawling, modern-style General Motors Technical Center campus in Warren and several buildings on the University of Michigan campus in Ann Arbor.

The schools at Cranbrook are attended by the children of many well-to-do metro Detroiters and include lower, middle, and upper-grade facilities. The schools were open in 1915 and are based on the British boarding school model. Associated with the schools is the Kingswood School for Girls.

Cranbrook was named by George G. Booth (1864–1949) for Cranbrook, England, his father's hometown. Booth was the publisher of the *Detroit News,* and he also founded the Booth Newspaper chain of papers located in major cities in southern Michigan. He was helped along in his newspaper career by his father-in-law, James E. Scripps (1835–1906), who had founded the *Detroit News* in 1873. Scripps also had an interest in newspapers in Cleveland, St. Louis, Cincinnati, and Chicago, and was helped establish the Detroit Institute of Arts.

The arts and crafts–style house that Booth built for himself in 1908 is the centerpiece of the campus and was designed by Kahn. The house, which can be toured, is filled with antiques, hand-carved woodwork, and tapestries. The 40-acre garden was designed by Booth and includes sunken and bog gardens, along with formal ones.

Perhaps the most well-known school at the campus is the

Statue at Cranbrook Educational Community near Birmingham.

Cranbrook Academy of Art, which offers graduate degrees in architecture, art, and design. It was founded in 1932. Nearby is the **Cranbrook Art Museum,** which displays the works of contemporary arts and includes a collection of works including pop artists Andy Warhol and Roy Lichtenstein and many notable Cranbrook alumni and instructors, like sculptor and faculty member Carl Milles and artist-designers Charles and Ray Eames, who studied and worked at the academy. The museum is open to the public.

The **Cranbrook Institute of Science** houses a planetarium and is visited by many metro Detroit schoolchildren annually. There's also a collection of scientific artifacts, including dinosaur bones, on display. The institute offers many programs for children (call for more information).

The complex also has the **St. Dunstan's Theatre,** a 206-seat playhouse used by a St. Dunstan's Theater Guild, which stages performances for the public. During warmer months, it moves its productions to an outdoor Greek theater.

The Pontiac dates to 1926 and was long a major General Motors brand, appealing to drivers who wanted something better than a Chevy but cheaper than a Cadillac, and it stayed in the center of the market for decades until it ended up on the chopping block in 2008 when GM sought government loans to bail out the corporation. The last Pontiac rolled off the assembly line in nearby Lake Orion in 2009.

Checking In

Best places to stay in and around Woodward.

There are a variety of accommodation options serving the Woodward corridor. See chapter 1 for downtown hotels, and chapter 5 for hotels in the Auburn Hills area, east of Pontiac. The Townsend Hotel in Birmingham is a standout along the corridor, but pricey.

Birmingham

The Townsend Hotel (248-642-7900; townsendhotel.com; 100 Townsend St.) The hotel, a Forbes 4-star and AAA Four Diamond hotel, is probably the most elegant in metro Detroit; its guests have included visiting celebrities and performers appearing in the area. The furnishings in both the rooms and public areas are elegant, with wood panel walls and ornate lighting fixtures. $$$$ There is a sleek bar, and the Rugby Grille in the hotel offers classic meals such as Dover sole, grilled lamb, lobster rappardelle, and pan-roasted local trout. $$$

Local Flavors

Taste of the town—restaurants, cafés, bars, bistros, etc.

Birmingham

Big Rock Chophouse (248-647-7774; bigrockchophouse.com; 245 S. Eton St.) It's a bit formal, requiring business dress. House specialties include short ribs, filet migon, and whitefish. But there are also lamb, venison, duck, veal, chicken, and buffalo entrées, along with some seafood. The bar/restaurant also offers an array of appetizers, including an interesting onion and ale soup, and foie gras. $$$

Brady's Tavern (248-642-6422; bradystavern.com; 31231

Southfield Rd.,Beverly Hills). A less expensive, less formal dining option, Brady's is nearby Birmingham, in Beverly Hills. The bar is comfortable, and you'll find a large selection of burgers, plus a few entrées, including ribs, beer-battered walleye, and prime rib. $$

Cameron's Steakhouse (248-723-1700; camerons-steakhouse.com; 115 Willits St.) Steak is the main attraction here, with butcher cuts offered, but there's also lamb, fish, and chicken. The bar is sleek and modern, as is the décor throughout. $$$

Forté Restaurant (248-594-7300; forterestaurant.com; 201 S. Old Woodward Ave.) Although the atmosphere is upscale and elegant, the menu has some midwestern favorites that are interpreted with flair and include sautéed walleye, fire-roasted pork tenderloin, beef, and duck. There are also pizzas from a brick oven and there is a small-plate menu. $$$

Mitchell's Fish Market (248-646-3663; mitchellsfishmarket.com; 117 Willits St.) Metro Detroit is home to several of these sleek chain restaurants, and they are a good bet for fish and seafood. Offerings include surf and turf, lobster, and fish. Fresh oysters are also served. $$

Olga's Kitchen (248-647-2760; olgas.com; 138 S. Woodward) This lunch spot is known for the soft, chewy bread used to wrap its take on the gyro. This is the original outpost of the local chain started by Olga Loizon in 1970. It now has 30 restaurants, mostly in malls and strip malls in southern Michigan. The Original Olga sandwich has spun into many variations, and Olga's makes a good spinach pie too. The Orange Cream Cooler, a sherbety drink, is a favorite. $

Peabody's Dining & Spirits (248-644-5222; peabodysrestaurant.com; corner of Woodward and 15 Mile) This Birmingham landmark has a cozy feel. There's a formal dining room, as well as a casual bar where you can settle down and watch a game on big-screen TVs. There's live jazz on the weekends. The entrées are basic American fare such as filet mignon, baby back ribs, sage chicken, and salmon. A top pick is the Roquefort-crusted flat iron steak. $$$

Streetside Seafood (248-645-9123; streetsideseafood.com; 273 Pierce St.) If you're tired of cavernous restaurants, you'll enjoy this intimate 55-seat New York seafood saloon, which features fish and seafood, including Great Lakes catches, and fresh oysters. The lake perch is a local favorite. There's a limited selected of chicken and steak dishes on the menu as well. $$

220 & Edison's (248-645-2150; www.220restaurant.com; 220 Merrill St.) This was one of the first bar/restaurants to open in the 1970s after Birmingham allowed liquor by the glass to be served in establishments, and it has long been a gathering and meeting place. The décor is aimed at making you feel comfortable, and it succeeds. The menu is a match with the décor and ranges from pizza to rack of lamb. There's a good selection of pasta dishes. Check out the past with chicken and spicy Italian sausage. $$$

Ferndale

Anita's Kitchen (248-548-0680; anitaskitchenonline.com; 22651 Woodward) The small Lebanese-style restaurant serves beer and wine, but the cooking is the real attraction, with such Middle Eastern favorites as baked kibbeh, layers of lamb with pine nuts, onions, and cracked wheat, served with yogurt. Open for lunch and dinner. $

Assaggi Bistro (248-584-3499; assaggibistro.com; 330 W. Nine Mile) There are traditional Italian favorites, but try the house specialty, a four-course dinner that includes soup or salad; a pasta dish; chicken Francese, trout, or Moroccan duck; and dessert. The bar offers an extensive wine list. $$

The Blue Nile Ethiopian Restaurant (248-547-6699; bluenilemi.com; 545 W. Nine Mile Rd.) This restaurant with a full bar has a different take on African foods, including chicken, lamb, and beef dishes, which are highly seasoned and served traditional style: injera, a tangy flat bread, accompanies the meal and is used in place of utensils (available on request); each dining party eats from the same platter. Open for lunch and dinner. $$

The Cork Wine Pub (248-544-2675; corkwinepub.com; 23810 Woodward) is a real find along this stretch of the Woodward corridor, just north of Ferndale in Pleasant Ridge. The pub has 150 different wines, and although the menu is not large, it does feature small plates that include pan-seared chicken, duck, and salmon. Make sure to check out the dessert menu for the chocolate cakes, banana espresso tart, and butterscotch pudding. There are also snacks, such as cheese and smoked fish. $$

The Fly Trap (248-399-5150; theflytrapferndale.com; 22950 Woodward Ave.). Billing itself as a "finer diner," there are classic American breakfasts and burgers and such, but you'll also find Asian, Italian, and African influences to some dishes, such as the North African spiced chicken breast with Monterey jack cheese served on sourdough bread. $

Howes Bayou (248-691-7145; howesbayouferndale.net; 22848 Woodward) Somewhat difficult to spot while driving along Woodward, but it's worth the effort once you're inside, where there's an intimate 20-seat bar. There's also seating outside during the warmer months. It's refreshingly unpretentious and so are the prices. There are po'-boy sandwiches for lunch, and other New Orleans–style dishes for dinner, such as catfish, chicken Creole, and shrimp and crawfish étoufée. $$

Hamtramck

Polish Village Café (313-874-5726; thepolishvillagecafe.com; 2990 Yemans) The café evolved from a beer garden operated in the building since 1925, and you can still feel that tradition alive in this family-style tavern. The menu is filled with Polish favorites and daily specials, lots of sausage and meatballs, pierogi, and potato pancakes. $$

Polish Yacht Club (313-925-5335; ivanhoecafe-pyc.com; 5249 Joseph Campau St.) The formal name of this place is the Ivanhoe Café, but years ago so many Detroiters started calling it the Polish Yacht Club that the name stuck, and most folks don't know it by any other name. The bar/restaurant has been serving Polish-style foods for more than 100 years. Dishes include the Polish Reuben, which is kielbasa and sauerkraut and cheese, and, of course, burgers. $$

Polonia Polish Restaurant (313-873-8432; polonia-restaurant.net; 2934 Yenmans St.) This is the real deal when it comes to Polish food. Even celebrity chef Anthony Bourdain showed up

Polish Village Café in Hamtramck.

here with his crew to film an episode of his television series, *No Reservations.* The Polonia has been serving its fare since the early 1970s, and the menu is filled with Polish favorites such as stuffed cabbage, pierogi, Polish smoked sausage with kraut, goulash, and potato noodles, pork chops, and potato pancakes. Regulars show up for the daily specials. Brewed-in-Poland Okocim beer is on tap, and wine and spirits are served. $$

Polonia Restaurant is a neighborhood favorite.

Under the Eagle (313-875-5905; 9000 Joseph Campau St.) The small, family-style restaurant has kielbasa and sauerkraut, stuffed cabbage, and a combination plate that will introduce newcomers to Polish food. $

Midtown

Atlas Global Bistro (313-831-2241; atlasglobalbistro.com; 3111 Woodward Ave.) This upscale restaurant serves the adventurous palate. There's an international feel to the menu, and the place has contemporary furnishings and stands out in area heavily populated with student burger bars. Entrées change seasonally and have included Moroccan grilled quail, and osso bucco. Reservations are suggested. $$$

Avalon Bakery (313-831-0008; 422 Willis St.) It's a good stop for coffee and fresh baked goods to go, or enjoy in-café seating. With a focus on organic ingredients and community enrichment, the bakery produces goods for many of Detroit's better restaurants. The line can get long but it moves quickly.

Cass Café (313-831-1400; casscafe.com; 4620 Cass Ave.). Catering to the theater and arts crowd, this lively place restores your faith in Detroit's revitalization. The restaurant and art gallery are in a sleek, newly remodeled structure that reflects the spirit of the growing arts community in the midtown area. Much of the artwork in the gallery is by better-known contemporary artists. There's a full bar in addition to the dining room. Entrées include tuna, roasted chicken, fish and chips, a vegetarian lasagna, and steak. $$$

Mario's (313-832-1616; mariosdetroit.com; 4222 Second Ave.) One of Detroit's classic Italian restaurants, it's been around since 1948 and, as one of the last supper clubs of its era, offers an elegant setting for a meal. Although the waitstaff is clad in tuxedos, there's no dress code. The bar serves hefty drinks and is a comfortable and friendly place to wait for a table, which you need to do on occasion. The restaurant runs a complimentary shuttle service to nearby entertainment and arts venues, making it a good place to start your evening on the town. $$$

Traffic Jam & Snug (313-831-9470; trafficjamdetroit.com; 511 W. Canfield) This started out as a student bar in the 1960s and has changed over the years as its original customers have gotten older and their tastes have changed from burgers and beer to roast duck and fine wines. However, its signature urinal from the 1960s hangs from an outside wall by the entrance, and the place still has a college-bar feel, with rough sawn paneling and brick walls decorated with an eclectic array of old photos of Detroit, animal heads, and antiques. The crowd ranges from college-age kids to people in their 60s and 70s, many of them Wayne State alums. While there are some upscale items such as duck confit on the menu, there are also Michigan favorites like fried smelt. Other items include Carolina crab cakes grilled and served over rice and accompanied by a capered remoulade. Detroit Delmonico, a 12-once steak; salmon topped with macadamia nuts; and fish and chips. They make their own bread and other pastry items, and they also brew their own beer. $$

The Whitney (313-832-5700; thewhitney.com; 4421 Woodward Ave.) The Whitney is billed as "Detroit's most iconic mansion," and it's an elegant place to dine. There's a full menu, which includes pork, fish, chicken, steaks, risotto, and cioppino. Also open for lunch. $$$

The Traffic Jam & Snug Restaurant in midtown.

Astoria Pastry Shop (248-582-8040; astoriapastryshop.com; 320 S. Main St.) This suburban outpost of the established Detroit location is a great alternative to the Starbucks down the street. Drool-worthy European desserts and cappuccinos will keep you abuzz with sugar and classy caffeine.

Bastone Brewery (248-544-6250; bastone.net; 419 S. Main St.) The bar/restaurant is in a 1930s-era building that has been restored to its art deco look. The menu is laced with Belgian-style dishes, including waterzooi, steamed mussels, and pomme frites. It also includes pizza, steak, and sandwiches. There are many Belgian-style beers offered. The Commune Lounge is downstairs from the Bastone, and has a contemporary industrial-design feel, and is more of a dance club. There are French and Belgian beers. $$

Bastone Brewery in Royal Oak.

Diners enjoy a meal at Blackfinn on Main Street.

Blackfinn (248-582-9460; blackfinnroyaloak.com; 530 S. Main St.) The classic American-style saloon is known for its martinis and DJ-style music. The menu is a bit up from normal pub fare and includes the requisite pizza and burgers. The burger menu is only served at the bar. Entrées include prime rib, steak, chicken, and fish. $$

Little Tree Sushi Bar (248-586-0994; 107 S. Main St.) The menu features Japanese, Thai, and Filipino offerings. The service is excellent, the bar well stocked, and there's usually jazz playing. There are live performances on occasion. $

Oak City Grille (248-556-0947; oakcitygrille.com; 212 W. Sixth St.) The small bar/restaurant offers live music on many nights. They serve mostly inexpensive pub foods, such as pizza, but get creative with crab cakes, almond shrimp, and sliced steak. $

O'Tooles Irish American Grill and Bar (248-591-9226; www.otoolesbar.com; 121 N. Main St.) The bar is a comfortable place to watch a game on TV or socialize. The menu has mostly pub food, burgers and such, but also a few wraps and fish and chips. $$

Oxford Inn (248-543-5619; oxfordinnroyaloak.com; 1214 Main St.) This casual establishment offers a nice bar for happy hour and a comfortable dining area. There are often daily specials such as beef tenderloin medallions, roadhouse-style frog legs, jambalaya, and Italian-style chicken. The wood paneling lends a cozy feel. $$

Red Coat Tavern (248-549-0300; 31542 Woodward Ave.) This place has a friendly look from the outside and it doesn't disappoint. The burgers are the main attraction, but there are other pub favorites, including pizza, prime rib, and fish and chips. There are often people waiting in line to get in. $

The Royal Oak Brewery (248-544-1143; royaloakbrewery.com; 215 E. Fourth St.) The brewpub produces its own beers, which are served in the large bar and during warmer weather on an outside patio. The fare includes fish tacos, blackened catfish, fish and chips, pizza, burgers, and chicken. $$

Town Tavern (248-544-7300; towntavernroyaloak.com; 116 W. Fourth St.) The 1930s-style tavern is a great place to order a martini and enjoy the wooden bar and décor. The menu is filled with classic American fare for lunch and dinner, and includes pepper-grilled shrimp, lobster macaroni and cheese, spaghetti, short ribs, and white fish. $$

Vinsetta Grill (248-543-2626; vinsettagrill.com; 28028 Woodward Ave.) Burgers are big here, and they let you build your own. They claim to have 300,000 to choose from. There are also ribs, steak, and seafood. $$

The Royal Oak Brewery.

Woody's Diner (248-543-6911; woodysdiner.com; 208 W. Fifth St.) The first floor is family friendly, while the second-floor bar attracts those into the bar scene, with its jukebox, which plays a large selection of music. The menu offers more than you'd expect from a diner, and includes wraps, burgers, roasted sandwiches, and entrées such as ribs, beef, pasta, stir-fry, and chicken. $

Watering Holes

Birmingham

The Corner Bar (248-647-2958; thecornerbarmi.com; 100 Townsend St., located in the Townsend Hotel) This isn't the place where locals meet for a beer after work; it's a sleek, upscale hotel bar that stocks premium alcohol and has a Euro-contemporary feel. The backlit bar creates a space where people want to gather. There are regular music performances on weekends, and recorded music on other days. The menu includes some light fare, mostly appetizers like chicken wings, salads, and small burgers. $$

Dick O'Dow's (248-642-1135; sessionite.com; 160 W. Maple Rd.) comes close to fitting the bill. The traditional Irish pub offers music, much of it Irish, on a regular basis, and has a full bar with many Irish beers. The food includes Irish dishes such as fish-and-chips, shepherd's pie, and Irish stew. It's packed on St. Patrick's Day. $$

Tallulah Wine Bar and Bistro (248-731-7066; tallulahwine.com; 155 Bates St.) For a more intimate venue, head to Tallulah. There's a wide selection of wines, including Michigan labels. It's a wine bar, so the menu is limited; entrées include pastas, trout, chicken, and hanger steak. It's generally a nice, quiet place to hold a conversation, and is a good meeting spot. $$

Hamtramck

The Belmont (313-871-1966; thebelmontbar.com; 10215 Joseph Campau St.) The Belmont has its devotees. Drinks are cheap, there are often local bands or a DJ, and it's a bit of a singles place. $

New Dodge Lounge (313-874-5963; newdodgelounge.com; 8850 Joseph Campau) You can get a burger here, but most people come

Tallulah Wine Bar and Bistro is a Birmingham gathering place.

for the bands in this older bar. Performers include local and smaller-scale touring bands. $

Paychecks (313-847-0909; paycheckslounge.com; 2932 Caniff) A top seller is Pabst Blue Ribbon, the traditionally blue-collar beer that's cheap, nostalgic, and easy to drink. There's a cover charge when the bands perform after 9 pm. $

Small's (313-873-873-1117; smallsbardetroit.com; 1033 Conant.) The music tends to be punk rock, and it books many local and small touring acts. There's a cover charge when the bands perform in the back room off the bar. Expect it to be loud and crowded. The jukebox has an eclectic mix of music. $

Midtown

Alvin's (313-638-6300; alvinsoncass.com; 5756 Cass Ave.) Located on the Wayne State campus, this has been a student hangout for more than 40 years. It has long been a live music venue for new acts, and attracts a younger to middle-aged crowd. $$

Bronx Bar (313-832-8464; 4476 Second St.) It's a classic down-and-dirty Detroit burger-and-beer rock bar that's crowded during lunch and fills up in the evenings with students attracted by the reasonably priced drinks and impressive jukebox. $

Motor City Brewing Works is a hangout for Wayne State University students.

Circa 1890 Saloon (313-831-1122; 5457 Cass Ave.) This students-and-locals bar has cheap beer, pizza, and pool tables, and has been around for more than 40 years. Daily specials and a friendly staff make it a dependable joint that won't break the bank. $

Magic Stick (313-833-9700; majesticdetroit.com; 4120 Woodward Ave.) This is where bowling collides with cutting-edge music. Housed in the Majestic Entertainment Center, a decades-old building that includes bowling in the Garden Bowl, and a restaurant, the Majestic Café. The Magic Stick hosts both touring acts and local groups trying to get started. The beer is cheap and you can get pizza by the slice, so expect a lot of students in the crowd. $

Motor City Brewing Works (313-832-2700; motorcitybeer.com; 470 W. Canfield) The microbrewery is a favorite of students, and the pizza kitchen serves a variety of brick-oven pizzas. The servers are cheerful and helpful and you could spend an entire evening sampling the beers. $

Northern Lights Lounge (313-873-1739; 660 W. Baltimore) The small lounge is on an out-of-the-way street close to W. Grand Boulevard, but it's worth seeking out for its old school nightclub feel and music from new groups. The martinis pack a punch. $

Royal Oak

Duggans (248-549-3659; 31501 Woodward) The Irish pub right on Woodward gets constant praise for its burgers. It's painted bright green, and is easy to find. With outdoor and rooftop dining areas, it's very popular during the annual Woodward Dream Cruise of vintage cars during the summer. (See sidebar, Dream Cruise, p. 106.) $

Goodnite Gracie Jazz & Martini Bar (248-544-7490; 224 Sherman Dr.) The name pretty much says it all. Happy hour is an event here, with drink specials and savings on appetizers. The music is funk, soul, R&B, and jazz. $

Gusoline Alley (248-545-2235; 309 S. Center St.) Something of a biker bar, with an emphasis on beer, customers can select from more than 100 types of bottled beer. Don't let its hole-in-the-wall exterior fool you; it's a great place inside. $$

Hi-Tops Ten & One Half (248-398-9526; 25422 Woodward Ave.) Sports, burgers, and beer. That's the main attraction of this place, where a dozen TV sets help fans keep up with the action. $

Luna (248-589-3344; lunaroyaloak.com; 1815 N. Main St.) The dance club is popular with the younger set, and there are specials on drinks. If you like it loud and hip, this is the place to go. $

Mr. B's Pub (248-399-0017; 215 S. Main St.) This outpost of the usually dependable local Mr. B.'s franchise offers basic American bar fare. On the menu you'll find pizza and burgers, but there's also steak and seafood. A mostly young, typically noisy crowd gathers here to hit the bar and watch games. $

Michigan Avenue Cruise

CORKTOWN, MEXICANTOWN, DEARBORN, INKSTER AND WAYNE, YPSILANTI

MICHIGAN AVENUE was one of the original roads laid out in Detroit in 1805, and it ran from Cass Avenue downtown all the way to Chicago, with many of the towns along the way serving stagecoach passengers in the early 19th century (when was a five-day trip from Detroit to the Windy City).

The Michigan Avenue cruise takes travelers through the heart of blue-collar and ethnic neighborhoods, many of which developed when Henry Ford built his massive Ford Rouge factory complex in Dearborn. The complex employed about 100,000 workers at its peak, and defined life for many working-class Detroiters.

Even prior to the rise of the auto industry, much of Detroit's industry was located on the Detroit River near the Michigan Avenue corridor, and it became the unofficial main street for much of the West Side of Detroit. The corridor from near downtown to Ypsilanti has been, and still is, home to many other Ford plants, General Motors facilities, and hundreds of other smaller plants that provided parts and services to the auto industry.

The neighborhoods have a distinctly blue collar feel to them; simple homes, many of them frame houses, and corner neighborhood bars

LEFT: St. Anne Catholic Church in Mexicantown.

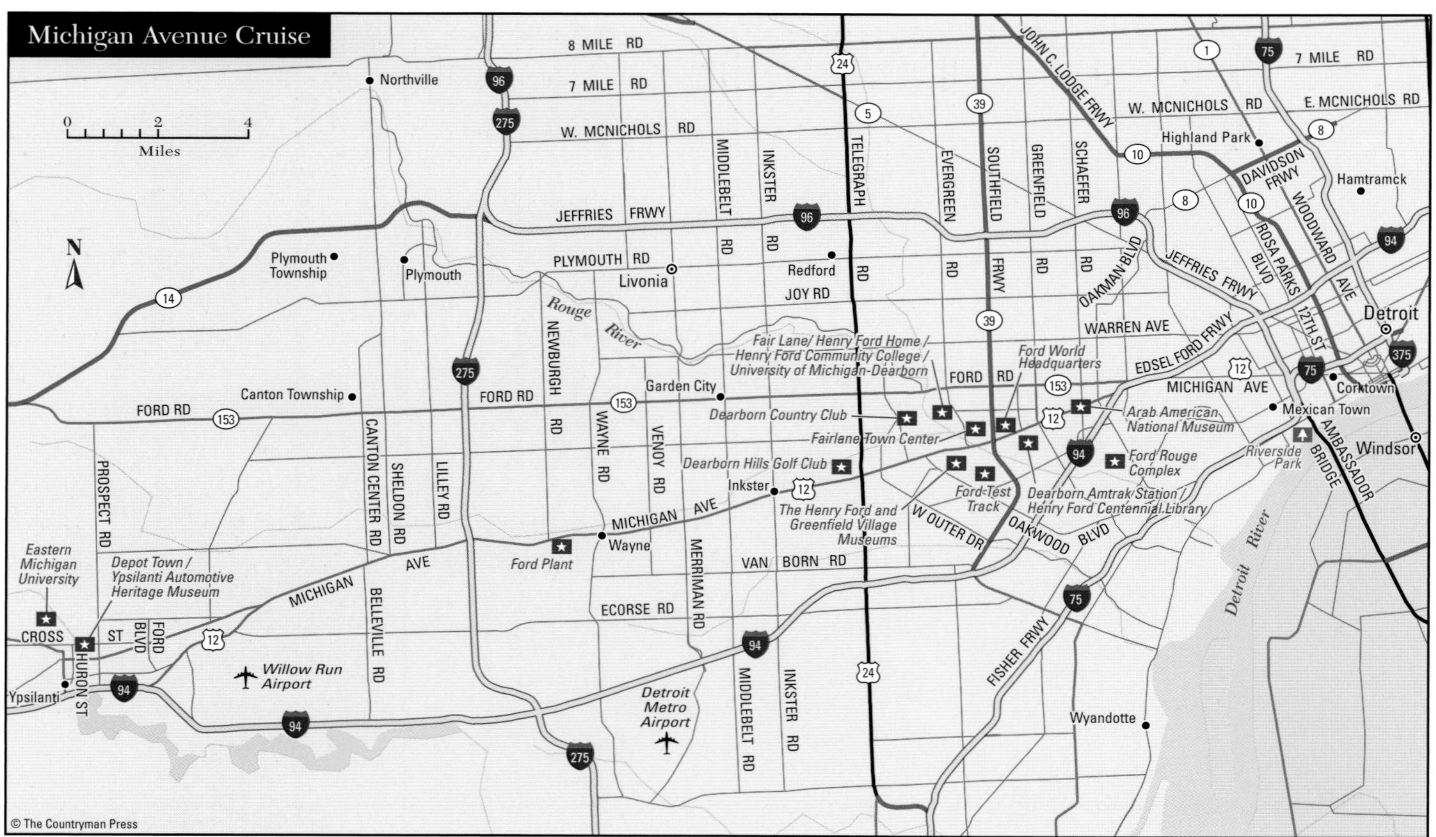
Michigan Avenue Cruise
0 2 4
Miles
N
8 MILE RD
7 MILE RD
W. MCNICHOLS RD
E. MCNICHOLS RD
JEFFRIES FRWY
PLYMOUTH RD
JOY RD
WARREN AVE
FORD RD
MICHIGAN AVE
VAN BORN RD
ECORSE RD
MIDDLEBELT RD
INKSTER RD
TELEGRAPH RD
EVERGREEN RD
SOUTHFIELD FRWY
GREENFIELD RD
SCHAEFER RD
JOHN C. LODGE FRWY
DAVIDSON FRWY
WOODWARD AVE
ROSA PARKS BLVD
12TH ST
OAKMAN BLVD
EDSEL FORD FRWY
FISHER FRWY
W OUTER DR
OAKWOOD BLVD
AMBASSADOR BRIDGE
NEWBURGH RD
WAYNE RD
VENOY RD
MERRIMAN RD
CANTON CENTER RD
SHELDON RD
LILLEY RD
BELLEVILLE RD
PROSPECT RD
CROSS ST
FORD BLVD
HURON ST
Northville
Plymouth Township
Plymouth
Livonia
Redford
Canton Township
Garden City
Inkster
Wayne
Ypsilanti
Highland Park
Hamtramck
Detroit
Corktown
Mexican Town
Windsor
Wyandotte
Riverside Park
Rouge River
Detroit River
Fair Lane/ Henry Ford Home / Henry Ford Community College / University of Michigan-Dearborn
Ford World Headquarters
Dearborn Country Club
Fairlane Town Center
Dearborn Hills Golf Club
The Henry Ford and Greenfield Village Museums
Ford Test Track
Dearborn Amtrak Station / Henry Ford Centennial Library
Arab American National Museum
Ford Rouge Complex
Ford Plant
Eastern Michigan University
Depot Town / Ypsilanti Automotive Heritage Museum
Willow Run Airport
Detroit Metro Airport
1
5
8
10
12
14
24
39
75
94
96
153
275
375
© The Countryman Press

dot the area. Old Catholic churches abound, their names marking the ethnic background of those who once lived in those neighborhoods.

Over the past 150 years, the corridor has been home to Irish, Germans, Polish, Ukrainians, and Hungarians who found jobs nearby, and it's now home to many Hispanics whose center is Mexicantown.

Driving the corridor is like being in a time machine. Once you get out of downtown, there are brick buildings lining Michigan that date to the late 19th century, and as you drive to Dearborn, you can easily spot the buildings from each successive decade.

CORKTOWN

Driving from the downtown area, you'll pass the often-photographed Michigan Central Depot in Corktown, at Michigan Avenue near Trumbull. Constructed in 1913 for the Michigan Central Railroad, it was a major rail depot, and was in operation until 1988. The rotting, hulking, structure about 2 miles from downtown has become a symbol of the city's plight, and is often photographed by media covering the city's purported demise. It has actually become a tourist destination in recent years for urban explorers taking photographic expeditions to the city. It's on the National Register of Historic Places, but the city has made plans to tear it down. Various renovation projects have been proposed for it, including turning it into Detroit Police headquarters, but none has seriously moved forward.

While the depot is the poster child for urban decay, a newer symbol of the city's resurgence that points to the possibilities for the future is nearby on Michigan, Slows Bar-B-Q, which is jammed most days (see listing under Restaurants, Corktown). Slows and other bars and restaurants along Michigan in the Corktown area are a welcome sign of vitality in a city where the promise of urban renewal is long overdue.

Corktown is bounded by Michigan Avenue, I-75, the Lodge Freeway, and Bagley and

The abandoned Michigan Central Depot in Corktown.

Porter Streets, and is a residential community, said to be the oldest neighborhood in Detroit. One block of homes on 6th Street dates back to the 1840s. The area takes its name from County Cork in Ireland, the origin of the Irish immigrants fleeing the Great Potato Famine of the 1840s. Many of these immigrants made their home in Corktown. Germans started moving in during the Civil War. The older homes are primarily frame row houses, but there are some larger brick Victorian townhouses, and some newer housing has been built over the years. Detroit never did have tenement houses as did New York or Boston, and the simple workingmen's cottages were the destination for immigrants. There are many such cottages stretching along the Detroit River, not just in Corktown. The district now has an active neighborhood association.

Perhaps its best-known intersection is Michigan and Trumbull, where the Detroit Tigers played in two different stadiums for more than 100 years. While Tiger Stadium has been torn down, several sports taverns that served the old ballpark are still popular with sports fans, who gather there before and after games. Nemo's runs shuttle buses to the sports arenas for patrons. (See Watering Holes, Corktown.)

MEXICANTOWN

Vivid colors are on display in Detroit's Mexicantown.

The next stop on Michigan Avenue is Mexicantown, and when you pass over the Jeffries Freeway (I-96) you'll start seeing many signs in Spanish. Turn south on Clark Street and take it off Vernor Highway, which is the heart of the district. The rough boundaries are Clark, Vernor, Porter, and Bagley Streets.

Detroit has long been a destination for Hispanics, many drawn to the city by the auto industry. Mexicantown is the cultural hub for the city's Hispanics, many of whom live in Mexicantown.

Mexicantown is one area of the city where community pride is evident, and there are ongoing efforts to keep the businesses thriving. Mexicantown itself has played a key role in that effort, notably with its annual Cinco de Mayo Festival.

The Ambassador Bridge as seen from Mexicantown.

The southwest region of Detroit has long been a working-class area, partly because of its close proximity to the giant Ford Rouge Complex in nearby Dearborn. But even before that, in the 19th century, it was home to workmen whose jobs were close by in plants along the Detroit River. While Corktown is known for its large array of workmen's cottages, there are also such structures here, many of them still lived in, stretching along the river. One neighborhood in the area, Delray, is nearly a ghost town now, but was once a Hungarian enclave.

Mexicantown's restaurants are a draw for visitors, and the many eateries in the district are often filled with suburban Detroiters (see listings under Restaurants, Mexicantown)

The center of life for many

Mexicantown's Sweet Spot

La Gloria Bakery (313-842-5722; 3345 Bagley) is a great stop for dessert or a breakfast or lunch treat. The bakery offers a substantial selection of churros, cookies, and other scrumptious goods. Open daily, 5 AM to 10 PM. $

Fort Wayne

The officers' quarters at Fort Wayne.

A short drive south from Mexicantown takes you to **Historic Fort Wayne** (313-833-8849; historicfortwaynecoalition.com/visitors.html; 6325 Jefferson Ave.). Early in the 19th century, there were fears of another war with the British, and Detroit would have been on the front line. That resulted in the construction of the fort in the 1840s on the Detroit River, less than a mile from Canada, which was then ruled by Britain. Fort Wayne was the third fort built in the region; Fort Ponchartrain de Détroit was established by the French in 1701, and Fort Lemoult was built by the British a few years later and eventually taken over by the Americans and renamed Fort Shelby.

During the War of 1812, the fort was surrendered to the British, who held it briefly before abandoning it. It was eventually demolished by the city of Detroit, but by the 1830s a group of Americans and Canadians were organizing in an attempt to free Canada from Britain. The short-lived conflict, called the Patriot War, was unsuccessful but it did prompt America to build Fort Wayne. It was eventually opened in 1851 and served as a training site for soldiers during the Civil War and the Spanish-American War.

It remained in the hands of the military until the early 1970s, serving in various capacities until it was turned over to the city of Detroit. Antiaircraft guns were manned there during World War II, and missiles during the 1950s Cold War. The fort also served as a military induction center during the Korean and Vietnam Wars.

There are buildings from various eras located on the 83-acre site and include barracks, officers' quarters, shops, a guardhouse, and stables. The fort is now operated by the Detroit Recreation Department and is home to the **Tuskegee Airmen Museum.**

Tours of the fort can be arranged, and there are reenactments scheduled during the warm-weather months.

Hispanics in the area is St. Anne Catholic Church, at 1000 Saint Anne Street, which was founded in 1701 and is the second oldest Roman Catholic church in the nation. The building dates from 1886 and is on the National Register of Historic Places. The Detroit River and Ambassador Bridge are nearby.

DEARBORN

The Ford Motor Company World Headquarters, at the corner of Michigan Avenue and the Southfield Freeway, towers over this town in more ways than one. The "glass house," as local residents call it, is the tallest building around, and the Ford Motor Co. logo on the building pretty much defines this city in the Detroit metropolitan area that stretches along Michigan Avenue in western Wayne County.

Ford Motor Company World Headquarters in Dearborn.

Dearborn became a village in 1836 and was named after a patriot, Henry Dearborn, but its most famous resident, Henry Ford, wasn't born until 1863. The city has a population of about 97,000 residents, and went from 2,470 in 1920 to 50,358 by 1930. That was the era during which Henry Ford built his massive Ford Rouge Complex on the banks of the Rouge River in Dearborn.

Between the headquarters building and other Ford facilities here, and the museum simply called The Henry Ford, a leading tourist attraction in the metro region, Dearborn is pretty much the home of Ford Motor Company.

Apart from its identification with Ford, Dearborn is also home to the largest Arabic-speaking population in the nation and to many mosques and Arab American groups and organizations.

The Ford Rouge Plant Complex

The Ford Rouge Complex was once the largest integrated factory in the world and included 93 buildings on a 1.5-by-1-mile site on the Rouge River in Dearborn off Miller Road near Michigan Avenue. Some of the buildings were designed by Detroit architect Albert Kahn, and took advantage of natural lighting. At the time, it was

The Henry Ford

The Henry Ford, a National Historic Landmark known in full as **The Henry Ford and Greenfield Village,** is thought to be the largest such indoor-outdoor museum complex in the world, and it is a top tourist attraction in the metro Detroit area, with its mix of historic buildings and vehicles, antique automobiles, and farm tools and equipment.

The Henry Ford is a top tourist destination in metro Detroit.

It's just what you'd think the garage and attic of an eclectic mechanical tinkerer with an interest in history would hold. That's because it was begun by the original Henry Ford, the farmer turned mechanic who fine-tuned the assembly line system and founded the Ford Motor Co. Entire homes and other historic structures were moved to the property in an effort to preserve them as Americana.

Not limited to a certain time period, The Henry Ford includes a wide range of exhibits, from the chair President Lincoln was sitting in when he was shot to pop culture items from Motown Records and everything in between.

While there are structures and memorabilia associated with notable figures, everyday people and their lives are also represented: the tools our great grandfathers used to hammer out metal products or farm the land, domestic implements for tending the home fires, toys that entertained the kids.

Plan a two-or-more-day stay if you want to get the full museum and village experience. And don't let winter stop you. There are sleigh rides in the snow, and at Christmas, special events are scheduled.

A stroll through Greenfield Village will take you to Henry Ford's birthplace, a typical frame 19th-century farmhouse; the Wright Brothers' bicycle shop and home, a one-room schoolhouse; an old tavern, which still serves food; a stone English cottage; several 17th-century New England frame homes; a slave home; Daniel Webster's home; typical 19th-century homes; a plantation home; a bridge tollhouse; various Ford factories; and Thomas Edison's Menlo Park laboratory.

The facility is a great place to take kids. The museum houses an IMAX Theater that shows scientific and nature films. The village has a steam locomotive that operates rides, and there's a carousel. There are food concession stands throughout the village, and one larger restaurant. There are also shops, many of which sell old-timey items made in the village.

There are many reenactors strolling through the village wearing period costumes; some ride horses or vintage bicycles, or drive antique cars. Others demonstrate traditional trades such as glass-blowing.

For kids, the one-room schoolhouse is a delight. They can see how children were educated in the 19th and early 20th centuries. Near it are reenactors playing with the toys of the era, including hoops, tops, and marbles.

One of the seven historical districts in Greenfield Village is Firestone Farm, complete with barnyard animals and actors who tell what it was like to work farms back in the day. Those interested in arts and crafts should visit the Liberty Craftworks district, where there are working blacksmiths, pottery makers, and other craftspeople.

From late May through early September there are many special annual events.

- In late May the village celebrates Memorial Day weekend with a Civil War Remembrance, which draws war reenactors who set up encampments in the village.
- Father's Day in June brings the Motor Muster and attracts owners of vintage cars.
- A Discovery Camp is held during summer for children, and includes craft-making projects.
- The Detroit Symphony Orchestra performs over the July Fourth holiday.
- An antique-car festival is held in mid-September and attracts auto buffs with hundreds of cars on display.

Another major draw at the Henry Ford is the vintage baseball games held over the summer. Players dress in uniforms similar to those used in the late 19th and early 20th centuries, and they use the rules of the day, which increased a batter's chances of hitting the ball. The game was a bit different in those days, partly because the players didn't use mitts, and the scores were higher.

continued next page

The complex was dedicated in October 1929 on the 50th anniversary of the invention of the light bulb by Thomas Edison and was attended by President Herbert Hoover, Will Rogers, Orville Wright, John D. Rockefeller, and Marie Curie. It was originally called the Edison Institute in honor of Edison, who was a longtime friend of Henry Ford, who had once worked at an Edison power plant in Detroit, and included the Henry Ford Museum, Greenfield Village, and Greenfield Village Schools, a type of trade school that also taught agriculture.

While The Henry Ford isn't owned by the auto company, there are still strong ties to it, and the museum offers tours of the nearby Ford Rouge Complex, which was once the largest industrial area in the world.

For information on ticket prices and calendar visit the museum's website, www.thehenryford.org.

RESTAURANTS AT THE HENRY FORD

Cotswold Tea (313-982-6001) is located in Greenfield Village, and the outside venue offers tea sandwiches, scones, cookies, pastry, and tea. It's open daily from mid-July through late August, weather permitting, and Saturday–Sunday from late August through early October.

The Eagle Tavern (313-982-6001) is located in Greenfield Village but was originally constructed in 1831 in Clinton, Michigan, as a stagecoach stop for travelers. The waitstaff is clad in period costume, and the interior reflects the 1830s era. The menu matches the décor, with many 19th-century dishes served, such as pork and apple pie, baked whitefish with maple butter, roast chicken with pear sage stuffing, noodles with dried cherries and walnuts, and beef cakes. Side dishes include bubble and squeak, onion pie, and baked cauliflower. Desserts are pumpkin pie, apple cider cake, and French Charlotte. Also on the menu are beer, wines, and brandies and other liquor, including Michigan corn whiskey. One wonders what Henry Ford would have thought of serving alcohol at the museum, as he was a teetotaler. $$

Mrs. Fisher's Southern Cooking (313-982-6001) is a lunch stand in the village that serves fried chicken, catfish, and hushpuppies. $

A Taste of History Restaurant (313-982-6001) is a cafeteria-style place that's a great destination for kids and offers sandwiches and salads. $

thought to be the one of the most humanely designed plants for workers.

Basically, the complex took in raw materials and turned out automobiles. Located on the Rouge River, it was accessible to Great Lakes ships carrying iron ore, coal, and timber needed by the complex. It was built between 1917 and 1928, and replaced Ford's Highland Park plant. Ironically, the site had been purchased by Ford, with an eye toward turning it into a bird sanctuary, but during World War I, then secretary of the Navy Franklin Roosevelt persuaded Ford to build boats for the war, and plants were erected on the site.

The complex grew to dominate much of Westside Detroit and the Downriver area, with road systems organized to take the more than 100,000 plant workers of that era to their jobs. New subdivisions in western Wayne County came into being, partly because of the complex. Dearborn was once a small village, but it grew into a city in 1927 with construction of the complex.

The complex reached its peak during the 1930s and in the late 1940s production started moving to other facilities in the metro Detroit area and other facilities nationwide. These days it still employs thousands of workers and is called the Ford Rouge Center. The 600-acre site produces steel, and there's a pickup truck plant. It was long the home of Mustang production.

In an effort to go green, Ford has covered the roof of its truck factory with a green layer of sedum, which is designed to retain rainwater and clean it before returning it to the groundwater system. The 10-acre roof is is a highlight of Ford Rouge tours conducted by The Henry Ford.

Attractions

In Dearborn.

Automotive Hall of Fame (313-240-4000; automotivehalloffame.org; 21400 Oakwood Blvd.) Located near The Henry Ford, the hall is filled with automotive artifacts, old cars, and interactive exhibits that focus on the auto industry. The hall also honors early automakers and their firms. Admission is $8 for adults, $6 for seniors and students, and $4 for children 5–12.

Arab American Museum (313-582-2266; arabamericanmuseum.org; 13624 Michigan Ave.) The museum is thought to be the only such one in the United States, and its focus is on the contributions of Arabic peoples to life in America. It includes a library and resource center, a gallery of displays, meeting rooms, and a museum store. Open Wednesday–Sunday. Admission is $6 for adults and $3 for children.

The Automotive Hall of Fame in Dearborn.

Ford World Headquarters (Michigan Avenue and the Southfield Freeway) Locals call the 11-story building "the glass house." Ford consolidated its offices here in 1956 when the building was opened, and it's home to Ford's far-flung global operations. Henry Ford founded the company in 1903 in Detroit, where his first factory was located, but later moved operations to a larger plant in Highland Park. Operations started shifting back to Ford's hometown of Dearborn in about 1917 when work started on the nearby Ford Rouge Complex. Much of the surrounding land was owned by Ford and it has been developed over the years. There are many other Ford facilities in the area, including design centers and the Ford's test track.

Henry Ford Centennial Library (313-943-2330; dearbornlibrary.org; 16301 Michigan Ave.) In the rush of traffic, one could easily pass this place, which is just across the street from the Ford World Headquarters, but it's worth seeking out for the modernistic architecture of the building and the statue of Henry Ford located here. The site was given to the city of Dearborn to commemorate the 100th anniversary of Ford's birth on July 30, 1963, and the Ford Foundation donated money for construction.

Dearborn has one of the nation's largest populations of people from the Middle East, and they have enriched the city's cultural and restaurant scene. For the most part, Dearborn eateries are pretty traditional places that cater to the mainstream tastes of Ford Motor Co. employees, but in past decades a number of Middle Eastern restaurants have opened along the Michigan Avenue business strip to cater to the large Arabic population in the city. There are many mosques in the city and in the nearby West Side of Detroit. In Dearborn, 30 per-

Henry Ford Estate Fair Lane

While Henry Ford's son, Edsel, moved to the Grosse Pointe area, Henry stayed put and built **Fair Lane** not far from where he was born in western Wayne County (313-593-5590; henryfordestate.org; 4901 Evergreen Rd.) The 1,300-acre estate is on the banks of the Rouge River in Dearborn, where Ford played as a child. He lived there with his wife, Clara, from the time it was completed in 1913 until his death in 1949. One of Ford's first jobs was at a Detroit Edison electric plant in Detroit, and he was fascinated with power plants, so the estate had its own electrical generating plant that also helped power the then village of Dearborn. The cornerstone of the plant was laid by Thomas Alva Edison. One story goes that when he died, the power plant broke down.

The estate was named after an area in County Cork, Ireland, from which Ford's family emigrated. Frank Lloyd Wright was hired to design the home, but when Wright withdrew from the project, the work fell to Marion Griffin, who stuck with the Prairie style favored by Wright but gave it her own touch. Griffin, a master drafter, was thought to be the first licensed woman architect and was deeply involved with Wright in developing the Prairie style.

Fair Lane has 56 rooms and is 31,000 square feet, but when a visitor is inside, the rooms have an intimate feel and you don't feel like you're in a mansion. There are extensive gardens designed by Jens Jensen, and part of the estate is a nature preserve. There is also a boathouse, used by Ford to store his electric boat for travel on the Rouge.

The estate was donated to the University of Michigan, which used much of the land for its Dearborn campus. The estate is currently closed to tours and its ownership was being transferred to the Edsel and Eleanor Ford House in Grosse Pointe Shores. Renovation work is being done and it's expected that the house will reopen for public tours in 2013.

cent of the population has Middle Eastern roots. Most of the Arabic-style restaurants do not sell alcohol. (See Restaurants, Dearborn.)

Arabic foods have almost become mainstream in metro Detroit, with most grocery stores stocking pita and flat breads and other Arabic specialty items. There's even a fast-food chain that has Americanized pita bread and offers roll-up-style sandwiches.

Ford Farms

Henry Ford was a farm kid who ended up owning vast acres of farmland near his estate and now world headquarters located at Michigan Avenue and the Southfield Freeway. Much of the area is now developed, but for many years the land was farmed by students at the Henry Ford Trade School. The high school was founded in 1916 and its curriculum including the industrial arts and agricultural study.

One of Ford's favorite crops was soybeans, which he envisioned as a material that could be used in the production of cars; soybean oil was used in painting Ford's automobiles. Soy was also used in the making of parts during World War II, and there's a well-known photo of Ford hitting a bumper made of soy-based plastics with a hammer to show how strong it was. At the time, some farmers were worried that farm animals would try eating the soy bumpers.

I was well aware of the project because, like many others drawn to Michigan by the auto industry, my father came from Arkansas to Detroit on a Ford scholarship of sorts to teach agriculture at the Ford Trade School. He was well versed in growing soybeans because they were being used in the South to help revive lands that had been depleted by the growing of cotton.

Ford's interest in soybeans for manufacturing came long before automakers started talking about going green and using sustainable materials. A recent Ford commercial brags that the company has long used soybeans as a material. To this day, Ford's acreage is planted with the crop.

Shopping

In Dearborn.

There are really two downtown shopping districts in Dearborn along Michigan Avenue, one located east of the Southfield Freeway that has more of a Detroit feel to it, the other west of the freeway, which has more of an old village atmosphere. That's partly because of how Dearborn formed in the 1920s. The eastern part of the city was once called Springwells, and had been a longtime industrial district bordering Detroit. Much of the land between the two districts is owned by Ford

Historic Ford Neighborhood

During his life, Henry Ford had his hand in a lot of projects in the metro Detroit area, including housing, as can be seen in the **Ford Homes Historic District** in Dearborn (fordhomes.org). The homes were built to house workers at his nearby tractor plant in the days when many people still commuted to work via streetcars.

The tractor plant started in operation in 1915 and employed about 400 workers, who were forced to rent homes for the then-high rate of $75 a month, and even then they had to catch crowded streetcars to get to work.

In about 1918 Ford got involved, but didn't want his name attached to the housing project. He suggested that the homes each look different so as not to look like they were factory made. He also wanted them to be large enough to accommodate families. The Dearborn Realty and Construction Co. was formed, and in 1919 bought 312 lots in an area bounded by the Michigan Central Railroad tracks, and Military, Nowlin, and Monroe Streets. The prices of the new homes ranged from $4,500 to $5,500, and work started on them in 1919 and continued through the early 1920s. The Ford homes are of colonial style and are staggered in their distance from the street.

Annual home tours are offered. Check the group's website for more information.

Motor Co. and was once the site of extensive farming operations, but has since been developed into shopping, office, and residential property. There is still plenty of open land.

New Yasmeen Bakery (313-582-6035; yasmeenbakery.com; 13900 W. Warren Ave.) This is a great place to sample Arabic sweets and baked goods. A specialty is the pita bread, a thin, flat bread with Middle Eastern roots that's been adopted by residents of the metro Detroit area. $

The Fairlane Town Center (800-992-9500; shopfairlane.com; 18900 Michigan Ave.) Near the intersection of Michigan Avenue and the Southfield Freeway, this was one of the first regional malls in Michigan, opening in 1976, and it has become a destination in the general area along with The Henry Ford. It's home to major retailers and has a food court and a movie theater. When it opened, its multilayered design with pedestrian ramps was called innovative, but some shoppers find walking through the mall to be a confusing experience.

Hewitt's Music (313-846-8850; hewittsmusic.com; 13936 Michigan Ave.) The store was founded in 1920 by Clarence Hewitt Sr., and sells new and used musical instruments; it has been an institution for many generations of student musicians in metro Detroit. They also offer music lessons.

Westborn Market (313-278-3815; westbornmarket.com; 21755 Michigan Ave.) There are three of these stores in the metro Detroit area, and they are a favorite of residents looking for quality meats, wines, cheeses, and produce. There are deli foods, and a nice selection of cut flowers. They have an extensive selection of wine.

Hitting the Links

The Dearborn Country Club (313-561-0800; 800 N. Military St.) As with many Dearborn institutions, the club was founded by Henry Ford, in 1925 for his friends and workers. The 18-hole golf course was designed by Donald Ross, and the country club was designed by Ford favorite Albert Kahn. The course has hosted the Tournament Players Championship. The club is private.

INKSTER AND WAYNE

Once you get out of the Dearborn city limits to the west on Michigan Avenue, you are in the more blue-collar suburbs of Inkster and Wayne. Inkster was a suburb that Henry Ford helped create for his African American workers, and it retains that character to this day.

Wayne stretches along Michigan Avenue and has long been a Ford town, with two Ford plants located in at, and employing many of the city's 19,000 residents. The city itself is fairly old and was founded in the 1820s and at first called Derby's Corners, but was later changed to Wayne in honor of General Anthony Wayne, an American officer who served in the War of 1812. Unlike many suburban Detroit communities, it has a traditional downtown and history. Community leaders have been working to revitalize the area, and some efforts are focused on the State-Wayne Theater, a historic art deco structure.

The State-Wayne Theater on Michigan Avenue in Wayne.

The prevalent culture is working class, and nowhere can you better sample that than in the shot-and-a-beer type taverns along the Michigan Avenue corridor (see Watering Holes, Wayne).

YPSILANTI

Pronounced Ip-sa-LAN-tee, the city of nearly 22,000 stretching along Michigan Avenue is a bit of a forgotten place, even though it has a rich history and a state university. Part of the reason for that is that it has long been in the shadow of its larger and better-known community, Ann Arbor, 6 miles to the west, where the University of Michigan is located.

Ypsilanti is the location of Eastern Michigan University, and has many historic homes that in the past few years have been discovered by urban professionals from Ann Arbor who like the area but could do without the Ann Arbor price tag. The area is larger than it appears, and there are another 50,000 or so residents in Ypsilanti Township.

First settled in 1823, "Ypsi" became a city in 1858, and figured heavily in the development of the auto industry, especially that of the Tucker, the ill-fated "car of the future" promoted by Preston Tucker, whose family owned a machine-tool company in the city.

Tucker's story was put on film in 1988 by Detroit-born director Francis Ford Coppola (Coppola's family left the state when he was still very young, but the filmmaker's middle name honors his birthplace, Henry Ford Hospital). Jeff Bridges starred in the movie, *Tucker: The Man and His Dream,* which recounts Tucker's efforts to build and market the 1948 Tucker Sedan. The car was a flop and so was the movie. However, the story tapped into suspicions on the part of the

Depot Town in Ypsilanti is a thriving area with taverns and shops.

American public that the Big Three auto companies could and should be making better products. The Tucker had advanced features that later became common on cars, such as disc brakes, but the company failed regardless.

During World War II, Ypsilanti was a booming place, partly because of the Willow Run plant, located nearby, that mass-produced B-24 Liberator bombers for the military. The plant was built and operated by Ford Motor Co, but was sold to Kaiser Motors and later to General Motors, which still operates it as the Willow Run Transmission Plant.

Another claim to fame is that it was the site of the first Domino's Pizza, which was founded in 1960 by Tom Monaghan and now has outlets nationwide.

A major attraction is Depot Town (www.depottown.org/), a

The Ypsilanti Farmer's Market attracts crowds to Depot Town.

Firefighting History

Located in Depot Town is the **Michigan Firehouse Museum** (734-547-0663; michiganfirehouse museum.org; 110 W. Cross St.). Dedicated to the preservation of firefighting history and promotion of fire safety, the site includes an original 1898 firehouse and a modern display area that houses antique fire trucks and historic artifacts. Kids love this place.

Open Tuesday–Saturday, 10–4, and Sunday 12–4. Admission is $5 for adults, children 2–16 $3. Check website for scheduled events.

Michigan Firehouse Musuem.

historic district centered around an 1838 train stop and commercial hub at East Cross Street near the Huron River. A popular green space called Frog Island Park is here, and in recent years bars, restaurants, small shops, and art galleries have sprung up in the district. Depot Town is also home to a seasonal weekly Farmer's Market, periodic fundraisers, and the annual Michigan Elvisfest, with concerts, tribute artists, and BBQ (www.mielvisfest.org/).

Shopping

In Ypsilanti.

Ypsilanti offers some interesting shops, if you're looking to spend more than just your time here.

Baron Glassworks (734-482-8829; baronglassworks.com; 838 Railroad St.) The shop features works of glass and also offers classes in furnace glassblowing and bead making.

Bowerbird Mongo (734-482-4595; bowerbirdmongo.com; 210 W. Michigan Ave.) There are more art objects than anything else here, and the shop is a delight to pottery collectors.

Materials Unlimited (800-299-9462; www.materialsunlimited.com;

Eastern Michigan University

Eastern Michigan University is less than a mile from the Depot area, and its more than 22,000 students provide plenty of customers for its bars and entertainment venues. The school was founded in 1849 as Normal College, one of many such named teacher-training colleges in Michigan back then. To this day EMU produces educators, but over the years its other departments have expanded and there are now about 23,000 students enrolled. Eastern's art school is fairly well known in the region. The sports teams play in the Mid-American Conference, and are called the Hurons. 89.1 FM is the college radio station, an NPR affiliate broadcasting "jazz, news, and blues." The **Ypsilanti Water Tower** is located near the campus, and has long been a landmark.

2 W. Michigan Ave.) This isn't your typical antiques store; the emphasis is on refurbished home fixtures and architectural details, including lighting, mantels, beveled glass, doors, plumbing fixtures, and hardware. There is also some period furniture.

Schmidt's Antiques (734-434-2660; schmidtsantiques.com; 5138 W. Michigan Ave.) This place has been in the same location since 1938 and specializes in English, French, and Spanish furniture from the 18th through the 20th centuries, along with some art items.

Checking In

Best places to stay in and around Dearborn.

Corktown and Mexicantown are well served by Detroit's downtown-area hotels (see chapter 1). The Dearborn hotels listed are convenient to the area's major attraction, The Henry Ford.

Courtyard by Marriott Dearborn (313-271-1400; marriott.com; 5200 Mercury Dr.) A chain hotel with modern furnishings and Internet connections. Nothing special, but adequate. There's a Courtyard Café inside that serves breakfast. $$

Dearborn Bed & Breakfast (313-563-2200; dearbornbb.com; 22331 Morley) The four-bedroom B&B near downtown Dearborn features Victorian-themed rooms, including one with a hot tub. There are many antiques and a fireplace in the public rooms on the first floor. $$

The Dearborn Inn (313-271-2700; marriott.com; 20301 Oakwood Blvd.) If you like history, this is the place to stay. It was built in 1931 on the grounds of the Ford Motor Co. and was basically the company hotel. Now a Marriott hotel, it's actually fairly affordable, with rates as low as $129 on weekends, and it's within blocks of The Henry Ford. The inn was another idea from Henry Ford and was designed by his favorite architect, Albert Kahn, as a hotel to serve those flying into the nearby Ford Airport. Ford actually built airplanes for a while and the inn is thought to be the first airport hotel. The airport is no longer around. Built in the Colonial Revival style, it is little changed since it opened. It was designed to function in conjunction with the museum and village, and a small colonial village of five homes was built in 1937 to recreate the structures lived in by Edgar Allan Poe, Walt Whitman, Barbara Fritchie, Oliver Wolcott, and Patrick Henry. Guests can still rent them. The facility is on the National Register of Historic Place and the Michigan Historic Register. $$$

Dearborn West Village Hotel (877-259-8970; dearbornwestvillagehotel.com; 20061 Michigan Ave.) The hotel overlooks The Henry Ford and is also close to Ford Motor Co. headquarters. It offers modern rooms, a pool, and a workout room. $$

The Henry, Autograph Collection (313-441-2000; marriott.com; 300 Town Center Dr.) The Marriot hotel is all you would expect from a top-flight hotel,

The Dearborn Inn once was an airport hotel.

with new, modern rooms, a pool, fitness area, restaurants, free Internet access in rooms, and quality service. There are two grand ballrooms. The hotel is 3 miles from The Henry Ford and 2 miles from the Ford World Headquarters. $$ The Gallery Restaurant (313-253-4475), is in the hotel and is open for breakfast, lunch, and dinner. Entrées include chicken, steak, beef, and salmon. Henry's Bar & Grill serves pub-style fare. $$

Local Flavors

Taste of the town—restaurants, cafés, bars, bistros, etc.

Corktown

Slows Bar-B-Q (313-962-9828; www.slowsbarbq.com; 2138 Michigan Ave.) This is more than a restaurant; it has become the poster child for the revitalization of downtown Detroit, attracting attention from the New York Times in its restaurant section. It has defied its location, which is near the hulking shell of the old Michigan Central Train Depot, an abandoned station and office building that's a favorite subject of the news media looking to portray Detroit as a decaying city. The building has received a sleek-looking renovation, and Slows has become a destination restaurant for suburban residents, rather than just a place to eat before or after a sporting event, like many other downtown places. One of its owners, Phillip Cooley, has become a community activist, advising others looking to revive downtown. As for the food, Slows was named one of *Bon Appetit* magazine's best new BBQ places in July 2009; was on the Travel Channel's *Man v. Food*; and was named one of

Slows Bar-B-Q on Michigan Avene in Corktown is evidence of Detroit's resurgence.

America's best BBQ joints by *Budget Travel* magazine. The menu includes baby back ribs, pulled pork, catfish, surf and turf, and Texas-style beef brisket. You can make a meal of the Southern-style sides alone. $$

Dearborn

Al Ameer (313-582-8185; alameerrestaurant.com; 12710 W. Warren Ave.) The décor is more American than Arabic, but this is a good place to introduce yourself to Middle Eastern fare, which you'll find a lot of in Dearborn. The menu includes many American dishes such as fried chicken, but entrées include raw kebbie, a dish of raw lamb topped with onions. For the less adventurous, try the hommus with meat, lamb, beef, or chicken. Hommus is made from chickpeas and spices. Vegetarians will appreciate the tabbouli and fattoush salads. $$

Al-ajami Restaurant (313-846-9330; 14633 W. Warren Ave.) Traditional Middle Eastern fare and some American dishes, including steak and lamb. They serve family trays of Arabic foods, which is a good way to sample a bit of everything. $$

Andiamo Dearborn (313-359-3300; andiamoitalia.com; 21400 Michigan Ave.) The upscale Italian-style place is one of 12 restaurants in the Detroit-based Andiamo chain. The décor is sleek and contemporary. There's a large wine list, and the menu is extensive, with many appetizers, soups, and salads. There's pasta, of course, but there are some interesting Italian variations when it comes to entrées. Try the *pollo con funghi arrosto,* which is free-range chicken stuffed with mushroom mousse and served with potatoes and vegetables. Other dishes include veal, steak, beef, and lamb. $$$

Bistro 222 (313-792-7500; bistro222.com; 22266 Michigan Ave.) Chef/owner Michael Chamas has brought some sophistication to the Dearborn restaurant scene, with this sleekly designed restaurant with deep-redwood tones. The menu is a match, with its blend of American, Italian, and French dishes. There's shrimp scampi,

Bistro 222 is a sophisticated choice on Michigan Avenue in Dearborn.

but also lake perch, a local favorite. For meat lovers, there's a delightful blend of beef and veal with cheese and tomato sauce. There's a full wine cellar. Chamas learned his skills at the Prescott Hotel in San Francisco under Wolfgang Puck. $$$

Cheli's Chili Bar (313-274-9700; chelischilibar.com; 21918 Michigan Ave.) The Detroit Red Wings hockey team has a near-cultlike following, and if you don't have tickets or the team is playing an away game, there are bars that cater to fans. This one, owned by former Red Wing Chris Chelios, is one of the most popular ones, and with its hockey-themed interior it is packed during games. The menu is a bit up from standard burgers and includes ribs, calamari, pulled pork, beef brisket, soups, and of course chili. There's a second location in downtown Detroit. $$

Kiernan's Steak House (313-565-4260; kiernsteakhouse.com; 21931 Michigan Ave.) This has been a classic steakhouse and bar since it opened in the mid-1960s. It's a comfortable place to meet and socialize. There's no loud music, and the focus is on drinks and food. The menu is filled with hearty meals, steak, ribs, and seafood all done in a traditional American style. The bar is classy and a great place for a martini. If you're looking for more entertainment, try Silky's Martini & Music Café, which is part of the steakhouse. Customers will find local pop and rock bands along with some jazz. $$

Miller's Bar (313-565-2577; millersbar.com; 23700 Michigan Ave.) There are other things on the menu, but you may just as well order a cheeseburger and fries or onion rings, because that's what draws most folks to this place, which has been a Dearborn tradition since 1941. Taking a cue from Henry Ford, the burgers are built assembly-line-style, and you pay on the honor system, telling the cashier what you created. You can get a grilled chicken sandwich or grilled cheese, if you really must diverge from the hamburgers. $

Mexicantown

Armando's Mexican Restaurant (313-554-0666; mexicantown.com; 4242 W. Vernor Hwy.) It's open until 4 AM on weekends, and is a favorite for the bar crowd downtown. A top draw are Cuban sandwiches and seafood tacos. $

El Rancho Restaurant (313-843-2151; 5900 W. Vernor Hwy.) It's a low-keyed place, with a homey feel to it, but it offers traditional foods, such as steak, chicken, and shrimp fajitas. $

Restaurants in Mexicantown.

El Zocalo Mexican Restaurant (313-841-35400; elzocalo detroit.com; 3400 Bagley) This place has a more extensive menu. One great appetizer, perhaps adapted from Greektown, is the *queso flameado,* flaming Mexican cheese served with Mexican sausage and sauce. They offer standard dishes like tacos and burritos, and other tempting offerings, including menudo, a beef tripe soup. $$

Evie's Tamales (313-843-5056; 3454 Bagley) This small, family-run place could easily be overlooked by first-time visitors, but shouldn't be, especially if you have a taste for tamales and other traditional Mexican food, like *menudos.* $

Los Galandes (313-554-4444; 3362 Bagley) The menu offers the traditional Mexican fare, but it specializes in seafood, including shrimp. There's music and dancing on some nights. $$

Mexicantown Restaurant (313-841-5811; mexicantown restaurant.com; 3457 Bagley) Try the flaming fajitas, marinated steak, tomato, onion, and green pepper served on a sizzling plate. For lunch, a good option is the Mexican sandwich, composed of tortillas, rice, beans, and either beef or pork. There's also a calamari and octopus salad for the more daring. There's a full bar. $$

Mexican Village Restaurant (313-237-0333; 2600 Bagley) This is the oldest restaurant in Mexicantown, and people keep coming back. Try the *pollo en mole,* chicken cooked in a dark, sweet sauce. It's a bit spicy for some tastes. The Mexican sampler will give you a chance to introduce yourself to Mexican foods. $$

Xochimilco Restaurant (313-843-0199; 3409 Bagley) A favorite haunt for locals. The atmosphere is homey, the portions are large. The bar is known for its botanas and margaritas. $

Brownie's Diner in Wayne is a throwback to the 1950s.

Wayne

Brownie's Diner (734-721-6160; 34250 Michigan Ave.) This little throwback to the 1940s is a longtime local favorite; it's kid-friendly and offers classic dishes such as roast beef sandwiches and other diner fare. $

Ypsilanti

Haab's (734-483-8200; haabs restaurant.com; 18 W. Michigan Ave.) It's a local favorite and has been around since 1934 when Oscar and Otto Haab opened it. The restaurant has housed a bar or restaurant since the 1850s. The 30-foot-long mahogany bar dates to 1906 and there's still a portion of a wall that divided the women's and men's sections of the tavern. The menu is composed of American favorites, and includes seafood, fish, chicken, and beef. A top seller is the London broil marinated in burgundy, herbs, and spices. $$

Haab's Resturant has long been a fixture in Ypsilanti.

Watering Holes

Corktown

Casey's Pub (313-963-2440; 1830 Michigan Ave.) This place has been a favorite of Tiger fans for more than 25 years and is a friendly place to watch a ball game while having a burger and a beer. Make sure to bring cash; they don't take credit cards here. This is also the home base of many who show up each March for the annual St. Patrick's Day Parade on Michigan Avenue. $

Corktown Tavern (313-964-5103; 1716 Michigan Ave.) This is a music-driven place that attracts a dance crowd and is an example of the newer nightlife resurging in Corktown. Many local bands find a place to try out their music here. $

Gaelic League and Irish American Club (313-964-7474; gaelic leagueofdetroit.org; 2068 Michigan Ave.) The club is home to many Irish-related activities in the metro Detroit area, and on many weekends it features Irish entertainment, including music and step dancing. It's involved in the annual St. Patrick's Day Parade. Alcohol is served. A membership form is available at their website. $

Nancy Whiskey Pub (313-962-4247; 2644 Harrison) This is one of Detroit's hidden gems, a blues bar that attracts music devotees of all ages. The original bar was destroyed by fire several years ago, and to the relief of its devotees, it rebuilt. The best way to get there is to turn off Michigan onto Rosa Parks Boulevard/12th Street, go over the Fisher Freeway (I-75), and turn east on Spruce. The bar is at the corner of Spruce and Harrison. It's mostly a drinking and music bar, but you can get a burger, if you can get the attention of the usually very busy waitstaff. Various amateur musicians wander in and play during jam sessions. $

Nemo's (313-965-3180; nemosdetroit.com; 1384 Michigan Ave.) The menu is basically burgers and beer, but sports talk is the centerpiece in the nearly century-old building with a cool old tin ceiling. While patrons with tickets shuttle back and forth between the sports venues and the bar, many use the place to watch the games and soak up the atmosphere. $

Dearborn

Bailey's Pub N' Grille (313-277-3212; 22091 Michigan Ave.) This is the kind of place people come to hunker down after a hard day at the plant or office. The menu is basic pub food, burgers and nachos. $

The Biergarten (313-561-7711; 22184 Michigan Ave.) An affordable burger-and-beer place that can get crowded on weekends. There are beer specials and karaoke nights. $

Double Olive (313-359-5533; 22027 Michigan Ave.) Strong martinis, including chocolate ones, are the draw. Darts and pool tables are other attractions in this busy bar. $

Howells Bar & Grill (313-565-6322; 1035 Mason St.) A classic small, friendly, corner neighborhood bar with burgers and beer. Forget the plastic, though; last time we checked, this was a cash-only establishment. $

Post Bar Dearborn (313-277-3524; 22065 Michigan Ave.) It's a place to unwind after work, and attracts a younger crowd, especially on weekends when the dance floor can be packed. The menu isn't huge, but you can get dinner here. $

Wayne

Jake's Again (734-728-1570; 3519 S. Wayne Rd.) This sports bar is a favorite of locals out for a burger and a beer. Sporting the University of Michigan school colors, it's a good place to settle back and watch a game. The menu is mostly pub food. $

US 12 American Bar & Grill (734-722-3170; 34824 W. Michigan Ave.) The bar takes its name from Michigan Avenue, which bears the designation US 12. Don't come overdressed to this place, which attracts a younger crowd intent on drinking beer. There's some pub food, but it's not a family-friendly place. $

Ypsilanti

Corner Brewery (734-480-2739; cornerbrewery.com; 720 Norris) This is a cleaned-up version of a college-town barn, with its own beer and pub food such as burgers and pizzas. The ceilings are high and there's plenty of natural light, so you don't get that cramped bar feeling. $

The Elbow Room (734-956-0526; elbowroomypsi.com; 6 S. Washington St.) It's about live music and beer. The entertainment tends toward the cutting edge, with mostly local performers including The Squidling Brothers Ringmaster Zeb, Collateral Damage, Heroes on Parade, and the Green Room Rockers.

The Tap Room is a popular watering hole in Ypsilanti.

Tap Room (734-482-5320; taproomypsi.com; 201 W. Michigan Ave.) The historic tavern building dates to the 1890s and has long been a favorite local hangout. Although it has changed some over the years, it still has a classic neon sign featuring a martini glass, an old wooden bar, and paneling and historic fixtures. There's music some nights; call ahead. The menu is mostly pub food. $

East Jefferson Cruise

THE EAST SIDE, GROSSE POINTE, ST. CLAIR SHORES

THE CORNER OF WOODWARD AVENUE and Jefferson has long been the dividing line between Detroit's East and West Sides, each of which has a different character. While the riverfront on the West Side, and an area south of it, Downriver, have long had a working-class feel, parts of the East Side along the river and into Grosse Pointe are notably upscale in character.

A cruise from Detroit's East Side to the Grosse Pointe area takes visitors past upscale waterfront homes and old historic neighborhoods. There are some first-class restaurants along the river, along with some traditional watering holes. Jefferson has long been used as a community road by professionals who live in the Grosse Pointe area and commute to offices downtown.

THE EAST SIDE

Visitors can get a good look at the Detroit River just off Jefferson from the William G. Milliken State Park (313-396-0217; michigan .gov/dnr; 1900 Atwater St.). Fishing is allowed from the banks, and there are picnic facilities, and a lighthouse to view.

LEFT: A historic home in Detroit's Indian Village.

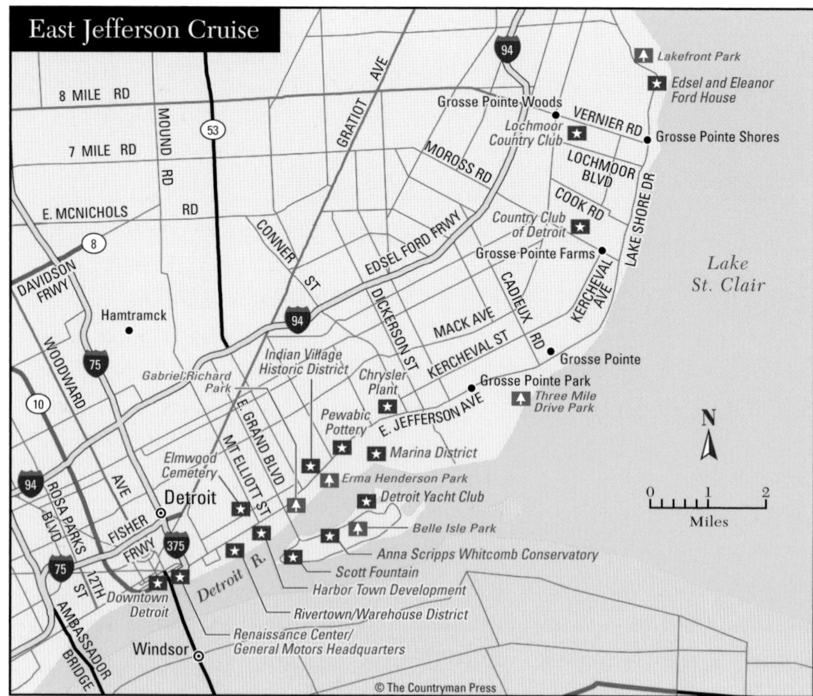

One of Detroit's showcase developments, Stroh River Place (300 River Place), is along E. Jefferson and on the river. The 25-acre mixed-use complex includes offices, businesses, apartments, and restaurants. It's the former headquarters of the Stroh Brewery Company.

For old-time Detroiters, Stroh's beer was a symbol of Detroit, and generations were devoted to the brew until it was sold to Miller, much to the distress of its devotees. Like many large industrial cities, Detroit had dozens of breweries until Prohibition. Stroh's was founded in Detroit in 1850 by the Stroh family, shortly after they arrived from Germany, and was brewed in the city until 2000, when it was sold. Although it's still on shelves, it doesn't have the allure in Detroit that it once did.

A short detour about a half mile north of E. Jefferson on Mt. Elliot Street takes you to historic Mt. Elliot and Elmwood Cemeteries, two of the oldest in Detroit and the final resting place of many of the city's founders.

Worth a visit on Detroit's East Side is Belle Isle (www.fobi.org), a

The MacArthur Bridge connects Belle Isle Park with the mainland.

982-acre island in the Detroit River that has been Detroit's playground since the 19th century. It was first settled by the French, who called it Hog Island, and for a time it was a private estate, but by the 1880s a bridge connected it to the mainland and the island had become a park. Well-known landscape architect Frederick Law Olmstead created a design for the island, and some of that work was carried out. In the days before air-conditioning, the island was a perfect place to go to escape Detroit's hot, humid summer nights.

These days, Belle Isle is a destination for joggers and bicyclists. It's also a good place to watch ships plying the Great Lakes trade, many of them iron ore freighters. From the island's south end, there's a good view of downtown Detroit.

The island is home to the Dossin Great Lakes Museum (313-833-1733; www.detroithistorical.org/main/dossin/index.aspx; 100 The Strand). The museum pays tribute to Detroit's maritime heritage, and has exhibits and artifacts from Great Lakes ships. On display is the anchor of the famous Edmund Fitzgerald, the last ship to sink in the Great Lakes, in 1975. Call ahead to arrange a tour.

Detroit's skyline as seen from Belle Isle.

Heidelberg Project

When Detroiter Tyree Guyton returned home from the Army in the late 1960s, he noticed that the homes on Heidelberg Street in his East Side neighborhood had deteriorated after the 1967 racial riots that hit the city, and in the 1980s, with the help of his grandfather and some neighborhood kids, he started decorating the homes with fanciful colors, designs, and decorations.

The block began to look like a fairyland, but not everyone appreciated the artwork. During the 1990s, under two Detroit mayors, six highly decorated homes were demolished by the city.

However, since then, the initiative has gained a new appreciation among both art lovers and urban renewal experts. By 2006, the 20th anniversary of the project's start, a community festival was held to celebrate the works. That was followed by two books about the project.

The Heidelberg Project (313-974-6894; www.heidelberg.org) is located in a traditionally African American neighborhood on Heidelberg Street near Mack Avenue on Detroit's East Side. There are 22 art sites featured in a one-block-long section.

There are also notable historical structures on the island, including Scott Fountain, Anna Scripps Whitcomb Conservatory, and the Detroit Yacht Club. Scott Fountain was built with a bequest from a 19th-century Detroit businessman, James Scott, in 1925. It has a 510-foot diameter and its central spray reaches 125 feet.

The Scripps Whitcomb Conservatory (313-331-7760; bibsociety.org) was designed by Detroit architect Albert Kahn and built in 1904; it was later named in honor of Anna Scripps Whitcomb, who left her 600-plant orchid collection to the city. It has formal perennial gardens, annual flowerbeds, a rose garden, and a lily pond. It is maintained by the Belle Isle Botanical Society. Call ahead for hours.

Established in 1868, The Detroit Yacht Club (313-824-1200, dyc.com) is a members-only social and athletic club located on its own private island adjacent to Belle Isle. Lots of little Grosse Pointe girls grow up dreaming about getting married here, and it's the location of various other special events and fundraisers.

Continuing east on Jefferson, make a turn onto Burns, Iroquois, or Seminole Streets to tour Indian Village, a historic district of more than 350 homes, most dating to the early 20th century. The large homes in various styles were built by well-to-do Detroiters, with Edsel Ford, the son of Henry Ford, being an early resident. Some of the homes are more than 12,000 square feet, and were designed by well-known architects of the time. Home styles include Federal, neo-Renaissance, Tudor Revival, neo-Georgian, beaux-arts, Gothic Revival, and Colonial Revival.

Many of the Indian Village homes are decorated with Detroit-crafted Pewabic tiles made in an art deco style. Examples can be found just east of the village at Pewabic Pottery (313-822-0954; pewabic.org; 10125 E. Jefferson Ave.) The pottery shop is a National Historic Landmark, and has been in the same building since 1907. It was founded by Mary Chase Perry Stratton (1867–1961), an artist who was involved in the arts and crafts design movement of the late 19th century. The name "Pewabic" comes from a copper mine in Michigan's Upper Peninsula near Houghton, where Stratton lived as a child, and it refers to the pottery's glossy glaze. The word itself is from the Native American Ojibwa people, who used it to describe the color of copper.

The ceramic tiles produced in this style were used in many Detroit buildings, both public and private, and can be seen in the Buhl Building in downtown Detroit, at the Detroit Institute of Arts, the Detroit Public Library, and the Detroit Zoo. Guided tours of the Pewabic building are available, as are hands-on workshops; call for fee and scheduling information. Self-guided tours are free and available Monday–Friday 10–4.

Nearby on the riverfront is the Whittier Apartments (415 Burns Dr.), which was constructed from 1921 through 1927 and was once a top-tier hotel, attracting well-known visitors. Over the years it has had its ups and downs, but now serves as an apartment building. It was added to the National Register of Historic Places in 1985.

The Pewabic Pottery shop on Jefferson Avenue is a Detroit institution.

Jefferson Avenue Presbyterian Church (8625 E. Jefferson) is worth a brief stop. The neo-Gothic structure was built in 1926, while the church itself dates to 1854. There's a historic plaque.

Just behind the church is Erma Henderson Park, E. Jefferson and Iroquois, which is named for a Detroit city councilwoman. The park features a public marina.

Detroit's East Side offers some primo opportunities for dining riverside (see Restaurants, East Side).

GROSSE POINTE

Once travelers pass Alter Road, they're in Grosse Pointe, one of the region's more affluent areas, and E. Jefferson becomes Lake Shore Drive. Technically Grosse Pointe is comprised of five communities that share variations on the name and are stretched out along Lake Shore Drive on Lake St. Clair until the road hits St. Clair Shores. "The Pointes" include Grosse Pointe Park, Grosse Pointe, Grosse Pointe Farms, Grosse Pointe Shores, and Grosse Pointe Woods. Most Detroiters simply call the entire area Grosse Pointe or the Pointes.

Lake Shore Drive is lined with mansions that receive the cool summer breeze off Lake St. Clair. It's also dotted with marinas where yachtsmen moor their sail- and motorboats, and the lake is typically crowded during summer months.

In the 19th century, the Grosse Pointe area was a summer resort

A mansion on Lake St. Clair on Windmill Pointe in the Grosse Pointes.

Hitting the Links

The Country Club of Detroit (313-881-8000; ccofd.com; 220 Country Club Drive, Grosse Pointe Farms) The 18-hole course is a private club. One of the first courses in the Detroit area, it was founded in 1897 by a group of Detroit business leaders. The club grew quickly in the 20th century as golf became more popular.

Lochmoor Country Club (313-886-1010; lochmoorclub.com; 1018 Sunningdale Dr., Grosse Pointe Woods) The club was founded in 1917 when a group of well-to-do Grosse Pointe families bought 135 acres of farmland. Among the early members were Edsel Ford, the Dodge brothers, and Eddie Rickenbacker, the World War I flying ace. The club is private.

A home on Windmill Pointe in Grosse Pointe.

destination where well-to-do Detroiters spent their summers, but with the advent of the automobile it eventually became the favored address for upper-middle-class and wealthy people, many of whom had made their fortunes in the auto business. One of the lone holdouts was Henry Ford, who built his Fair Lane estate in his hometown of Dearborn, but his son Edsel built an elaborate mansion in Grosse Pointe on the lake.

While there are many large homes to gaze at, there isn't a lot to do in the Pointes; there are no restaurants or bars located along the lake, and parking can be difficult if you want to stroll near the water. Nearby Mack Avenue is Grosse Point's business strip. But don't expect too much in the way of restaurants or entertainment in the Pointes, which have long been synonymous with wealthy WASP culture in the Detroit area.

There are businesses on nearby Kercheval, where there are some restaurants. One area, called The Hills, offers the most services. You

The Fords in Grosse Pointe

If there's one family that looms over Detroit, it's the Fords. The Ford logo is still around after more than 100 years, and the family is still involved in running the auto company; another family member owns the Detroit Lions.

Many of the Fords have lived in Grosse Pointe, but not Henry—he built his estate, Fair Lane, in his hometown of Dearborn. However, his only son, Edsel, opted to build his dream home on the shores of Lake St. Clair in Grosse Pointe. Edsel had four children, and many of his descendants still live in the Detroit area and are active in the company and the community.

Tours of the **The Edsel and Eleanor Ford House** (313-884-4222; fordhouse.org; 1100 Lake Shore Rd.) are offered, and travelers can get a glimpse into the past when auto barons built large houses in the Detroit area. The home on Gaukler Pointe was designed by Detroit architect Albert Kahn, and resembles a cluster of Cotswold village cottages with stone roofs, vine-covered exteriors, and lead-paned windows.

Edsel Ford (1893–1943) was the only son of Henry Ford, the founder of Ford Motor Co., and was president of the company from 1919 until his death in 1943 from a stomach ailment. Unfortunately, his name was used for the auto manufacturer's biggest mistake, the Edsel, in the 1950s. The model was a failure.

However, Edsel had some notable accomplishments. While his father tended to be conservative when it came to auto styling and color, the son liked sports cars, and prompted redesigns and the use of a V-8 engine in Ford cars. The company had produced the

have to be an insider to know its location. There's actually no hill at The Hills; it's formally called Kercheval on The Hill, and it is a business district in Grosse Pointe Farms.

The Pointes show up in books, movies, and on television on occasion, with references to its so-called preppy lifestyle. The 1997 movie *Grosse Pointe Blank* starring John Cusack was set in the communities but was actually filmed mostly in Chicago. The area also serves as a backdrop to Michigan writer Jeffrey Eugenides' novels *The Virgin Suicides* and *Middlesex.*

Model T for more than ten years, but when sales started to lag, it began producing the Model A in the late 1920s. Edsel had an affinity for the style of that time, which is evident from a tour of his home. One room is done totally in the art deco style. The gardens are somewhat unconventional and were designed by Jens Jensen, a Danish immigrant, as a modern landscape that takes advantage of American wildflowers.

The home is furnished with many 18th-century antiques, and like the exterior, much of it is done in an English style, with wood paneling imported from England in many rooms, and a Gothic chimney in the English baronial hall that came from an English estate.

If the walls could talk in Edsel's study, it would be interesting to hear what they witnessed when he spent his evenings here, talking to other industrialists of his era. The room has been kept the same as it was at the time of his death. With its Elizabethan oak paneling, it has the feel of a gentleman's club of a bygone era. It's decorated with many photos, and also has a model of his favorite sailboat, *The Acadia.*

Edsel was also active with the Detroit Institute of Arts, and came to the rescue of a controversial set of murals done there titled *Detroit Industry* by Mexican muralist Diego Rivera, an avowed Marxist, in the 1930s (for more on the controversy, see Detroit Institute of Arts listing, p. 89)

There are tours of The Edsel and Eleanor Ford House and its grounds; call ahead to schedule. The house tours are $12 for adults, $11 for seniors, and $8 for children 8–12. Garden tours are $5. Light lunches are served in the Cotswold Café on the grounds.

While the Pointes have a reputation as being the most upscale suburbs in metro Detroit, Oakland County communities like Birmingham, Bloomfield, and Franklin have attracted increasingly wealthy residents in recent decades.

Just east of The Edsel and Eleanor Ford House is the Grosse Pointe War Memorial (313-881-7511; warmemorial.org; 32 Lakeshore Drive), which was built in 1910 as the private residence of Russell A. Alger Jr., a politician of his era. The home was known as The Moorings, and it was bequeathed to the community in 1949. It

Grosse Pointe War Memorial.

serves as a community center for the Grosse Pointe area and is on the National Register of Historic Places.

Lakeshore Drive runs to the edge of Lake St. Clair, and if you can find a place to park, walking, running, or bicycling along the lake is popular. It's a good way to see the mansions that line the lake.

ST. CLAIR SHORES

Lakeshore Drive eventually turns back into East Jefferson Avenue when you pass into St. Clair Shores, a Detroit suburb of about 60,000 that has many private marinas on Lake St. Clair and is another popular destination for boaters in the metro Detroit area. It's a working-class suburb, and while there are nice homes near the lake, it's nowhere near as exclusive or expensive as the Grosse Pointes.

Just northeast of St. Clair Shores in Harrison Township is Metropolitan Beach, the largest beach on Lake St. Clair in the metro Detroit area. Metro Beach (800-477-3172; www.metroparks.com; 31300 Metro Parkway) is part of the Huron-Clinton park system that has 13 facilities on 25,000 acres surrounding the Detroit area. Hikers, bicyclists, and runners are attracted to the 770-acre park, which has a beach and a 1,600-foot boardwalk overlooking a mile-long shoreline. Nature trails take hikers through meadows, marshland, and a grove of cottonwood trees. The park is home to more than 230 commonly seen birds. There's also a boat launch. A Metroparks sticker is required for entrance.

Local Flavors

Taste of the town—restaurants, cafés, bars, bistros, etc.

East Side

Sindbads at the River (313-822-7817; sindbads.com; 100 St. Clair) This place has been a favorite of boat owners since 1949, when it first opened at the site of an old speakeasy. Located near a boat docking facility, it appeals to mariners. It has a well-worn, cozy feel and has a view of the river. The bar is large and attracts an eclectic crowd of patrons, ranging from suburbanites to city dwellers. The menu is nothing special, but it's adequate and has standard favorites, including fried fish, burgers, and steak. $$

The Rattlesnake Club offers fine dining along the Detroit River.

Rattlesnake Club (313-567-4400; rattlesnakeclub.com; 300 River Place) Located in Stroh River Place, the restaurant is the creation of Jimmy Schmidt, a well-known Detroit chef, and the menu focuses on traditional American dishes, including steak, short ribs, game birds, and pasta creations. There are creative appetizers such as oysters in champagne sauce served with caviar. The atmosphere is casual, and the place has a clean, modern look. $$$

Rumors on the River (313-331-1012; 8900 E. Jefferson) A friendly tavern, a favorite for folks as an after-work gathering place. Sandwiches are served. $

Grosse Point

Blue Pointe Restaurant (313-882-3653; 17131 E. Warren, Detroit) The Muer family is legendary in the metro area for operating some of the best fish and seafood restaurants, and this place is run by David Muer. The recipe for successful fish is to make it simple, broiled, pan fried or deep-fried, and that's what they do here with such dishes as perch and whitefish. $$

Bucci Ristorante (313-882-1044; ristorantebucci.com; 20217 Mack, Grosse Pointe Woods) Under the ownership of chef Bujar Mamuslari, the small, neighborhood restaurant has evolved into one with a European flair, in line with the owner's background in many Old World kitchens. The wine list complements the dishes, which include sea scallops, pasta, chicken, and Italian sausage in a traditional ragout; and perch. $$$

Cadieux Café (313-8828560; cadieuxcafe.com; 4300 Cadieux Rd., Detroit) The small tavern is a favorite of Detroiters and a throwback to a different era, when many bars had an ethnic flavor. In this case it's Belgian; the café offers Flemish foods and feather bowling. At one time it was a Prohibition speakeasy and the social hub for the Belgian community. It was recently featured on Anthony Bourdain's *No Reservations* TV show on the Travel Channel. In the episode Bourdain sampled the beer stew and mussels. The game of feather bowling involves rolling balls to get them as close to a feather as possible, and is usually played by teams. The menu is big on mussels, but also includes a Belgian dip sandwich. As expected, there are many Belgian beers. $$

The Cadiux Café near the Grosse Pointe communities.

City Kitchen (313-82-6667; city-kitchen.com; 16844 Kercheval Ave., Grosse Pointe) There's a wood-burning pizza oven inside the well-crafted interior that includes leather-upholstered booths, oak tables, and a zinc bar. It's sleek, and so is the menu, which includes pizza hot from the oven, steak, and seafood. Try the lake perch, which is sautéed with capers and lemon, or the beef tenderloin tournedos. They've come up with a good idea here: light-portion meals. $$$

Da Edoardo (313-881-8540; daedoardo.com; 19767 Mack Ave.) Edoardo Barbieri, the founder, was an Italian immigrant, but he didn't pass through Ellis Island, like many others. He was a soldier in the Italian army during World War II and was fighting in North Africa when he was captured by the Americans and shipped back to the United States as a prisoner of war, and eventually ended up working in the mess hall at Fort Wayne. He returned to Italy after the war, married, and eventually returned to America, set-

The Hill on Kercheval Avenue.

tling in Detroit. The restaurant is still family-owned. The menu is filled with traditional Italian fare and includes veal, seafood, steak, lamb, chicken and beef. There are also pizzas and pasta. $$

Dirty Dog Jazz Café (313-882-5299; dirtydogjazz.com; 97 Kercheval, Grosse Pointe Farms) The small but elegant place is reminiscent of night-clubs from the 1940s and '50s but has a more upscale feel. The intimate space is well suited to listening to jazz. The menu isn't large but it's adequate, and includes fried oysters, salmon, calamari, and Korean beef. The bar is the place to be. The music is top notch, with performers such as Thornetta Davis, Jason Marsalis, Freda Payne, Johnnie Bassett, Kimmie Horne, and Bobby Lyle. $$$

The Hill Seafood & Chop House (313-886-8101; thehill grossepointe.com; 123 Kercheval Ave.) The bar/restaurant offers fine dining, and a sleek place to have cocktails. But while the décor is upscale, the atmosphere is casual and comfortable, with low lighting. The menu includes steaks, chops, seafood, chicken, and some pasta dishes. The Lake Superior whitefish is a good pick. $$

Rustic Cabins Bar (313-821-6480; 15209 Kercheval St., Grosse Pointe) Not every place in the Grosse Pointe area is upscale, and anyway, everybody gets the occasional hankering for a cheeseburger and a beer. One patron during the 1940s was writer Jack Kerouac, who spent several months living in Grosse Pointe with his then wife, Edie, and worked in a factory, one of the best jobs he ever had. To get away from the upper-middle-class lifestyle of his wife's family, he would escape to the Rustic Cabins for a beer and listen to jazz. He had good taste: the bar is comfortable and has a satisfyingly "up North" feel. $

Rustic Cabins in Grosse Pointe.

200
IMPORTED FROM DETROIT
CHRYSLER

Oakland County

AUBURN HILLS; ROCHESTER; TROY; THE BLOOMFIELD AREA; FARMINGTON AND FARMINGTON HILLS; NOVI

OAKLAND COUNTY is located north of Wayne County and is one of the largest counties in terms of landmass in the state, and also in population, with about 1.2 million residents, second only to Wayne (population 1.9 million). Apart from Pontiac (see chapter 2) and Troy, there are no large cities, and the county has about 62 different political entities.

A number of Fortune 500 companies are located in the sprawling county, and the region has a reputation of being very well-to-do. It ranks as the fourth-most-affluent county in the nation, but among its suburbs there are numerous blue-collar enclaves.

The Chrysler Corporation is headquartered here, in Auburn Hills, and Oakland County is also home to many General Motors executives, who can easily commute via I-75 to GM headquarters in the Renaissance Center downtown, or to GM's nearby Warren Technical Center.

The county also has inland lakes and recreation areas that are popular boating and swimming destinations in the summer.

The difference between Wayne and Oakland Counties is

LEFT: Chrysler World Headquarters in Auburn Hills.

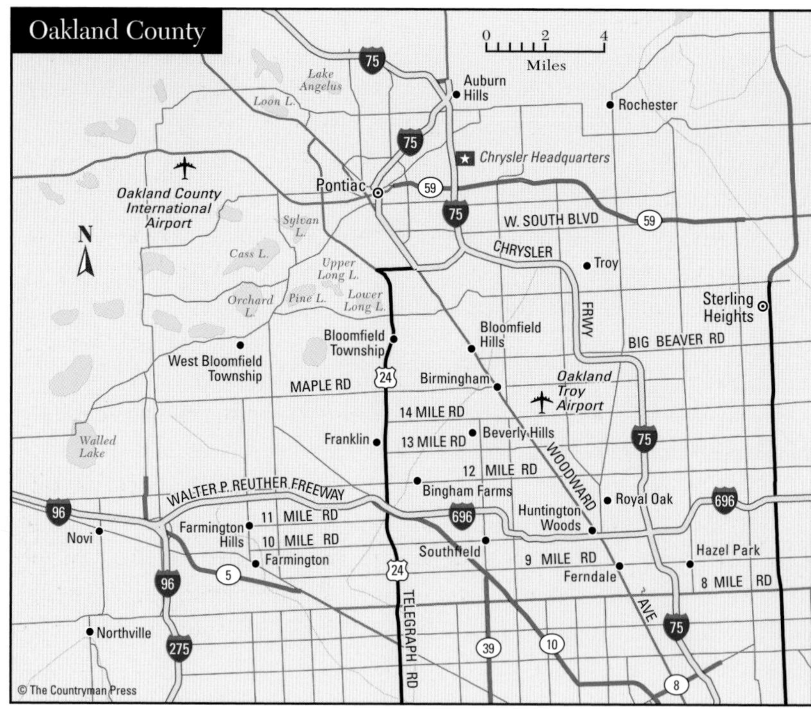

palpable, and visitors can see it immediately during a stop in the upscale communities of Rochester and Troy. Henry Ford set a conservative, even somber tone for his workers, traditionally associated with western Wayne County, decades ago. For years, Ford white-collar workers were just that, clad in the Ford uniform of white shirts and dark ties. Oakland County is home to more GM and Chrysler executives, who traditionally wore more colorful clothing and dined at more expensive restaurants.

To this day, visitors will find more trendy restaurants and wine bars in Oakland, and the patrons there will typically be more stylishly dressed than in Wayne. One shopping destination that keeps Oakland County's fashion-conscious up to snuff is the Somerset Collection (see Troy).

To keep track of what's in and what's out, many Oakland County residents subscribe to *Hour Detroit*, a monthly lifestyle publication that not only lists and reviews restaurants but also does lush photo stories on homes, mostly in Oakland County (see listing in chapter 11).

Located in central Oakland County, the city was founded in 1983 out of the former Pontiac Township and Auburn Heights, and it is home to the Chrysler Corporation headquarters, the Palace of Auburn Hills, where the Detroit Pistons play, BorgWarner, a large auto supplier, and Oakland University.

The small city of about 20,000 is accessible to Detroit because I-75 is in the center of the community. Many of Oakland County's numerous communities don't have direct freeway access, partly because residents have opposed their construction and partly because the county's many lakes hinder such construction. Great Lakes Crossing is a major attraction for its outlet shopping, movie theater, and (mostly chain) dining.

The Chrysler Headquarters and Technology Center is basically the city's professional hub and a major taxpayer. The complex is located on 504 acres, and has 5.3 million square feet of space for its nearly 10,000 employees. The campus replaced Chrysler's old headquarters in Highland Park, which had served as the nerve center of the corporation since it was formed in the 1920s.

The building's design was much touted when it opened in the mid-1990s because its design was said to foster better cooperation between departments. It also put the design studios in the same place as the business and technical operations, making it different from either Ford or GM, where the design studios and engineers are located in separate facilities from the business operations.

The main building is topped by the Chrysler logo and has rounded-off exterior corners that make it look like a car body. The complex is composed of the Chrysler Group World Headquarters, a 15-story building that includes the offices of its corporate executives, accounting, legal, and marketing and sales staffs; the Chrysler Auburn Hills Technology Center, which houses vehicle product teams and design studios, plus a 170,000-square-foot Pilot Plant; and Chrysler Auburn Hills Scientific Laboratories, which conducts auto testing.

The Walter P. Chrysler Museum (wpchryslermuseum.org; 1 Chrysler Dr.), which is near the intersection of Featherstone and Squirrel Roads, is in the complex and is open to the public. There are many vintage cars on display, along with exhibits about how Chrysler Corporation got its start.

A major attraction is The Palace of Auburn Hills (248-377-0100; palacenet.com), 6 Championship Dr., which is the home court of the

The Walter P. Chrysler Museum is open to the public.

Detroit Pistons basketball team, and also a major music performance venue. It's located off I-75; take the Lapeer Road exit and expect lots of slow-moving traffic on game and event nights.

Auburn Hills has the look of one big corporate park, with office buildings and many chain hotels and restaurants catering to Chrysler workers and Oakland University students. Nearby Rochester has a cheerful downtown area with shopping, hotels, and restaurants, and would be a good choice for those needing to stay near the Chrysler complex. Nearby Troy also offers many hotels and restaurants, and is a large center for corporate offices.

ROCHESTER

The city of about 10,000 residents is a destination for many Oakland County residents in that it has a traditional downtown shopping district, with many of the businesses, including restaurants, located in older brick buildings. It's named for Rochester, New York, where many of its settlers came from in the early 19th century, and it is located near the Clinton River and Paint Creek, a trout stream.

Some of the notable buildings on Main Street include the Rollin Sprague Building, which dates to 1849 and has been a bakery for many years, and the Rochester Opera House, dating from 1890, which has been refurbished.

Rochester offers plenty of shopping and dining options.

The Western Knitting Mills building on Water Street was constructed in 1896 and for many years produced gloves. These days, the restored building houses the Rochester Mills Beer Co. brewpub (see Restaurants) and offices.

The nearby Municipal Park behind City Hall, at 400 Sixth Street, is good for a stroll. There are walkways and playgrounds along Paint Creek, tennis courts, and ice skating when the ponds freeze over.

TROY

I-75 bisects this city of about 81,000 residents and makes it easily accessible to the metro region. It has become a favorite location for corporations, including Bank of America, the Budd Company, Delphi Corporation, DuPont Automotive, Flagstar Bank, J.D. Power and Associates, Kelly Services, the Kresge Foundation, and the Woodbridge Group.

Most of the office complexes in Troy are located along the Big Beaver Road corridor, which is very busy during rush hour. There are about 125,000 workers in the city, more than its population. The residential areas are found mostly to the north and south of Big Beaver, and are mostly composed of affluent subdivisions where the family household income average is over $100,000. *Newsweek* placed

Troy's two high schools on its list of the thousand Most Outstanding High Schools in the nation.

The Somerset Collection (248-643-6360; thesomerset collection.com; 2800 W. Big Beaver Rd.) is a major attraction with its upscale shops. It's really two malls, one south of Big Beaver Road and one north of it, that are connected by name and a walkway bridging the busy roadway. There's a food court on the top of the north building. There are also hotels and restaurants located in and around it.

Most accommodations are large chain hotels located along the Big Beaver business corridor, and along I-75 nearby (see Hotels, Troy).

The Sommerset Collection mall in Troy is a top attraction in the community.

THE BLOOMFIELD AREA

The West Bloomfield Township community is another affluent Oakland County suburb where the median income is about $99,000 per household. The township is known its large number of inland lakes, including Cass, Pine, and Orchard, where many large homes have been constructed along the water. There are few direct routes through the township, and most traffic is carried by Orchard Lake Road, which runs north-south and is very crowded during rush hour.

West Bloomfield has a large Jewish population and many Jewish cultural institutions are located here, including the Jewish Community Center of Metropolitan Detroit, several Jewish schools, and the Jewish Historical Society of Michigan. A touchstone for the Jewish community is the Holocaust Memorial Center, Zekelman Family Campus, in nearby Farmington Hills (248-553-2400; holocaustcenter .org; 28123 Orchard Lake Road) The center maintains a large library and various exhibits that pay tribute to victims of the Holocaust. It's said to be the first freestanding museum of its kind here in the States.

Meadow Brook Hall

A major attraction in Rochester is **Meadow Brook Hall and Gardens** (248-364-6200; meadowbrookhall.org; 480 S. Adams Rd.). The Tudor Revival mansion was constructed by Matilda Dodge Wilson, the widow of auto baron John Dodge, between 1926 and 1929. The hall and grounds were later donated to the State of Michigan for use as a university; it is now the site of the **Oakland University** campus. There are tours held throughout the year, with a special holiday tour in November and December. Numerous events are held at the mansion, including weddings.

Matilda Dodge Wilson was one of the richest women in the world after the death of her husband in 1920, and she spent $4 million to build the elaborate 88,000-square-feet manor home. The estate was built on a 320-acre farm, but eventually expanded to 1,500 acres.The 110-room structure is reminiscent of an English country home, and its setting in gently rolling hills helps heighten that genteel effect. Most of the metro area is flat as a pancake until you get into the Rochester area. The ceilings are of ornate plaster and there are many wood carvings, and Tiffany stained glass.

The Meadow Brook Theatre (248-377-3300; mbtheatre.com; 207 Wilson Hall), on the Oakland University campus, offers major professional theater productions, which have included *Dracula: A Rock Opera, The 39 Steps,* and a yearly production of *A Christmas Carol.*

Visits are guaranteed to be both educational and moving. The museum is open to the public, closed on Saturdays and Jewish holidays.

The Bloomfield Hills and Bloomfield Township communities and a small enclave, Franklin, are home to some of the metro Detroit area's most wealthy residents. Bloomfield Hills is one of the top five richest communities in the nation. The median household income is more than $200,000, and about half the homes are worth more than $1 million. Its residents include many sports and entertainment figures.

Telegraph Road and Woodward Avenue are the major arteries serving the communities, and the major crossroads, going east-west, are Maple, Lone Pine, and Long Lake Roads, but don't expect to see many of the palatial homes, as they are set far back from the roads and are tucked into woodlands. Bloomfield Township has a large number of inland lakes, and many of the homes are built on them.

Most of the area's restaurants and hotels are located along the well-developed Telegraph Road corridor.

FARMINGTON AND FARMINGTON HILLS

The area in western Oakland County is large and affluent, and filled with subdivisions, but there are also a number of corporate offices and auto-related facilities. The city of Farmington is surrounded by Farmington Hills, and has a small, historic downtown. Located in Farmington are Gale, a publishing company; Chrysler Financial; and the Nissan Technical Center.

The city of Farmington is a historic rural community that became encircled by suburban Detroit but has retained its own identity, partly because of a large number of historic buildings. Farmington was settled in the 1820s by a group of Quakers from Farmington, New York, led by Arthur Power. The site of the first Quaker meetinghouse on

The Governor Warner Museum in Farmington.

Grand River Avenue near Farmington Road is marked by a state historic plaque.

One of the best examples of historic structures here is the Governor Warner Museum (248-474-5500; ci.farmington.mi.us/Services/CityClerk/GovernorWarnerMuseum.asp; 33805 Grand River Ave.), a Victorian Italianate structure built in 1867 that sits on three acres. It was the residence of Fred M. Warner, a Farmington businessman who established 13 cheese factories and served as Michigan's governor from 1905 to 1911. Tours are available on Wednesdays and one Sunday a month.

Historic Mill

For several generations of metro Detroiters, the **Franklin Cider Mill** (248-626-2968; franklincidermill.com; 7450 Franklin Rd., Franklin) at the corner of 14 Mile and Franklin Roads, has been an annual stop during autumn for fresh cider and doughnuts. The mill opened in 1837 and was the first gristmill in Oakland County. In 1914 it was turned into a cider mill. The place can get crowded on fall weekends. $

NOVI

Just west of Farmington is the city of Novi. Formerly a rural township, Novi has become one of the fastest-growing cities in Michigan in recent years, partly sparked by the construction of a large regional mall here, and it's now a mix of housing, office space, and retailing. Its office parks are home to both domestic and foreign auto-related suppliers. The Suburban Collection Showplace draws a variety of expositions, trade shows, and other events. The city has good access to the great metro Detroit region because it's bisected by I-96 and borders a complex freeway interchange, where I-275, M-10, and I-696 converge.

The city is very spread out and suburban, although there has been an attempt to create a traditional downtown near Grand River Avenue and Novi Road. However, the real town center is Twelve Oaks Mall (248-348-9400; shoptwelveoaks.com; 27500 Novi Rd.) Located near the Novi Road exit off I-96, the mall has more than 180 stores, and is anchored by Macy's, Lord & Taylor, Nordstrom, J.C. Penney, and Sears. Over the years many other retailing locations have opened near the mall. The mall has also attracted a large number of restaurants and hotels.

Checking In

Best places to stay in and around Oakland County.

Novi

Baronette Renaissance Detroit-Novi Hotel (248-349-7800; thebaronette.com; 27790 Novi Rd.) The hotel's 149 rooms have been renovated, and are done in a contemporary style, with wireless Internet access. The rooms are fully equipped with cable TV and coffee makers. There's also an outside garden terrace. $$ Toasted Oak Grill & Market restaurant is located in the hotel (see listing in Restaurants).

Doubletree Hotel Detroit/Novi (248-344-8800; doubletreenovihotel.com; 42100 Crescent Blvd.) Located along the I-96 corridor, it's a good option for those doing business or traveling in the metro Detroit area. The rooms and suites have work areas and wireless Internet connections, along with large-screen TVs with cable service. $$

Hilton Garden Inn (248-3840; detroitnovi.hgi.com; 27355 Cabaret Dr.) With its location near Twelve Oaks Mall and not far off I-96, the 148-room hotel is a convenient place to stay if you're in Novi to shop or to do business in the nearby office parks. The General Motors Proving Grounds is 15 miles away, and the Nissan Technical Center, 2.5 miles. The contemporary rooms come with special work areas and wireless high-speed Internet access. $$

Residence Inn by Marriott Detroit/Novi (248-735-7400; marriott.com; 27477 Cabaret Dr.) A good option for longer stays. It's an all-suite hotel, and the rooms offer kitchens, work areas with high-speed Internet, and cable TV, including TV Japan. There are one- and two-bedroom suites, all with a contemporary feel. $$

Sheraton Detroit Novi Hotel (248-349-4000; starwoodhotels.com; 21111 Haggerty Rd.) It's located along the I-275 corridor near Eight Mile, and is another good home base in the metro area, as its close to downtown Detroit via the freeway system, and to the Dearborn area, where Ford Motor Co., has its headquarters. The rooms and suites are business-friendly and feature work areas and Internet connections. $$

Rochester

Royal Park Hotel (248-652-2600; royalparkhotel.net; 600 E. University Dr.) an upscale, out-of-the-way establishment that's a real find for business travelers. The Paint Creek is nearby, and the hotel is surrounded by green space. It's a four-star, four-diamond hotel, with 143 rooms, a banquet room and a conference center. The décor is English manor house and is decorated with cherry wood and marble. $$$ The Brookshire Restaurant (248-453-8732) is on-site and offers breakfast, lunch, and dinner; entrées include chicken, fish, seafood, duck, and steak. $$$ The Commons Bar offers pub food and there's live music on the weekends. $

Troy

Candlewood Suites Extended Stay Hotel (248-269-6600; candelwoodsuites.com; 2550 Troy Center Dr.) If a business project keeps you in the area for an extended period, this a good choice. There are studio, one-bedroom, and two-bedroom suites, all furnished in a contemporary style. The rooms have full-sized refrigerators, dishwashers, microwaves, and a stove top, plus kitchen dishes, utensils, and cookware. The television set has a DVD player. There are also large workspaces. $$

Detroit Marriot Troy (248-680-9797; marriott.com; 200 W. Big Beaver Rd.) Located in the heart of Troy's corporate business district. The hotel is contemporary and the rooms modern. $$

Embassy Suites (248-879-7500; hilton.com; 850 Tower Dr.) Just off I-75 (the Chrysler Freeway), it's a short drive to Auburn Hills if you're coming to do business with Chrysler. The rooms are modern, with contemporary furnishings, and there are some suites with two bedrooms and two baths. $$

Somerset Inn (248-643-7800; somersetinn.com; 2601 W. Big Beaver Rd.) Within walking distance of the upscale Somerset Collection complex of shops and restaurants, this is a good choice for business travelers who are looking for something to do after the workday. The hotel has 250 contemporary rooms, and there's a ballroom, foyer, and meeting room space. $$$

Local Flavors

Taste of the town—restaurants, cafés, bars, bistros, etc.

Auburn Hills

Alfoccino (248-340-1000; alfoccino.com; 2225 N. Opdyke Rd.) is only 1.5 miles from The Palace, and with its large bar and dining area, is a good stop after a game or event. The traditional Italian dishes are joined by favorites such as ribs, chicken, and white fish. $$

O'Malley's Tavern (248-373-6690; omalleysauburnhills.com; 1500 Opdyke Rd.) The Irish-style tavern serves pub food, burgers and pizza, and is a good place to watch a sporting event on TV. $

Bloomfield Area

Hogan's (248-626-1800; hogansdining.com; 6450 Telegraph Rd., Bloomfield Hills) Despite the chic neighborhood it's in, the bar/restaurant is a causal, friendly place with a sports bar theme. There are chicken wings for the sports fans, and pasta, ribs, chicken, steak, and fish as well. $$

The Lark (248-661-4466; thelark.com; 6430 Farmington Rd.) West Bloomfield is the location of one of Detroit's most exclusive and expensive restaurants, one of those once-a-year places, and it's an evening to be anticipated. *Bon Appetit* magazine said of it: "European style, Midwestern in substance and enlightened innovation add up to perfection . . . a restaurant that seamlessly blends the best of the Mediterranean and Middle America." But the style comes with a price; meals start at about $70. The dishes include fish, lamb, beef, duck, lobster, walleye, and seafood. The dishes are varied in their influence. Check out the Portuguese copper cataplana of large wild shrimp, clams, mussels, and smoked linguica sausage with tomatoes, garlic, and fresh herbs. The house specialties are rack of lamb, curried duck salad, lobster, and steaks. Reservations are required, and there's a dress code, coats and ties preferred. There is a large wine selection. $$$$

New York Bagel (248-851-9210; 6927 Orchard Lake Rd.) At one time there were many bagel factories in the Jewish enclaves of metro Detroit, but they have dwindled to a few. When traveling to the West Bloomfield area, I make sure to stop for lunch at this small shop, which features fresh bagels and lox. It's small and hard to find on busy Orchard Lake Road, but it's worth the effort. $

Stage Deli (248-855-6622; thestagedeli.com; 6873 Orchard Lake Rd.) A great spot for lunch, serving traditional deli foods. The Stage isn't your normal lunch counter; they serve beer and wine and also full meals, but of course the centerpiece is still corned beef, bagels and lox, gefilte fish, and herring. The menu is large and varied, and includes Lake Superior whitefish, walleye, salmon, rainbow trout, shrimp, and fried clams. $$

Farmington Hills and Farmington

Café Cortina (248-474-3033; cafecortina.com; 30715 W. 10 Mile, Farmington Hills) The owners, Rina and son Adrian, have a reputation of helping patrons with the menu. The northern Italian dishes are served in a relaxed, casual atmosphere, with many tables near a fireplace. Outside, the owners plant their own garden, where they cultivate the herbs used in their dishes. There's a large wine list. $$

Ginopolis' on the Grill (248-851-8222; ginopolis.com; 27815 Middlebelt, Farmington Hills) Greek family-owned restaurants were once common in Detroit and its suburbs, but they've become less so. Pete and Johnny Ginopolis keep the tradition alive with their grill and sports bar. The place is large and usually bustling, especially when one of Detroit's sports teams are playing and fans are at the bar. Patrons can have a burger or other selections from the menu at the bar, or they can sit in the dining rooms. There are many appetizers for those who like to nosh while watching a game. There are favorites, like fish and chips, meat loaf, baked chicken, and grilled lamb chops. The specialty is Montgomery Inn rib dishes, including ribs and shrimp and chicken and shrimp. They also do well with Greek-style lamb. $$

John Cowley and Son's Pub and Coolhenry Restaurant (248-474-5941; johncowleys.com; 33338 Grand River Ave.)

John Cowley and Sons in Farmington.

The Irish pub is on the corner of Grand River Avenue and Farmington Road, in the heart of the city's downtown, and is where local residents hang out after work. In the evenings, its two floors are crowded with diners eating fish and chips, burgers, and other pub fare. The atmosphere is friendly. It's a major gathering place for the Irish on St. Patrick's Day. The pub was founded in 1972 by a couple from Ireland, John and Marie Cowley, and the establishment is still family-run. $$

Novi

Bonefish Grill (248-347-1635; onefishgrill.com; 43304 W. 11 Mile Rd.) While there are some other grilled dishes, you better come here with a taste for fish, baked, grilled, or fried. The bar is a cozy place, and there's a large wine selection. You don't often see grouper on the menus in Detroit, but it's offered here and is a good choice. There's also Norwegian salmon, rainbow trout from Idaho, and shrimp and scallops. For those not inclined to seafood, there's steak and chicken too. $$

Cherry Blossom (248-380-9160; cherryblossom.biz; 43588 W. Oaks Dr.) Cherry Blossom gets high marks from Japanese Americans in the metro area, especially for its sushi bar, and is a good bet for lunch and dinner. It's a favorite of many Japanese who work in nearby auto-related industries, many of whom gather for happy hour at the bar. There's karaoke on the weekends. The menu offers traditional dishes, such as *kain su,* crab meat with cucumber, seaweed, and vinegar dressing; *tako nuta,* octopus and green onion with nuta sauce; *futomaki,* barbecued eel, egg, spinach, shitake mushroom, kanpyo, and crab stick in a roll; beef teriyaki; *tonkatsu,* a pork cutlet breaded in panko and deep friend; and fried shrimp. $$

Famous Dave's (248-735-1111; famousdaves.com; 43350 Crescent Blvd.) Although it's a national chain, you get that down-home feeling in this place, with its smoked BBQ. The Texas beef brisket and pork ribs are the classics on the menu. There's also chicken and pork. The atmosphere is casual and family-friendly. There's a full bar. $$

Gus O'Connor's (248-465-9670; gusoconnors.com; 42875 Grand River Ave.) No Michigan city is without an Irish pub it seems. And although this one's in a mall-like setting, the owners have done a decent job of replicating the traditional pub feel, especially at the wood-paneled bar, where there are plenty of Irish beers. The menu offers mostly pub food, but there are also entrées including steak, ribs, and salmon. Try the Irish trinity, a Guinness stew, and chicken potpie. $$

Toasted Oak Grill & Market (248-277-6000; www.toastedoak.com; 27790 Novi Rd.) The dining room has an elegant air; the bar has a laid-back, comfortable feel. Familiar dishes are given a creative twist, such as the cider-brined pork chops, Angus skirt steak, and filet mignon with black truffle butter. One standout is the Lake Huron trout, served with spinach, spring peas, and mustard seed vinaigrette. $$

Rochester

Rochester Chop House (248-651-2266; kruseandmuerrestaurants.com; 306 S. Main St.) Check out Kabin Kruser's Oyster Bar, in front of the restaurant, for a more casual dinner. Inside the main dining room, the Chop House offers seafood, fish, steak, chicken, and pasta. Among the fish dishes are two Michigan favorites, whitefish and perch. $$$

The Rochester Chop House.

Red Knapp's in Rochester seves old-style malts.

Red Knapp's Dairy Bar (248-651-4545; 304 S. Main St.) A casual, kitschy lunch option in downtown Rochester. Kids love this established little 1950s-style diner with its cursive neon sign, horseshoe-shaped bar, and small vinyl booths. They mix great milkshakes and malteds here, and serve signature flat, big-as-your-plate burgers. $

Rochester Mills Beer Co. (248-650-5080; www.cplanet.com; 400 Water St.) Located in the historic Western Knitting

The Rochester Mills Beer Company is located in a historic mill building.

Mills building, the brewpub has original hardwood floors, columns, and exposed brick walls. Along with its beers, the menu offers burgers, pizza, and pasta. During the warmer months, there's an outside patio. $

Troy

The Capital Grille (248-649-5300; thecapitalgrille.com; 2800 W. Big Beaver Rd.) Located in the Somerset Collection mall, this fine dining establishment offers steak, seafood, fish, and pasta, and some enticing appetizers such as pan-fried calamari with hot cherry peppers. The bar is a great gathering place for happy hour, and offers upscale pub food such as lobster and crab burgers. $$$

Mon Jin Lau (monjinlau.com; 1515 East Maple Rd. at the Stephenson Freeway) The Chin family has owned and operated this restaurant since 1969 and it's highly recommended by Asian Americans in the Detroit area, who say it has some of the most authentic sushi around. It's a hangout for many of the advertising people who have offices nearby. The menu ranges from traditional Asian dishes to newer styles that infuse many traditions from the East. Happy hour is a special time, when sushi meets martinis at the large bar in the contemporary building. During warmer months, there's an outside patio decorated with palms, bamboo, and lanterns. $$

Picano's Italian Grille (248-689-8050; picanos.com; 3775 Rochester Rd.) This restaurant offers Italian favorites in a casual atmosphere. Offerings include pasta, chicken, veal, steak, and lamb. The veal is a favorite. As for an appetizer, try the eggplant; it's not often seen on menus in the metro area. $$

Tre Monti Ristorante (248-680-1100; tremontitroy.com; 1695 E. Big Beaver Rd.) The restaurant/bar is located in a European-style bar behind the San Marino Club, a fraternal organization, and offers an elegant interpretation of Italian dishes. The house specialties are *chitarra frutti di mare, costoletta di vitello,* and *la spigola spummante.* Entrées include pasts, chicken, seafood, and fish. $$

The Wilcox House

6

Western Wayne County

PLYMOUTH AND NORTHVILLE

THE CITIES OF PLYMOUTH AND NORTHVILLE are distinctive enclaves in the metro Detroit area. Picturesque and historic, with their traditional downtowns they retain a small-town feel.

PLYMOUTH

Downtown Plymouth.

The city of Plymouth is an older community (many buildings date to the late 19th century) with a small but thriving downtown. The center of activities is Kellogg Park, which is a town square affair, with a fountain at its center. The annual Plymouth Ice Festival in January (plymouthicefestival.org) attracts thousands of spectators to see professional and amateur carvers sculpt figures from large chunks of ice.

The community is relatively affluent and there are a number of corporate facilities located here, including auto supplier Johnson

LEFT: A historic home near Plymouth's Kellogg Park.

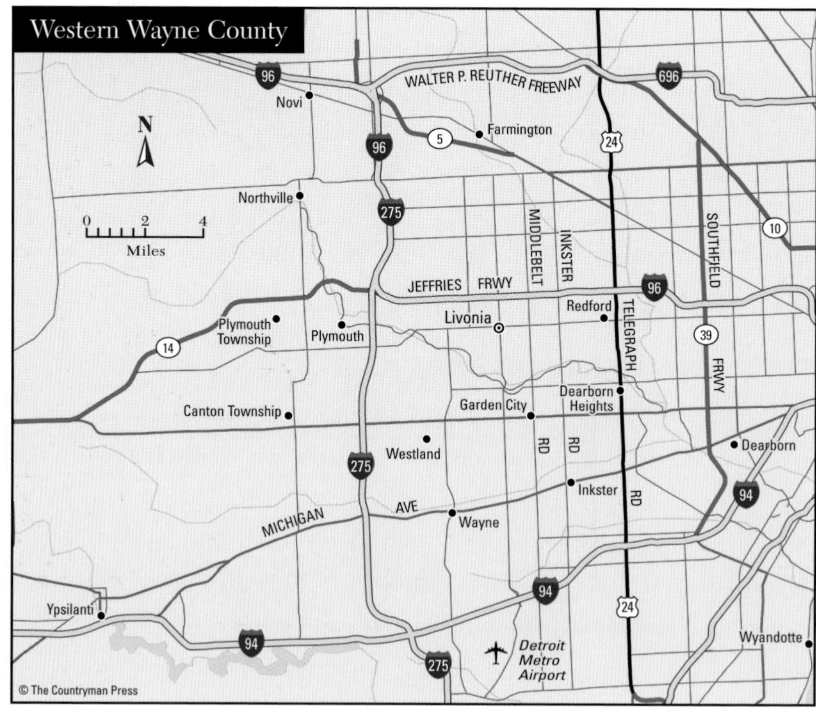

Controls. Yazaki has its North American facility in nearby Canton Township.

The city evolved from a settlement started in 1825 when New England farmers Benjamin and William Starkweather purchased a 240-acre farm in the area. Plymouth thrived as a farm community, but with the coming of the railroads, it saw dramatic growth, with several rail beds running through the town. To this day, drivers must often stop to wait as trains run through the community. It was also home to the Daisy Manufacturing Co., which was founded in 1882 and made BB guns until here until moving to Rogers, Arkansas, in 1958. The old factory has been turned into upscale condos.

The best way to see Plymouth is on foot. There are large parking structures in the downtown area. Start in Kellogg Park, where in the warmer months musical performances and art shows are scheduled. Near the park is the Penn Theatre (734-435-0870; penntheatre.com; 760 Penniman Ave.). The theater opened in 1941 with a showing of *Week-End in Havana,* and has managed to stay in operation, despite it only having one screen in an era of multiscreen movie houses. For

The Penn Theatre in Plymouth still serves as a movie house.

some strange reason, the original owner didn't like popcorn, and it wasn't served until 1950. By 2003 the movie house fell on hard times and was temporarily closed. In 2005 a community group purchased it and put it back into operation.

Although Plymouth is a small community, the Plymouth Historical Society Museum (734-455-8940; plymouthhistory.org; 155 S. Main St.) hosts some fairly large exhibits, including one that traces the city's growth from a railroad depot to a city. It has a substantial collection of Lincoln material, and also has a focus on the Ford Village Industries. At one time Ford had several plants located along the Rouge River, using it as a power source, and ran them as a social experiment, thinking that people could spend part of their time on farms and other hours in a small factory.

NORTHVILLE

The small city of 6,459 and the surrounding Northville Township share a distinction with nearby Plymouth and Farmington (see chapter 5), in that they were classic small rural towns before they were surrounded by Detroit's suburbs.

Downtown Northville.

The city's roots date to the 1820s, when settlers, many of them from New York State, came to the area and started farming. By 1827 Northville had a post office, a doctor, a tailor, a tavern, and blacksmiths. During the Victorian era, there was a small building boom, and a number of Queen Anne–style homes were built, many of which are still standing. In 1919 Henry Ford came to town and established a valve plant in Northville, which hastened growth. The city is also home to Northville Downs (northville downs.com), a harness raceway.

The downtown has many small specialty shops, and restaurants, and is a popular destination for metro Detroiters who come to walk the quaint streets, and look at many of the historic buildings. During summer concerts are held on Friday nights in the town square.

Checking In

Best places to stay in and around Western Wayne County.

The I-275 corridor that runs through Plymouth and Northville has many chain hotels and motels, especially at the exits (see chapter 5 Hotels, Novi).

Local Flavors

Taste of the town—restaurants, cafés, bars, bistros, etc.

Northville

Deadwood Bar (deadwoodbar andgrill.com) Located just outside downtown Northville, the place has a North Woods feel and a menu to match. It's part of a small Detroit-area chain that includes The Moose Preserve Bar & Grill in the Bloomfield area, Camp Ticonderoga, The Beaver Creek Tavern in Westland, and the Iroquois Club in Bloomfield Hills. All are decorated with outdoors motifs and have similar menus. Deadwood has handcrafted birch-bark décor, antler cocktail chairs, and a high wood ceiling. The menu

Hines Drive Cruise

For drivers, and especially for bikers and bicyclists, Hines Drive in western Wayne County offers an 18-mile dream cruise along the two-lane blacktop road that follows the Rouge River through parklands between Dearborn Heights and Northville.

If you're driving, don't get carried away when it comes to speed. The limit is 40 miles an hour; you can push it to about 45 before you get stopped. There's a Wayne County Sheriff's Department substation at Hines Drive and Newberg Road, and the deputies set many speed traps. I drive this road a lot and often see people getting pulled over.

A motorycle parked along Hines Drive in western Wayne County.

But what's the hurry? During warmer months especially, this is a pleasure drive, so take your time.

There's a separate asphalt trail for bicyclists that follows the road and has parkland on each side. There are numerous places to stop, with picnic tables and restrooms, and a quick exit will take you to local restaurants. You'll find bikers hanging out at certain spots together with softball players and bicyclists.

A popular stopping place for motorcyclists along Hines Park is the **Lakepointe Yacht Club** (734-591-1868; 37604 Ann Arbor Rd., Livonia). There aren't any boats docked here, although it is located on Newburgh Lake, which isn't a lake, exactly, but an impoundment of the Rouge River. The bar/restaurant has long been a destination for bikers cruising Hines, dating back to the 1950s. There is a "no colors allowed" sign on the door, aimed at dissuading bikers from wearing gear signifying their association with any club or group, to keep the vibe friendly. But don't let that intimidate you; the crowd includes many businesspeople and construction workers lunching on burgers, fried fish on Fridays, and sandwiches. There's an outside deck. During the cruising season you will see a number of motorcycles parked outside. $

is filled with hearty fare, including half-pound burgers, buffalo, and steaks. $$

Genitti's Hole-in-the-Wall (248-349-0522; genittis.com; 108 E. Main St.) A destination restaurant for metro Detroiters, the place started life as a grocery store in 1971, and in 1979 it shifted gears and became a restaurant. It has expanded several times over the years, taking over adjoining buildings. Dinner here is a seven-course affair that includes Italian wedding soup, bread, pasta, an antipasto salad, Italian sausage, and Italian steak with baked potatoes, baked chicken, and cannoli for dessert. And dinner isn't the only event at Genitti's; after the meal interactive comedy shows are often scheduled. $$$

Table 5 (248-305-6555; table5.net; 126 E. Main St.) A local favorite, the bar is lively; the dining room more subdued. The "Bites at the Bar" menu includes more than chicken wings: a favorite is a platter of tomatoes, pancetta, greens, roasted red peppers, and pesto, and there are other such plates to share. In the dining room, entrées include steak with polenta cakes, and pan-fried walleye. The building dates to 1867 and has exposed brick walls, and also large windows, giving patrons a good view. $$

Genitti's (top) and Table 5 restaurant are both in Northville.

Plymouth

Box Bar (734-459-7390; 777 W. Ann Arbor Trail) Across from Kellogg Park, Box Bar has long been the hangout of residents who flock to the park for musical or other events. Burgers are the mainstay, and there are many types of bottled beer in the cooler. $

Compari's On the Park (734-416-0100; comparisdining.com; 380 S. Main) The sleek bar invites you to order a martini and have a chat. The upscale menu includes mostly traditional Italian pasta dishes, but it moves up a bit with such offerings as veal cherry and a Sicilian combo, pork chops and Italian sausage. There are also fish dishes, including white fish and salmon. $$

Fiamma Grille Steak & Seafood (743-416-9340; www.fiammagrille.com; 380 S. Main St.) Elegant, white-tablecloth-type dining downtown; the menu has something of an Italian flair but the focus is on midwestern fare, with such dishes as woodland tenderloin, lamb chops, Piedmontese filet mignon, seafood and fish. They also offer small plates. One favorite is the Lake Superior whitefish. $$

Hermann's Olde Town Grille (734-451-1213; hermannsotg.com; 195 W. Liberty St.) Also in the Old Village area, Hermann's is a local favorite, with its large moose painted on an outside wall, and a moose head inside behind the bar (no you're not seeing things; it moves). It's more of a friendly tavern than a restaurant, although there is food. Most of the action is at the long polished wood bar. Some nights it can be loud. It's basically a burger and pizza place, although there are some wraps offered, and of course the required Michigan bar food, chicken wings. $

Nico & Vali Italian Eatery (734-207-7880; nicoandvali.com; 744 Wing St.) This casual Italian place is a favorite of Plymouth residents, and features soups, salads, pizza, sandwiches, pasta, and panini. $

Sean O'Callaghan's (734-459-6666; seanocallaghanspub.com; 821 Penniman Ave.) One of the more authentic Irish pubs in the metro area. Many of the bartenders are right from Ireland and know their Irish whiskeys. Near Kellogg Park, the place has the look and feel of an old pub, and some of the furnishings were imported from the old country. It's a Victorian pub look, with mahogany woodwork and handcrafted stained glass. The menu stays true to its Irish roots, and includes shepherd's pie, Irish stew, corned beef and cabbage. and fish and chips.

Station 885 (734-459-0885; stations885.com; 885 Starkweather) Located in an older area of Plymouth called Old Village, it pays tribute to the community's railroad heritage and has a model train on the walls. The cozy bar/restaurant has a fireplace and a comfortable feel. The menu is nothing special, but it is heavy on local favorites, including lake perch, walleye, steak, ribs and prime rib, and chicken. There is also lighter fare, such as pizza and pasta. $$

WYANDOTTE
MICHIGAN
SHOPPING
DINING
& CULTURE
PC&K

Downriver

WYANDOTTE, GROSSE ILE, FLAT ROCK

THIS IS ONE of the most interesting areas of metro Detroit, with its riverfront feel, French Canadian roots, and transplanted southerners; it offers a diversity of restaurants and activities.

Traditionally home to chemical plants and steel mills, the Downriver area was long spurned as a residential district. Because of that, it has not experienced the suburban sprawl that has marked other metro regions over the last 30 years.

Wyandotte is the site of America's first Bessemer steel mill.

The largest town is Wyandotte, the birthplace of the actor Lee Majors, Lucille Ball, and writer Tom McGuane. Its downtown is lined with 1860s structures and gives visitors a glimpse of what downtown Detroit looked like during the 19th century. Just south of Wyandotte is Grosse Ile, an island in the Detroit River that has many large waterfront homes and the Ford Yacht Club, which gives boats access

LEFT: Downtown Wyandotte.

Historic homes near the Detroit River in Wyandotte.

not only to the river but to nearby Lake Erie. Flat Rock is the southernmost community in Wayne County, and is located on the river.

WYANDOTTE

Wyandotte was named for the Wyandot tribe of Native Americans, part of the Huron Nation of Michigan. As with other tribes, they signed a treaty with the U.S. government and were removed from the land and eventually resettled in Oklahoma. During 1763 Chief Pontiac plotted an attack on Detroit from the Wyandotte area.

Because of its frontage on the Detroit River, the city became a center for smelting iron ore mined in Michigan's Upper Peninsula and shipped to the city on the Great Lakes. The ore was smelted in huge furnaces, which became known as Bessemer steel mills. The steel was used to make rails for railroads, and iron stoves, and nearby Ford Motor Co. also became a customer.

The city was also home to Wyandotte Chemical, which started in 1893 as Michigan Alkali Co. and made baking soda, soda ash, and lye. It later made soaps and cleaners and eventually became part of the chemical company BASF, and it still has a facility in the community.

Making a Meal of Muskrat

One long-standing Downriver tradition is eating muskrat meat during lent, a custom that was handed down by the early French Canadian residents who settled the marshy areas along the shorelines of Detroit, south to Toledo in the early 18th century. Most lived by hunting and fishing, and the muskrats inhabiting the low, swampy areas became common table fare, especially during winter.

The early settlers, who were mostly Catholic and therefore required to eat fish on Friday, were eventually dubbed Muskrat French; they received special permission from the pope to eat muskrat rather than fish during lent, since muskrats were more plentiful in late winter and could be seen as related to fish, living mostly in water. The origin of the ruling is in doubt. Some say it dates to the War of 1812 and came from an archbishop, not the pope, while others say permission was granted during the Great Depression in the 1930s. The Detroit Archdiocese has been unable to find any documentation in its archives dealing with muskrats.

Whatever the history, it has left many in the Downriver area with a taste for muskrat, whether they are of French origin or not. Some say it tastes like chicken; others say it recalls duck. During lent, many Detroit-area Catholics gather in kitchens, halls, and a few restaurants to partake of the delicacy.

Several years ago, the State of Michigan got involved, causing a public outcry when it attempted to regulate the sale of muskrat. The state insisted that the meat be purchased from state-approved and inspected sources, but there were no inspection procedures or official sources in operation. Downriver legislators got involved, and the state backed down.

If you're in metro Detroit during lent, you can sample muskrat at **Kola's Kitchen** (313-281-0662; 4500 13th St., Wyandotte). $

Apart from French Canadians, Wyandotte has a strong Polish enclave, with many of it residents descended from a large wave of Polish immigrants that started coming in the 1890s to work in the shipyard and chemical industries. By 1899 Our Lady of Mount Carmel Roman Catholic Church (ourladyofmountcarmel.org; 976

Superior Blvd.) formed, and services were held in Polish. The church opened in 1900, and has many historic stained-glass windows.

GROSSE ILE

The island is the largest in the Detroit River, and is home to about 10,000 residents, many of which live in waterfront homes and have boats. The island is connected to the mainland by a bridge, and it's basically a residential area with a yacht club on the south end. Boating and fishing are popular activities in this area, partly because the river empties into Lake Erie just downriver from the island. There are also golf courses on the island.

The Ile is home to many large estates; a drive around the island offers a view of these residents, and of the lake freighters in the Detroit River.

Ford Yacht Club (734-676-8422; fordyachtclub.com; 29500 Southpointe Rd.) is a major attraction. The private club was formed in the late 1940s by a group of Ford Engineering employees, and it has a clubhouse, and boat slips.

FLAT ROCK

The community of about 8,000 is the southernmost in Wayne County, and borders Monroe County. It has long been heavily involved in the auto industry, with Ford Motor Co and Mazda Corp. owning plants in the city. It's also home to the Flat Rock Speedway, a longtime drag-racing destination for metro Detroit. The city is located along the Huron River, and that power source led Henry Ford to build a lamp factory along its banks in 1925.

Many white southerners migrated to metro Detroit for factory jobs, especially during the Great Depression, and they brought their musical tastes along. This tradition is alive at the Huron Valley Eagles Club (huronvalleyeagles.com; 13636 Telegraph Rd.). The club has been hosting bluegrass bands since the early 1980s. Local bands play, and the club brings in national acts such as Bill Monroe, the Osborne Brothers, Ralph Stanley, Doyle Lawson, and the Lonesome River Band. The performances are generally on Saturday night, and visitors will find local players hanging around the place. The décor is simple, but there are meals and drinks offered. There's a cover charge. Most shows start at 8 PM on Saturdays. Check the website for upcoming acts. $

Local Flavors

Taste of the town—restaurants, cafés, bars, bistros, etc.

Grosse Ile

Lloyd's Bar & Grill (734-675-3117; 8961 Macomb St.) The local gathering place serves some of the best food on the island, including steaks, pasta, burgers, and ribs. They make their own potato chips. $

Wyandotte

Polonus Restaurant (734-283-3530; 1744 Biddle St.) This is a gathering place for many of Wyandotte's Polish American families, and local residents show up on a regular basis for hefty portions of traditional favorites such as kielbasa, potato pancakes, and pierogi, all served in a cozy family setting. $

MICHIGAN
JI SAW
SUNDAY I 3
THA KS TO
STOP
PUMP
THIS & THAT

Ann Arbor

THE QUINTESSENTIAL COLLEGE TOWN

THIS CLASSIC MIDWESTERN liberal college town is only about 40 miles from Detroit, but it may as well be a thousand miles. While Detroit has struggled with urban decay and declining factory employment, Ann Arbor, which is home to the University of Michigan, has a thriving, diverse economy and a well-educated populace.

The university dominates the town, which has a population of slightly more than 114,000, of which more than 36,000 are students. The university employs more than 30,000 people, of which more than 12,000 work in the school's medical center. The city is also home to the corporate headquarters of Domino's Pizza and Borders Books.

The city's small-town atmosphere, access to cultural events at U-M, and many restaurants make it an attractive place to live, and some residents make the daily commute to Detroit and its suburbs.

Top attractions are the U-M campus, the downtown shops, restaurants and taverns along the Main Street corridor, Kerrytown, a restored shopping district just out of downtown, and the Ann Arbor Farmer's Market during summer months. Ann Arbor, known to locals as A2 (short for "A squared"), is in Washtenaw County, but its specialty shops and restaurants also make it western Wayne County's downtown.

LEFT: Downtown Ann Arbor.

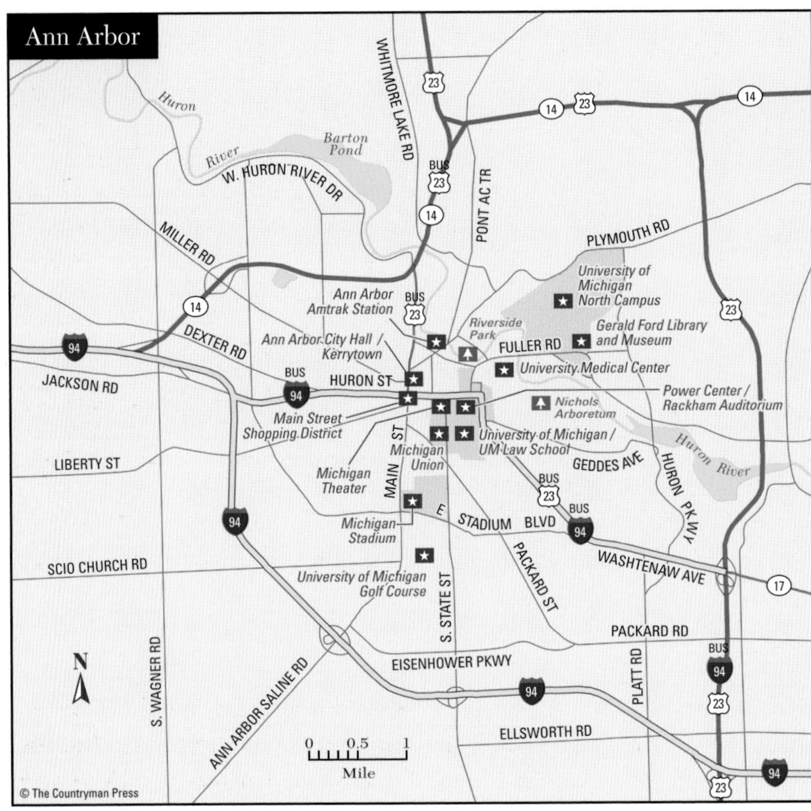

Perhaps the biggest attraction in town is U-M football on Saturdays during the fall. The school's newly renovated stadium holds about 110,000 fans, and when the Wolverines are playing at home, the town is invaded by alumni and others, many wearing the maze and blue colors of the team. There are about as many fans showing up for games as there are Ann Arbor residents, and parking can be difficult on game days. Unless you're a fan, avoid going to the city on those days.

In July, the annual Ann Arbor Street Art Fair attracts thousands to the downtown area for the artwork and related activities. The fair is mostly spread along Main Street, which is the main drag downtown, and home to many restaurants, shops, and galleries.

Ann Arbor was founded in 1824 by two land speculators, and by 1827 it had become the county seat for Washtenaw County. Shortly after the community was incorporated as a village in 1833, a group of

Ann Arbor has a strong arts community.

speculators set aside 40 acres and offered it to the State of Michigan as the site of the state capital. Lansing won out as the capital, but the state accepted the land as a home for the new University of Michigan, which was then located in Detroit. The city became a transportation hub by the 1840s, with the arrival of the Michigan Central Railroad, and new settlers started arriving in the late 19th century.

Because U-M, with its related research activities, has been the economic engine of Ann Arbor, property values have stayed stable with respect to Detroit, and there are few empty storefronts in the downtown area. Ann Arbor does have ties to the auto industry, mostly with respect to research and engineering, not production. Nearby Ypsilanti, 6 miles east of Ann Arbor, with its Willow Run plant that built bombers during World War II, and other plants, is more of a factory town than Ann Arbor, and has more of a blue-collar population.

Ann Arbor often shows up on lists of the best places to live. That's partly because of the cultural activities based at U-M and the downtown's lively street scene, but also because of Ann Arbor's surrounding natural resources. The Huron River runs through the city and offers some of the best canoeing and kayaking in the state, and the Huron-Clinton park system, which encompasses Washtenaw and several other counties, offers many acres open to outdoor recreation.

Art on the Street

A major event in the city is the **Ann Arbor Street Art Fair** (734-994-5260; artfair.org), which is held annually in late July and attracts thousands of visitors, who choke the major arteries of downtown Ann Arbor. Main Street is where artists, both homegrown and far-flung, set up stands and show their works. The first fair was held in 1960 and it has expanded over the years, with hundreds of artists selling everything from jewelry to prints, oil paintings to pottery. There are also street performances by musicians and mimes. If you're planning to go, plan out the logistics beforehand; parking is difficult, but there are shuttle buses that serve visitors to the event.

A series of state recreational lands just west of Ann Arbor adds to that. The Huron is a top bass-fishing destination.

Ann Arbor is known for its liberal political climate, partly because it's a college town, but also because of its reputation during the 1960s and '70s as a hotbed of antiwar sentiment during the Vietnam War. The activist movement Students for a Democratic Society got its start here in the early '60s, and the city was the site of many protest demonstrations during that era. But at the same time, it has a small-town, traditional vibe, with many well-kept neighborhoods and historic homes built in the late 19th and early 20th centuries. Add to that the historic brick buildings downtown, and you have Middle America and left-wing politics converging in a tree-filled town right out of the movies.

The best way to get a taste of Ann Arbor is on foot, by taking a walk along Main Street, where there are many restaurants, bars, shops, and art galleries. One note on parking, the city is particularly aggressive in its enforcement of on-street meter parking, so it makes sense to park in a lot, most of which are city-owned and aren't expensive. The city is pedestrian-friendly and very accommodating to bicyclists, with well-marked bike lanes.

A recommended first stop is the Ann Arbor Area Convention & Visitors Bureau (734-995-7281; visitannarbor.org; 120 W. Huron St.). Open Monday–Friday, 8:30 AM–5 PM, it offers maps and other useful information for visitors to the city.

University of Michigan at Ann Arbor.

THE UNIVERSITY OF MICHIGAN

The more than 35,000-student school looms over Ann Arbor, just like the auto industry does in Detroit, and has more than 30,000 employees ranging from academics to maintenance people, and sits on more than 700 acres. Ann Arbor residents simply call it "the U." The campus has more than 584 buildings, some dating from the 19th century, many of which are worth seeing. The school also offers venues for the arts and music, and other events that attract visitors to the campus.

The Central Campus is best seen on foot or bicycle and is bounded by North University Avenue, South University Avenue, East University Avenue, and State Street. This is the site of the original school when it was moved from Detroit to Ann Arbor in 1837, and it's a delight to walk through, partly because the school buildings are interspersed with businesses, including inviting coffee shops and small pubs. When school is in session, the sidewalks are crowded. The school year runs from late August through mid-May.

A May visit to the campus is especially nice. Lilacs perfume the air, and there's less hustle and bustle when the students have gone home.

One building to see is the Burton Memorial Tower (230 S. Ingalls St.), often referred to simply as the "clock tower." It's a popular meeting place for students, and its ten floors can be seen from quite a distance. The tower has 55 bells that chime on the hour. The tower was designed by Albert Kahn, a well-known Detroit architect, and built in 1935.

Another prime destination is the Power Center for the Performing Arts (734-764-2538; music.umich.edu; 121 Fletcher St.). The center opened in 1971 and its auditorium has been used for performances by students as well as visiting musicians. The modern classical structure is also used for corporate presentations.

Just off campus, check to see what's playing at the Michigan Theater (734-668-8397; michtheater.org; 603 E. Liberty), a classic, ornate movie palace that opened in 1928 and still has its original pipe organ. Movies are shown here, and lectures and other events are held in the space as well. The annual Ann Arbor Film Festival held in late March screens works by independent and experimental filmmakers.

But perhaps the most prized structure, especially by football fans, is Michigan Stadium, at the intersection of Main Street and Stadium Boulevard, near the main campus. The stadium, which is called "the Big House" holds about 110,000 fans, and is thought to be the third-largest stadium in the world. Because it's open air, by late November the whipping winds can make it a pretty cold place. The stadium was first used in 1927, but has been renovated over the years, most recently in 2010.

On-Campus Attractions

Alumni Center (734-764-0384; alumni.umich.edu; 200 Fletcher St.) The center houses offices and the Founder's Room, where various events are held.

Lydia Mendelssohn Theatre (734-763-3333; www.music.umich.edu; 911 N. University Ave.) Musical, theater, and dance performances. The 640-seat proscenium theater is decorated with oak paneling, giving it an intimate feel.

Michigan Union (734-763-5750; 530 S. State St.) is a good place to buy U-M paraphernalia, and is the hub of student activities. The building dates to 1917.

Rackham Building (734-647-7548; 915 E. Washington St.) is the center of graduate education at the university, and was opened in 1938 and renovated between 2000 and 2003.

U-M Law School Library (734-764-1358; 625 S. State). Worth seeing for its neo-Gothic architecture, the library, formally the William W. Cook Legal Research Library, dates to 1931 but looks much older, with its stained-glass windows and complex archways.

Shopping

In Ann Arbor.

Shoppers on Ann Arbor's Main Street.

The best way to see downtown Ann Arbor is by walking. There are dozens of restaurants and bars on Main and, during the warmer months, lots of outdoor sidewalk seating, great for people watching. The city and merchants have done a good job of preserving the look and feel of the turn-of-the-century buildings, mostly two-story brick buildings. The Main Street business district stretches roughly from East Huron Street to West William Street.

Many of Main Street's storefronts house art galleries and decorative-arts shops, and the quality of the works you'll find here is a reflection of the thriving arts community based at both the University of Michigan and nearby Eastern Michigan University. Many of the galleries host shows of works by local artists.

Here are some of the shops worth stopping at during a stroll on Main Street.

Alex Gulko Custom Jewelry (734-741-0652; alexgulko.com; 337 S. Main St.) Custom-designed rings and other jewelry all crafted on-site by Alex Gulko.

Clay Gallery (734-662-7927; claygallery.org; 355 S. Main St.) Ann Arbor artists offer their ceramic works here, which include sculpture and usable pottery.

Four Directions (734-996-9251; fourdirectionsa2.com; 211 S. Main St.) Native American artifacts and items from the Southwest are featured. There is also pottery, candles, and drums. The rock and mineral offerings are a draw.

Alex Gulko Custom Jewelry is among the shops on Main Street.

Kid-Friendly in Ann Arbor

Ann Arbor Hands-On Museum (734-995-5439; aahom.org; 220 E. Huron St.) This is a great place for kids, with its 250 interactive exhibits that appeal to preschool through middle school ages. There's a special gallery for preschool children, who can dress up like firefighters and play on a child-size fire truck. There's also a Michigan Nature Room that allows children to experience native plants, flowers, and animals, including a nature wall with lake fish. Media Works is an exploration of the science of television, telecommunications, and other newer technology. Open daily. Admission is $9 for ages 2 and up.

Matthaei Botanical Gardens and Nichols Arboretum (734-647-7600; www.lsa.umich.edu/mbg; 1800 N. Dixboro Rd.) The 700-acre natural area is managed by U-M, and includes gardens, research areas, and natural preserves in the Ann Arbor area. There is also a conservatory and greenhouse. Most of the areas can be used by the public, and tours are conducted. Stop at the Visitor Center for information. Near it are several special gardens, including the Gaffield Children's Garden. The trails in the gardens form loops and return back to the Visitor Center. Admission to the Conservatory is $5 for adults and $2 for children.

Graphic Art Wholesalers (734-769-5100; 224 S. Main St.) University of Michigan sports teams have a loyal following, and this is the place to go for sports posters and photos. There are also many framed artworks for sale.

A HAVEN FOR BOOK LOVERS

Ann Arbor is a high-tech town, and most places have wireless Internet available, but it's also a college town, and that means books, and bookstores—quirky ones, mainstream chains, and small independently owned shops.

Crazy Wisdom Bookstore and Tea Room (734-665-2757; www.crazywisdom.net; 114 S. Main St.) Those interested in New Age and alternative ideas and practices will find a home here. There are 200 categories of books on such things as acupuncture, Zen, and yoga. There are also cards, crafts, incense, ritual items, candles, and yoga supplies. The shop also hosts many programs and authors.

Dave's Books (734-665-8017; www.biblio.com; 516-B E. Williams) Stop by to browse through their collection of rare books ranging from art texts to history and old Bibles.

Dawn Treader Book Shop (734-995-1008; www.dawntreaderbooks.com; 514 E. Liberty) The shop deals in rare and antiquarian books, maps, and prints, and also buys used and rare books, especially scholarly texts in the sciences and humanities and modern first editions. It has about 70,000 titles, including modern paperbacks.

Nicola's Books (734-662-0600; www.nicolasbooks.com; 2513 Jackson Ave.) Located in the Westgate Shopping Center, the independently owned shop hosts book signings and related events, and stocks a number of hard-to-find books.

West Side Book Shop (734-995-1891; 113 W. Liberty St.) Book lovers could spend an entire day inside this place, browsing through the

The West Side Book Shop has many vintage books.

endless stacks of used and rare books. The owners have a good grasp of the value of old volumes, and are happy to share their knowledge.

Checking In

Best places to stay in and around Ann Arbor.

There aren't a lot of hotels/motels in the downtown area, and most accommodations can be found along the freeways leading to Ann Arbor, I-94, US 23, and M-14.

Bell Tower Hotel (734-769-3010; belltowerhotel.com; 300 Thayer). One of the few options for on-campus lodging. The building is older, but it has been refurbished, and the 66 guest rooms are clean and many have a rich English décor. There are suites available. It's a good place to stay if you're doing business at the university; the rooms have wireless Internet connections and there are conference rooms available. Mercy's Restaurant (734-996-3729) adjoins the hotel lobby. The menu is French-Asian and the dining room is a sleek, contemporary affair. There's a bar.

Campus Inn (734-769-2282; campusinn.com; 615 E. Huron St.) A good location near the university, the inn's 208 rooms have been redecorated and the top-floor rooms offer a good view of the surrounding campus and Ann Arbor. The bathrooms are marble. The public rooms are heavy on mahogany. There's a presidential suite that was actually stayed in by one President Gerald Ford, a U-M graduate. Victors Restaurant and Bar (734-769-2282) is in the hotel, and it offers breakfast, lunch, and dinner. The menu isn't large but features standard favorites like fish and chips, burgers, seafood, steak, and chicken.

Local Flavors

Taste of the town—restaurants, cafés, bars, bistros, etc.

Bella Ciao (734-995-2107; 118 W. Liberty St.) Open daily for dinner. This is a small place, but it scores big when it comes to its Italian menu, which is more than just pasta. There's pancetta-wrapped shrimp with lemon-sautéed spinach and grilled polenta. Duck, beef, Amish chicken, and veal are also

Deli Delirium at Zingerman's

It's not stretching it to say that one of Ann Arbor's major attractions is a deli: **Zingerman's Delicatessen** (734-663-3354; zingermansdeli.com; 422 Detroit St.) The term "deli" hardly serves to describe the restaurant/store, which has nearly a cultlike following, especially among U-M alumni and students. Some businesspeople headed to Ann Arbor often plan their day around eating at the deli. On Saturdays, there's often a line going around the block to get one of their legendary corned beef sandwiches.

It was founded in 1982 by Paul Saginaw and Ari Weinzeig in its present location, and at first offered a small selection of specialty and traditional Jewish foods, and since then it has expanded its menu and founded a successful mail-order business and also another Ann Arbor restaurant.

Zingerman's has a near-cult following.

The deli bakes its own specialty breads, which it uses in its sandwiches and also markets to regional food stores. It offers farmhouse cheeses, estate-bottled olive oils, varietal vinegars, and smoked fish and meats. There are about 100 different sandwiches, all with a vast selection of different breads, which for first-time patrons makes a visit a daunting experience. The best way to make it less intimidating is by going to the deli's website and printing out the menu before you go. You can also pick up a menu inside. There's usually a long enough wait to make a decision. $$

on the menu. There is a large wine list. $$$

Casey's Tavern (734-665-6775; caseys-tavern.com; 304 Depot St.) Open daily for lunch and dinner. Billed as "Ann Arbor's neighborhood bar," this popular tavern serves good burgers and offers weekly specials. It's near Kerrytown and the Amtrak Station and is a good place to wait for the train. $$

The Chop House (888-456-3463; thechophouserestaurant.com; 322 S. Main) The Chop House offers some of the best dining on Main Street. The high-end, elegant steak house has a great view of Main Street. There's a full menu, with entrée offerings that include steak, chops, venison, lamb, veal, and seafood. There's an extensive wine list. $$$

Casey's Tavern in Ann Arbor.

Conor O'Neill's Irish Pub (734-665-2968; conoroneills.com; 318 S. Main St.) While it's a traditional pub, the food isn't just burgers and fries. Offerings include fish and chips, shepherd's pie, corned beef and cabbage, and barbecued pork. The owners have done a good job of

The Chop House.

Conor O'Neill's on Main Street is an Ann Arbor gathering place.

The Gandy Dancer.

replicating an authentic tavern, especially the exterior. There's a large selection of beers from Britain and Ireland. Two favorites are Murphy's Irish Stout and Boddington's Cream Ale. $$

The Earle (734-994-0211; theearle.com; 121 W. Washington St.) is another top-notch choice, and offers more than 900 wines. Its décor is a bit old school, but it has a cozy, well-worn feel to it that's comforting. The seating is comfortable, in contrast to more upscale places, and it's a cheery place during the happy hour. Some could make a meal out of several appetizers that include calamari, escargot, beef tenderloin, ginger shrimp and crab cakes. There are French and Italian style entrées, including duck breasts, beef bourguignon, scallops, Delmonico steaks, chicken, trout and whitefish. A favorite is cassoulet, which is a stewlike dish with white beans, pork, pancetta, garlic sausage, onions, carrots, tomatoes and garlic. $$$

The Gandy Dancer (734-769-0592; www.muer.com; 401 Depot St.) has long been a destination restaurant for many in southeast Michigan. Near Kerrytown, it's located in a historic 1886 railroad depot that still has the original cobblestones and red oak ceiling. It's operated by the Muer family, which has been in the restaurant business in Michigan for generations. The emphasis is on seafood, and menu offerings include lake perch, whitefish, salmon, sole, crab, and shrimp. Try the seafood mixed trio, which includes salmon, crab cakes, and shrimp. There are also steaks, chops, pasta, and house-baked desserts. $$$

Gratzi (734-663-6387; 326 S. Main St.) The menu is fairly wide, ranging from burgers to Italian dishes and steaks. It's a great place for people watching on Main Street. Diners won't find many students patronizing this upscale steak house, unless they're eating there with visiting parents. Entrées include steak, beef wellington, pork chops, lamb, veal and seafood. There are half dozen types of appetizers to pick from, and range from calamari to oysters. While the atmosphere is elegant, its large windows on Main Street allow for good people watching. $$$

Grizzly Peak Brewing Company (734-741-7325; grizzlypeak.net; 120 W. Washington) If you're in town visiting somebody from the university, this is a great destination. The brew pub atmosphere appeals to booth students and older folks, with its microbewed beers and a pub-style menu. $$

Knight's Steakhouse (734-665-8644; www.knightsrestaurants.com; 2324 Dexter Rd., Ann Arbor). This place is out of the downtown mix, but is worth finding. The family-owned restaurant is in a nondescript building. Inside, it's an old-style steak house. The meat itself comes from the Knight family meat market. The meals are solid and heavy on beef, although there is some seafood and pasta. Come hungry to this place. $$$

The Heidelberg Restaurant (734-663-7758; theheidelberg.com; 215 Main) There were once many German restaurants in Ann Arbor, due to its strong German heritage, and the Heidelberg keeps the tradition alive. The German offerings on the menu are a bit sparse, and most of the fare is traditional America food including steak, fish and chips, country fried steak, and burgers. There is a large selection of German beers. $$

Metzger's German Restaurant (734-668-8987; metzgers.net; 305 N. Zeeb Rd.) Open daily for lunch and dinner. The family-owned German restaurant has been a fixture in Ann Arbor for several generations and serves up traditional dishes such as sauerbraten, Bavaria veal, chicken livers, and prime rib. There are German wines and liquors. $$

Pacific Rim (734-662-9403; pacificrimbykana.com; 114 W. Liberty). When an Ann Arbor restaurant owner says another place other than his or hers is the best place in town, it's advice that is worth listening to. The recommendation was to Pacific Rim. The Asian-based menu is particularly interesting. A good starter is the Monsoon Platter, which includes Saigon spring rolls filled with shrimp and served with a Vietnamese-style sauce. For an entrée, try the Japanese-style sablefish, which is marinated in miso and sake and pan roasted. Another interesting dish is Thai basil pesto fettuccini, which is served with a Chinese black bean sauce. Other offerings range from duck to rib eye stakes, all with an Asian kick to them. $$$

Zingerman's Roadhouse (734-663-3663; zingermansroadhouse.com; 2501 Jackson Ave.) The same care and thoughtfulness that prevails at Zingerman's Deli are evident at this upscale restaurant/bar, which takes classic American dishes and kicks them up a notch. For example, the macaroni and cheese is made with homemade béchamel sauce, raw milk, Vermont cheddar, and artisanal macaroni from Tuscany. Menu mainstays include grilled Carolina white grits, BBQ, pulled pork, chicken fried steak, smoked pork ribs, and steak. Most of the meat comes from a local producer. There are also burgers. $$$

For lunch

Jolly Pumpkin Café & Brewery (734-913-2730; 311 S. Main) With an emphasis on burgers, pizza, and its own beer, this is a natural student hangout. There are some interesting sandwiches, including chickpea panini and grilled chicken with Brie. The Mediterranean pizza with goat cheese and Greek olives is interesting. $

Parthenon Restaurant (734-994-1012; parthenonrestaurant.com; 226 Main) is a popular, noisy place on a well-traveled corner and is a great place for lunch, featuring Greek and Italian food. The gyros are a good bet, with thinly sliced lamb or beef on flat bread, with tomatoes and salad. $

Prickley Pear Café (734-930-0047; 328 Main St.) The small place features southwestern fare that ranges from chicken to seafood, with plenty of salsa on tap. $

The Prickly Pear on Main Street is a good lunch stop.

The Fleetwood Diner (734-995-5502; 300 S. Ashley) Relive college days at the diner, which has been a fixture downtown for several generations and serves up an array of student fare including burgers, hotdogs, corned beef hash, and traditional breakfast meals. During warmer months there are outside tables and chairs and you'll find an array of hipsters of various ages talking politics. $

The Fleetwood in Ann Arbor is a student hangout.

Entertainment

Go out on the town

There's a lively music scene in Ann Arbor, with bands often playing in the student bars around town, and there's also venues where jazz can be heard.

The Ark (734-761-1800; theark.org; 316 S. Main) Perhaps the mainstay of the music scene here, The Ark hosts music events more than 300 nights each year, and attracts many national performers, especially in the folk and blues vein. The Ark started as a coffee shop where folk music was performed in 1965 and is now a nonprofit dedicated to the preservation of folk, roots, and ethnic music. Over the years, many notable performers have played here. In late January, The Ark hosts an annual folk festival that is usually sold out. Performers have included the Avett Brothers, Citizen Cope, Vienna Teng and Alex Wong, The Spring Standards, The Paper Raincoat, Anais Mitchell, and Theo Katzman.

Hill Auditorium (734-763-3333; www.ums.org; 825 N. University Ave.) Since opening in 1913, the 33,538-seat venue has staged many concerts, with acts ranging from Jimmy Buffett to Leonard Bernstein. Performers in recent years have included everything from country to string quartets. During one season they had Rosanne Cash, The Hot Club of San Francisco, and the Hot Club of Detroit celebrating Django Reinhardt's 100th birthday, Carolina Chocolate Drops, the Cleveland Orchestra, and Breakin' Curfew.

The Ark is a top venue for folk singers and other musical acts.

Kerrytown Concert House (734-769-2999; kerrytownconcerthouse.com; 415 N. Fourth Ave.) The 110-seat concert hall is home to intimate jazz, classical, and singer/songwriter and poetry performances. Works by local artists is also displayed. An annual Edgefest is held in October.

Outdoor Recreation

Bicycling

Because of its large student population, there are many cyclists in and around Ann Arbor. The city has designated bikeways. For a map, visit the City of Ann Arbor website (www.a2gov.org). The website also has a map of Washtenaw County bike paths. A popular ride is along Huron River Drive, a two-lane blacktop road that follows the Huron River.

Fishing

The Huron River is great for bass and carp fishing. During summer months you'll see many fly anglers in the river catching large carp on fly rods. Colton Bay Outfitters (734-222-9776; coltonbay.com; 4844 Jackson Rd.) offers fly-fishing trips on the Huron River.

Golfing

Barton Hills Country Club (734-663-8511; 730 Country Club Rd.) is a private club that dates to 1919 and is worth seeing because it's located in Barton Hills, one of Ann Arbor's most exclusive neighborhoods. It has an 18-hole course designed by Donald Ross.

KERRYTOWN

The historic district is a downtown unto itself, and is located on the spot where the original village of Ann Arbor was located in the 19th century. Older structures have been renovated and new ones added and observers have a hard time telling the old from the new, it's that seamless. During warmer months the nearby Ann Arbor Farmers Market on Saturdays brings local farmers to the area.

Visitors will be entertained by the Kerrytown bell tower on top of the market building, which has 17 chimes in different tones. The bells were cast in the 1920s for a Massachusetts church, and in the late 1990s Kerrytown restored the bells and built the tower. The bells chime at noon on Wednesdays and Fridays and at 11:30 AM on Saturdays.

Travelers could spend most of an afternoon browsing through the shops and food markets, and there are plenty of restaurants nearby to have lunch or dinner. Kerrytown is probably the most concentrated area of upscale goods in the state.

Local Flavors

Taste of the town—restaurants, cafés, bars, bistros, etc.

Kosmopolitan (734-668-4070; 415 N. Fifth Ave.) The breakfast and lunch counter offers burgers and such but also Korean dishes such as b-bim, bulgogi, and twigim. $$

Kerrytown is filled with shops, restaurants, and markets.

Sweetwaters Coffee & Tea (734-622-0084; sweetwaters cafe.com; 407 N. Fifth Ave.) Offers coffee, tea, baked goods, and quiche. It's a good place for a light lunch. $

Yamato Restaurant (734-998-3484; 403 N. Fifth Ave.) A good choice for light fare served traditional-Japanese style. Sushi and sashimi are on the menu. The small place offers lunch and dinner. $$

Shopping

In Kerrytown.

Durham's Tracklements (734-322-9250; www.tracklements .com; 212 E. Kingsley, first floor) This is the placed for custom-smoked provisions, including salmon, rainbow trout, Finnan haddie, gravlax, and bluefish. The shop does all its own smoking. They also offer mail-order delivery.

Elephant Ears (734-622-9580; elephantearsonline.com; 415 N. Fifth Ave., first and second floors) If you're looking for some quirky clothing for kids and adults that come in vivid colors, check this place out. They also offer bedding and footwear. Much of the clothing is made from whimsical prints.

Everyday Wines (734-827-WINE; everyday-wines.com; 407 N. Fifth Ave.) This is a dreamland for frugal wine lovers who want to sample products from around the world. There are some great deals, especially if you purchase by the case.

Found (724-302-3060; foundgallery.com; 407 N. Fifth Ave.) The shop offers antiques and is a showcase for contemporary artists who create jewelry out of found objects such as typewriter keys and bottle caps and other eclectic items.

Fustini's Oils & Vinegars (734-213-1110; fustinis.com; 407 N. Fifth, second floor) There's a wide selection of aged balsamic vinegars and fresh olive oils.

Hollander's Kitchen & Home (734-741-7531; hollanders.com; 410 N. Fourth) The store offers a vast array of hard-to-find kitchen wares, general home goods, utensils, cookbooks, and tablecloths. The shop has been around since 1991 and offers many workshops on cooking and the decorative arts. Don't forget to check out the first floor, where it offers decorative papers, bookbinding supplies, and classes. It has more than 1,500 papers in stock and also offers hand bookbinding tools and supplies.

Mathilde's Imports (734-214-1248; 407 N. Fifth Ave.) A source for hard-to-find clothing from Latin America, Europe, Southeast Asia, and the United States. Most items are from small design houses.

Monahan's Seafood (734-662-5116; monahanseafood.com; 415 N. Fifth Ave., first floor) If it swims, they've got it. There's also a small restaurant that serves shrimp, fried calamari, salmon, and chowder. The place has the feel of an old-time fish market and the products are attractively displayed. They're also a good source of information about how to cook fish and other products.

Mudpuddles (734-662-0022; 415 N. Fifth Ave.) Games, books, and toys for children.

A shop in Kerrytown.

Princess Designs (734-663-2628; princessdesignsjewelry.com; 407 N. Fifth) A jewelry store that offers semiprecious stones and designs. There are more than 5,000 necklaces.

Sparrow Meat Market (734-761-8175; sparrowmeat.getwebnet.com; 415 N. Fifth Ave.) The shop offers free-range pork, organic lamb, free-range chicken and duck and homemade sausage.

Spice Merchants (734-332-5500; spicemerchants.biz; 407 N. Fifth Ave.) There are 150 different types of spices and 85 blends of tea to choose from.

V2V (734-665-9110; 415 N. Fifth Ave.) This place offers women's clothing, accessories, formal wear, bridal gowns, and some home wares.

9

Windsor

THE CITY ACROSS THE RIVER

THE CANADIAN CITY on the Detroit River grew up with the Motor City and has a common French Canadian heritage. It is also heavily reliant on the auto industry, with Chrysler and Ford plants located here, but the similarity stops there. When you enter Windsor (which, by a geographical oddity, is actually south of Detroit), you feel as though you've just left a gritty industrial metropolis and driven into a small English city, even though the Canadian city has 216,000 residents.

If you cross the Ambassador Bridge, one of your first sights is of the ivy-covered walls of the University of Windsor, which looks out on the Detroit River. Known as the "City of Roses," Windsor is a vibrant place, with flourishing older neighborhoods and a lively downtown. It has been spared much of the urban decay suffered by Detroit.

The city has long been a destination for Detroiters. During Prohibition in the 1920s, bootleggers crossed the Detroit River and brought liquor across the border to thirsty Americans, making alcohol smuggling the second-largest business in the city, after autos. These days Windsor is a haven for teenagers looking for a bar to party in, as the drinking age is 21 in Michigan, and 19 in Windsor. Gambling and restaurants are also a draw. For smokers, it's the place to find and buy

LEFT: The Windsor skyline.

Rolling the Dice in Windsor

Caesars Windsor Hotel & Casino (800-991-7777; caesarswindsor.com; 377 Riverside Dr. East) The casino perched on the Detroit River lures many Detroiters across the border for a change of pace. Apart from slot machines, poker, blackjack, and roulette, the casino offers elegant overnight accommodations, restaurants, and entertainment. $$$ There are six restaurants to chose from, including the **Artist Café** for fine dining $$; the **Augustus Café,** which serves breakfast, lunch, and dinner, and offers pasta, pizza, and sandwiches $; and the **Legends Sports Bar,** which serves burgers and other pub food and pizza. $

legal Cuban cigars. Those looking for cheaper prescription drugs also fill them at Canadian stores.

People cross the Detroit-Windsor border on a regular basis. (For information on getting to Windsor from the metro area, see "Routes to Canada," in the Transportation section, pp. 46–48.) There are duty-free stores at both the Ambassador Bridge and Detroit-Windsor Tunnel that sell liquor, beer, wine, and specialty food items. The alcohol and other items are cheaper, but there are restrictions on how much and what you can bring back to Michigan. The exchange rate varies. Before you go, check with U.S. Customs (313-442-0368; www.cbp.gov) to see what restrictions are in place.

Windsor's riverfront parks are a particular destination during the three-week Summerfest (summerfestwindsor.org) held mid-June through July, which includes a Riverfront Fireworks Party, with fireworks shot off over the Detroit River. Windsor's Riverwalk follows the River from the Ambassador Bridge to the Hiram Walker Canadian Club Distillery. The Odette Sculpture Park is located along the trail, and has 31 acres filled with contemporary sculptures.

Checking In

Best places to stay in and around Winsor.

There are numerous hotels in downtown Windsor, many with views of the Detroit River and the city's skyline.

Holiday Inn & Suites Ambassador Bridge Windsor (519-966-1200; www.his-windsor.com; 1855 Huron Church Rd.) Fully equipped, modern rooms and suites, with wireless Internet and cable TV. $$

The Radisson Riverfront Windsor Hotel (519-977-9777; www.radisson.com/windsor-hotel-on-n9a5k4/onwindso) gives guests a good view of downtown Detroit's skyline and Windsor's Riverfront. The rooms are large, have a contemporary feel, and are equipped with wireless Internet and cable TV and have a work area. A bar and restaurant are on the main floor. $$

Local Flavors

Taste of the town—restaurants, cafés, bars, bistros, etc.

A popular destination for dining in Windsor is Little Italy on Erie Street, which has many Italian restaurants and shops. Within five blocks alone on Erie Street there are 16 restaurants. But a wide range of cuisines are represented in the city.

Blue Danube (519-252-0246; bluedanuberestaurant.com; 1235 Ottawa St.) If your tastes run to Austro-Hungarian fare, check out Blue Danube. The restaurant has been around for more than 30 years, and it serves such favorites as chicken paprikash, a thick stew, and turkey schnitzel served with dumplings. Seafood dishes are also offered. The wine list includes local labels. $$

La Casalinga (519-258-9979; lacasalinga1.com; 653 Erie St. East) Pasta, fish, and chicken are the specialties, and one eye-catcher is the chicken breast filled with spinach and ricotta cheese. There's a large wine list. $$

Il Gabbiano Ristorante (519-256-9757; ilgabbiano.com; 875 Erie St.) This is an elegant little place with a large wine list and some interesting offerings on the menu. The house specialties include risotto del giomo, parpadelle fresco, noodles, spinach and salmon with a light tomato sauce; linguine alla bella donna, with sweet peppers, artichoke hearts, olives, capers and tomato; and surf and turf. $$

Rathskeller
RATHSKELLER
DAKOTA INN
17324

Where Detroiters Eat and What They Drink

CONEY ISLANDS, DELIS, DRIVE-INS, AND MORE

WHILE THE METRO AREA has its upscale and ethnic restaurants, Detroit has its share of neighborhood eateries and diner-type joints that see heavy traffic. Many of them are family-owned and -operated, and have been around for decades. They are the locals' favorites.

Perhaps because Detroit is a factory town, where workers took various shifts, many around-the-clock restaurants were established to serve them. No Detroit dining experience has endured longer than the Coney Island, which here is a generic term for any Detroit-area restaurant that serves hot dogs covered with chili and onions.

Detroit's original Coney Island restaurants, the Lafayette and the American, were founded in 1917 by the Keros brothers, Gust and Bill, in downtown Detroit at the corner of Lafayette and Michigan Avenue. The brothers eventually split the restaurant in half, one side becoming the Lafayette Coney Island and the other the American Coney Island, both of which still exist today and have become landmarks, although they are no longer owned by the Keros family.

I know these restaurants well because my wife is Greek American

LEFT: The Dakota Inn Rathskeller is a longtime favorite of Detroit-area residents.

and her grandfather knew the Keros family. At one point, when Detroit was much busier, you could double-park in front of the restaurants and hold up two fingers, which meant bring a Coney Island and a Coke out to the car. If you did it twice, that meant two Coneys and two cokes.

My wife's grandfather worked for the Lafayette Coney Island and lined up on that side of the family feud. To this day I've never been in the American, as though anybody would care or notice.

The Keros family still owns the Kerby's Koney Island chain in the Detroit area. Many other Greeks eventually got into the Coney Island trade, and there are numerous such restaurants in the Detroit area. One of the best is the Senate Coney Island in Livonia and another restaurant owned by the same family in Northville.

FAVORITE EATERIES

Coney Islands

Kerby's Koney Island (www.kerbyskoneyisland.com) has 24 locations in the metro area, and most of them are crowded with hot dog lovers. The menu includes Greek salads and gyros sandwiches, along with breakfasts. $

Senate Coney Island (734-422-5075; www.georgessenateandconeyislandrestarant.com; 34539 Plymouth Rd., Livonia) Located in the Plymouth Road corridor, which is home to a Ford plant and Roush Racing, a major supplier to NASCAR. Workers from those facilities fill up the parking lot of the Coney Island, and it's a great place to spot Mustang muscle cars. A popular breakfast special brings crowds in the morning, and lunch brings in even more customers. Coney Island hot dogs smothered in chili, onions, and mustard is the specialty, but there is also American fare and Greek dishes, such as stuffed grape leaves, gyros sandwiches served on flat bread, and Greek hamburgers. Try a bowl of the chili or the Greek lemon and rice soup. The owner, George Dimopoulos, is a Greek immigrant who came to this country in 1969 and has run the place since the early '70s. As with many suburban restaurants, it had its roots in Detroit. The original Senate opened at Michigan Avenue and Livernois in 1937 and was owned by Dimopoulos's uncle and aunt. $

Delis

At one time there were many Jewish delis in the metro area. Now their numbers have dwindled as large chains take over the restaurant business, but there are a few holdouts. The Stage Deli in West Bloomfield is the best. (See entry, chapter 5).

The Bread Basket (www.breadbasketdelis.com) has various locations in the metro area. The corned beef sandwiches are so large you have a hard time finishing them. Locations at: Redford (313-387-4767; 26667 W. Eight Mile); Livonia (734-422-1100; 11320 Middlebelt Rd.); Waterford (248-683-2244; 101 N. Telegraph Rd.); Warren (586-754-0055; 2201 E. Eight Mile Rd.); Detroit (313-865-DELI; 15603 Grand River Ave.); Detroit (313-836-DELI; 17740 Woodward Ave.); Oak Park (248-968-0022; 26052 Greenfield Rd.) $

Drive-ins

Detroit has many small pull-up places to grab a snack or a meal, some of which are part of local chains. If you grew up in the 1950s and '60s, check out the Daly Drive Inn (734-427-4474; www.dalyrestaurants.com; 31500 Plymouth Rd. in Livonia). Although there hasn't been a carhop for decades, the places are set up for it, making you think that a teenage greaser in a hot car will be cruising in at any moment. The Daly Drive Inn was "retro" before the word became popular. The menu has changed little in 50 years and still revolves around burgers, fries, and milkshakes. They are real, honest-to-goodness milkshakes made from scratch. A good bet is the chee-chee, which was once called a melted cheese and chili. $

Fish and Chips

Scotty Simpsons Fish & Chips (313-533-0950; 22200 Finkell, Detroit) Located in one of the city's most distressed neighborhoods, Brightmoor, the storefront restaurant has defied all odds and does a brisk business, one of the few surviving establishments in the area. The restaurant was started in 1950 by James Simpson, when

Scotty Simpson's Fish and Chips in Detroit is a local favorite.

Brightmoor was a thriving blue-collar neighborhood, and it has changed little in terms of décor, not that the regular diners seem to mind. Don't bother asking for a menu, it's pretty much as the name says: fish and chips. $

Soul Food

Beans & Cornbread Soulful Bistro (248-208-1680; beanscornbread.com; 29508 Northwestern Hwy., Southfield.) The down-home food and upscale atmosphere has made this a favorite place for metro Detroit residents who eat here on a regular basis. The menu has many southern staples, such as pork chops in redeye gravy, catfish, shrimp, gumbo, and greens for the health conscious. $$

Steve's Soul Food Restaurant (313-894-3464; 8443 Grand River Ave., Detroit) has been a longtime favorite of folks looking for southern foods. The cafeteria-style restaurant serves up large portions of fried chicken, pork, black-eyed peas, greens, cornbread, and other traditional southern fare. $

Southern Fires (313-393-4930; southernfiresrestaurant.com; 575 Bellevue, Detroit.) This upscale soul food restaurant is in a modern contemporary building, with good seating. It does a large carryout business, serving steak, meatloaf, short ribs, perch, catfish, salmon, pork chops, ribs, and fried and roasted chicken. The sides have that savory southern-comfort-food feel to them, and include fried corn, baked beans, black-eyed peas, sweet potatoes, and cornbread. $$

Traditional restaurant favorites

Beaver Creek Tavern (734-772-5330; www.beavercreektackleanddbeer.com; 1609 N. Wayne Rd.) Tucked away in the working-class suburb of Westland is a real find, especially for sportsmen and -women. There are waits to get seated in this family-friendly bar/restaurant. The décor is Northwoods Michigan and there are many hunting and fishing related items on the walls, along with a big fireplace. One item on the menu pretty much says it all about this place, that's the "Road Kill Grill," which includes roast venison, broiled quail, and wild boar sausage. A bumper sticker that says "I eat my road kill" comes free with the meal. There are also burgers, fish, and BBQ. $$

Dakota Inn Rathskeller (313-867-9722; www.dakota-inn.com; 17324 John R., Detroit) Open Wednesday–Saturday, but call ahead. Located in what was once a strong German neighborhood on Detroit's northeast side, the inn was opened in 1933 by Karl Kurz, the grandfather of the current owner, in what was then Detroit's German neighborhood. Kurz, like many others, worked at the Ford Motor Co. Highland Park plant but dreamed of having his own business. These days it serves genuine German food such as sauerbraten, roulade, knackwurst, bratwurst, and schweinefleisch. There's a large selection of German beers. $$

Giulio's Cucina Italiana (734-427-9500; www.giiuliositalian.com; 31735 Plymouth Rd.) You don't expect to find this place in Livonia, a northwest Detroit suburb that's not exactly known for its restaurants or entertainment venues. Giulio's has a small but diverse menu that includes veal, braised rabbit, lake perch, lamb chops, and pasta. There are hand-tossed pizzas. $$

Jack's Waterfront Restaurant (586-445-8080; jackswaterfront.com; 24214 E. Jefferson Ave., St. Clair Shores.) Located in a marina area on Lake St. Clair, the restaurant offers lakeside dining, with an emphasis on seafood and fish. Large windows offer diners a lake view from most tables. Offerings also include pasta, steak, chicken, and pizza. $$

Sweet Lorraine's (734-953-7480; www.sweeetlorraines.com; 17100 N. Laurel Park Dr., Livonia) Located in a popular shopping district in Detroit's northwest suburbs, this place has a devoted following. The casual-dining restaurant has been in business since 1984 and serves homemade soups, pastas, seafood, and vegetarian entrées. There's also steak and chicken. There's large wine list. $$

FAVORITE BEVERAGES

Local Soda Pop

While Detroit is known as a shot-and-a-beer town, metro Detroiters also have a special place in their hearts for two locally made soft drinks, Vernors ginger ale and Faygo. In our corner of the Midwest, soda is generally called "pop." If someone asks you if you want a pop, they aren't trying to start a fight, they want to serve you a beverage.

Founded in 1907, Faygo is a relative newcomer compared to Vernors, which has been around since 1866. According to company legend, its inventor, James Vernor, was a clerk at a Detroit drugstore, and was trying to come up with a recipe for a ginger ale that came from Ireland. He was working with his formula when the Civil War broke out, and he ended up joining the Union army. But back in Detroit, his concoction was aging in a wooden barrel. When he returned from the war in 1865, he opened the barrel and found that the concoction was perfect.

The firm's bottling company was located on Woodward Avenue, and from the 1940s to the 1960s, it operated a soda fountain at the front of its plant and also offered tours. Many a Detroit child got their fill of the ginger ale at the fountain after a plant tour.

Many parents thought that spicy-sweet Vernors had a medicinal quality, especially when served hot, and to this day, metro Detroit residents head to the store for bottles of Vernors when there's an ill child (or adult) in the house.

Faygo is still made in Detroit at a plant on Gratiot, and was the brainchild of two Russian immigrant brothers, Ben and Perry Feigenson, who established Feigenson Brothers Bottling Works, which offered low-cost soda with numerous flavors, including strawberry, grape, and fruit punch. The number of flavors expanded as the years went by, but it stayed a local company because the soda didn't have a long shelf life and it was difficult to distribute it to other parts of the country. That changed in the 1950s when a new formula was developed. It was family-owned for decades before being sold to the National Beverage Corporation.

Stroh's Beer

For over 100 years Stroh family members were the beer barons of Detroit, establishing their first brewery in 1850 in the city, and sparking local followers of the beverage to establish strong loyalties to the brand.

Unfortunately, that came to an end in about 2000, but that loyalty had been ebbing for years. The family was getting out of the beermaking business, and Stroh's, while still around and brewed by Pabst, just doesn't have the appeal in Detroit that it once did.

Information

THE NITTY-GRITTY FOR TRAVELERS to the metro Detroit region, including contact numbers and information on banking, media outlets, tourism resources, annual events, and recommended reading. But first, the ever important issue of the weather.

THE WEATHER HERE AND HOW TO DRESS FOR IT

Southeastern Michigan weather is a study in extremes: winter brings temperatures than can dip to below zero, and summers can see temperatures in the 90s. There are four distinct seasons, but not always on cue with the calendar. Spring is the most frustrating season because the region's weather is controlled by the Great Lakes. If the winter was cold and the lakes have frozen over, it often takes a long time for them to unthaw, making temperatures quite cool. The region gets an average of 45 inches of snow, and March and even early April can see heavy snowstorms. Often it goes from winter to near summer in a few days. March can be particularly frustrating with the freezing and thawing that constantly goes on. That cycle makes roads prone to potholes that crop up over night. The potholes can cause tires to blow out and can damage vehicles. Communities attempt to patch them, but they aren't always successful. Although spring officially arrives on March 22, don't depend on it. Spring can also bring sleet and freezing rain, which is often more difficult to drive in than snow.

According to the U.S. Weather Service, the average temperatures (in degrees Fahrenheit) are: winter (December–early March) average 30–40; spring (March–late June) 40s to 70s; summer (late June–late September) 70s–80s; and fall (late September–November) 70s–40s. In the summer, it can be hot and humid, with temperatures in the 90s, but usually when its gets real hot, the Great Lakes often dish up afternoon thunderstorms to cool things off. The fall is one of the best seasons in Michigan and Detroit, with moderate temperatures in the 60s and 70s. The reason is that the Great Lakes warm up in the summer and moderate the air temperature. The best radio stations for weather and traffic are WJR-AM (760) and WWJ-AM 950).

What to Wear

No matter what time of year you come, it's good to bring a sweater or jacket—fleece is a good bet. While summer tends to be warm, in the 70s–90s, the thermometer can quickly dip down into the 50s, especially at night. January is the coldest month, with temperatures averaging about 28 degrees but often plunging to near zero. Make sure to bring a heavy winter coat any time from late November until mid-March, and sometimes later. Actually, when it's cold and snowy it's more comfortable, especially for your feet, than when it warms up and the sidewalks are wet and slushy. Make sure to bring some type of boots in the winter, not the leather fashionable ones, but sensible lined ones. Don't worry about being a fashion plate; you'll fit in with the locals if you wear sensible gear. And don't forget a hat.

AREA CODES

The area code for Detroit and many inner-ring suburbs is 313; for western Wayne County and Ann Arbor, 734; for much of Oakland County and the northwestern portion of Wayne County, 248; in Macomb County, 586 covers the suburbs nearest Detroit, and a small portion of Detroit; for Windsor, 519.

AMBULANCE, FIRE, & POLICE

For emergency help in the region, dial 911.

Detroit and Wayne County

Detroit Police Department (313-596-2200; www.detroitmi.gov/Departments/PoliceDepartment/tabid/), 1300 Beaubien St., Detroit, police headquarters; there are other stations in the city.

Michigan State Police (313-456-6600; www.michigan.gov/msp/), 3050 W. Grand Blvd., Detroit.

Wayne County Sheriff's Department (313-224-2222; www.waynecounty.com), 1231 Saint Antoine St., Detroit. The sheriff's department handles police duties for the city of Highland Park and also administers the Wayne County Jail.

Metro Sheriff's Departments

Macomb County Sheriff's Department (586-469-5151; Macombsheriff.com), 43565 Elizabeth St., Mount Clemens. The department handles police duties for many smaller communities, and runs the county jail.

Oakland County Sheriff's Department (248-858-5000; www.oakgov.com/sheriff/), 1200 N. Telegraph Rd., Building 38E, Pontiac. The sheriff's department handles police duties for many smaller Oakland County communities, along with running the Oakland County Jail.

Washtenaw County Sheriff's Department (734-971-8400; www.ewashtenaw.org/government/sheriff/), 2201 Hogback Rd., Ann Arbor.

Metro Police Departments, no emergency

Ann Arbor 734-794-6911
Allen Park 313-386-7800
Beverly Hills 248-540-3400
Birmingham 248-644-3400
Bloomfield Hills 248-644-4200
Bloomfield Township 248-433-7755
Canton Township 734-394-5400
Clawson 248-435-5000
Dearborn 313-943-2240
Eastpointe 586-445-5100
Ecorse 313-381-0900
Farmington Hills 248-871-2600
Farmington, city of 248-474-4700
Ferndale 248-545-5272
Garden City 734-793-1700
Grosse Ile 734-676-7100
Grosse Pointe 313-822-7400
Grosse Pointe Farms 313-822-3200
Grosse Pointe Park 313-822-4416
Grosse Pointe Shores 313-881-5500
Grosse Pointe Woods 313-343-2400
Hamtramck 313-876-7800
Harper Woods 313-343-2530
Hazel Park 248-542-6161
Highland Park, contact the Wayne County Sheriff's office, 313-224-2222
Inkster 313-563-9856
Lathrup Village 248-557-3600
Livonia 734-466-2400

Lincoln Park 313-381-1800
Madison Heights 248-585-2100
Northville 248-349-5100
Northville Township 248-348-5800
Novi 248-348-7100
Plymouth 734-453-8600
Plymouth Township 734-354-3250
Pontiac 248-857-7890
Royal Oak 248-246-3500
River Rouge 313-842-8700
Redford 313-387-2500
St. Clair Shores 810-329-5710
Southfield 248-354-1000
Warren 586-574-4800
West Bloomfield Township 248-975-9200
Westland 734-722-9600
Windsor 519-255-6700
Wyandotte 734-324-4405
Ypsilanti 734-483-8932

Banks and Automated Teller Machines (ATMs)

Metro Detroit is served by all the major banks, including Comerica, Chase, Fifth Third Bank, Bank of America, National City, and Charter One. ATM machines are located in many gas stations, stores, at the casinos, and other public places.

MEDIA

Newspapers

Detroit is a two-newspaper town, except on Sundays, when the two papers print a combined edition. The papers are only delivered to homes on Thursdays, Fridays, and Sundays, but are available on newsstands daily. The *Detroit News* tends to be more conservative than the *Detroit Free Press*.

The *Detroit Free Press* (www.freep.com), a daily morning newspaper that serves southeastern Michigan and the state. You need to subscribe to see the daily paper online, but its website offers basic coverage of events. The paper is available at most newsstands, and on Thursday it publishes a section called Play that lists restaurants and covers cultural and musical performances for the coming week.

The *Detroit News* (detnews.com) this daily is known for its coverage of the auto industry and also is a good source of entertainment news, restaurant listings, and upcoming cultural events.

Magazines

Crain's Detroit Business (www.crainsdetroit.com) is a weekly business magazine read by many professionals in the metro area.

Hour Detroit (www.hourdetroit.com) is a slick four-color magazine devoted to lifestyle issues in metro Detroit. There are features on restaurants, who's who in Detroit, and entertainment. There are also home profiles with lush photographs.

The Jewish News (thejewishnews.com) keeps the metro area's large Jewish population up-to-date about issues.

Alternative press

Metro Times (metrotimes.com) is a free weekly alternative newspaper that's available in bars, restaurants, clubs, and other businesses. It's a refreshing newspaper that takes an alternative look at the issues facing Detroit, and is heavy with stories about clubs and other entertainment venues. There are restaurant reviews and in-depth stories on local musicians.

Ann Arbor media

Ann Arbor is served by the three local TV channels, but receives scant attention from them unless it's a large, national story. Detroit's two daily papers give minimal coverage to Ann Arbor.

AnnArbor.com (www.annarbor.com) is all that is left of the *Ann Arbor News*, which served the community for more than 100 years but closed for economic reasons. The website puts news and information online, and also prints several editions weekly. The paper can be found at various businesses. It also covers events in nearby Ypsilanti.

TV Stations

Detroit is served by three major local stations when it comes to news and information.

Channel 4 (clickondetroit.com) is the NBC affiliate and has a strong news presence in the city.

Channel 7 (wxyz.com) is the ABC affiliate and has much information at its website about the city.

Channel 2 (myfoxdetroit.com) is perhaps the weakest of the channels when it comes to local news and information, but its website does have local information and entertainment news.

Radio

There are a variety of radio stations in southeastern Michigan, including several National Public Radio stations.

Best for news

WWJ 950 AM (Detroit.cbslocal.com) is an all-news CBS affiliate that is very reliable when it comes to traffic and weather reporting, and also staffs many local news events. It also carries hookups with CBS network reports.

WJR 760 AM (www.wjr.net) bills itself as a news/talk station, but there's more talk than news. Many of their local broadcasters are veterans of the Detroit scene and can offer some good insights into what's going on in the city and region.

Best local music

WJLB 98 FM (fm98wjlb.com) is the city's top hip-hop and R&B station and has long been popular in the African American community. It's a good source of information about upcoming concerts and live performances.

WDET 101.9 FM (www.wdetfm.org) offers an urban version of National Public Radio and has a focus on new music, along with airing traditional NPR programming.

WRCJ 90.9 FM (www.wrcjfm.org) is an interesting animal in that it airs classical music during the day and jazz at night, without commercials. It's a nonprofit, listener-supported radio station licensed to the Detroit Public Schools but managed by Detroit Public Television.

CBC 89.9 FM (www.cbc.ca/Windsor/) is the Canadian take on National Public Radio, and its news programs give listeners a grasp of what's going on in Canada, and a different view of events in the United States. Much of the music played is by Canadian pop and rock artists.

WEMU 89.1 FM (www.wemu.org/listen.php) is a National Public Radio station broadcast from Eastern Michigan University in Ypsilanti and offers a more traditional NPR station and national programming not offered by the Detroit station. The station's signals are fairly strong in western Wayne County, but fade in Detroit.

WUOM 91.7 FM (www.michiganradio.org) is the Ann Arbor–based public radio station and has a strong focus on Michigan news.

TOURIST INFORMATION

Regional and statewide

Pure Michigan (www.michigan.org) is the State of Michigan's official travel information agency, and has listings for the metro Detroit area. The website gives users a good overall feel for southeastern Michigan and directs them to specific businesses.

Detroit

Detroit Metro Convention and Visitors Bureau (313-202-1800; visit detroit.com; 211 W. Fort Street, Suite 1000) The bureau is a good first place to visit if planning a trip. There's information about restaurants, lodging, transportation, and shopping in Detroit and the region.

Detroit Regional Chamber (313-964-0183; detroitchamber.com; One Woodward Ave., Suite 1900) Detroit's chamber of commerce provides information about Detroit's business community and economic development.

Ann Arbor

Ann Arbor Area Convention and Visitors Bureau (734-995-7281; visitannarbor.org; 120 W. Huron St.) Information about Ann Arbor's hotels, restaurants, shops, and attractions. A good source for travelers planning a trip to the area. The bureau offers useful maps of the downtown area.

Birmingham

The Birmingham Bloomfield Chamber (248-644-1700; www.bbcc.com; 725 S. Adams Rd., Suite 130) Serves the communities of Birmingham, Bloomfield Hills, and Bloomfield Township, as well as Beverly Hills, Bingham Farms, and Franklin.

ONLINE RESOURCES

Arab Detroit (arabdetroit.com) is a news outlet serving Detroit's large Arab American community and promoting outreach to the wider community.

Detroit Agriculture (detroitagriculture.org) is dedicated to the idea of helping the city's revival by using its unused lands for farming.

Detroit Area Art Deco Society (daads.org) Advocates preservation efforts and sponsors a variety of events promoting the architecture and style of the art deco period.

Detroit Irish (www.detroitirish.org) is a news source serving Greater Detroit and Michigan's Irish American community.

Detroit Public Library (detroit.lib.mi.us) offers general information about the city and the region.

Fabulous Ruins of Detroit (detroityes.com) gives users a photographic tour of the industrial buildings that are part of the city's past.

Forgotten Detroit (www.forgottendetroit.com) takes a look at the buildings constructed during Detroit's art deco heyday in the 1920s, some of which have been abandoned.

Historic Places in Detroit (nps.gov/nr/travel/detroit/detlist.htm) The National Park Service maintains a reliable list of places in Detroit that are on the National Register of Historic Places.

History Detroit (historydetroit.com) takes a look at the city's long past, and is a good source for information about the period of French rule of the region.

Inside Southwest Detroit (insidesouthwest.com) serves residents of the southwest Detroit area as well as visitors to the area.

North American International Auto Show (naias.com) is a site dedicated to the annual auto show held at Detroit's Cobo Center in January.

ANNUAL REGIONAL EVENTS

America's Thanksgiving Parade (theparade.org/thanks.php).The event has been held since 1924 and is one of the oldest in the nation. The parade route is along Woodward Avenue, the city's main street, and runs from Mack Avenue into the downtown area. Thousands of spectators line the streets to watch the colorful floats and other parade attractions.

Cinco de Mayo Parade (insidesouthwest.com) in southwest Detroit attracts thousands of spectators to the largely Hispanic neighborhoods near Mexicantown (see chapter 3). Held the first weekend in May, the parade includes many vintage cars entered by car clubs, as well as food, dancing, and music.

Corktown St. Patrick's Day Parade (detroitstpatricksparade.com). Held in mid-March, the parade attracts thousands to its route along Michigan Avenue in Corktown (see chapter 3), an area of the city settled by the Irish. The route runs from Sixth to 14th Streets.

Detroit Boat Show (boatmichigan.org) is held in February at the Cobo Center in Detroit. Michigan has one of the largest numbers of boat owners in the nation, and the event attracts many exhibitors.

Detroit Free Press Marathon (freepmarathon.com) held in mid-October is one of the top such events in the state, and attracts thousands of runners to the city. A half marathon and 5K run/walk are also held on race day.

Detroit Jazz Festival (detroitjazzfest.com) is held in early September. Thousands attend the free event, which takes place at various venues in downtown Detroit and attracts many nationally touring acts. The first festival was held in 1980 in an attempt to bring people to the downtown area and the event has evolved over the years into a major cultural institution that has many corporate sponsors.

Detroit River Days (riverdays.com) The late-June festival includes a range of Riverfront activities and showcases the downtown RiverWalk.

Highland Games (highlandgames.com) This summertime festival celebrating Scottish heritage is hosted by the St. Andrew's Society of Detroit and is held at Greenmead Historical Park in suburban Livonia. It features traditional games and physical contests as well as entertainment, including a lot of bagpipers.

Motown Winter Blast (winterblast.com) This winter festival takes place in February in the downtown area's Campus Martius Park.

North American International Auto Show (naias.com) The premier event is held at Detroit's Cobo Center in January.

Plymouth Ice Festival (plymouthicefestival.org) This ice-sculpting event held in January attracts thousands of spectators.

Summerfest (summerfestwindsor.org) Held across the river in Windsor, Ontario, for three weeks from mid-June through July; includes a popular Riverfront fireworks display.

RECOMMENDED READING

Detroit authors are varied, ranging from top-flight mystery novelists like Elmore Leonard and Loren Estleman to journalists and historians.

Mysteries

Detroit's best-known author is Elmore "Dutch" Leonard Jr., who has been writing gritty crime stories, many set in Detroit, for several decades, and even in his 80s is still writing. He's been referred to as the Dickens of Detroit because of his portrayal of Motor City characters. He was born in New Orleans, but his father worked for General Motors and the family eventually settled in Detroit in the 1930s; he graduated from the University of Detroit Jesuit High School in 1943. Leonard served in the U.S. Navy during World War II, and later obtained a degree from the University of Detroit, and went to work as a copywriter with an advertising agency. His first short stories were westerns published in magazines during the 1950s and '60s. More than a dozen of his 48 novels have been turned into films.

Although lesser known than Leonard, Loren D. Estleman is a prolific Detroit-area mystery writer who also produces westerns. His most popular books are in the 20-book Amos Walker private eye series, which have been published for more than 30 years. Most of the action in the series takes place in the Detroit area. Apart from the Walker series, he has written seven other books that deal with Detroit and its history. *Whiskey River* is a favorite, focusing on the story of a down-at-the-heels newspaperman who solves the real-life murders of Purple Gang members during Prohibition. The other Detroit books are *Thunder City, Jitterbug, Stress, Edsel, King of the Corner,* and *Motown.*

History

Scott M. Burnstein takes a long look at organized crime in Detroit in his *Motor City Mafia: A Century of Organized Crime in Detroit*. *The Violent Years: Prohibition and the Detroit Mobs* and *The Purple Gang: Organized Crime in Detroit,* both by Paul R. Kavieff, take a look at the lucrative liquor trade and gang activities.

The Detroit Almanac, by *Detroit Free Press* journalists Peter Gavrilovich and Bill McGraw, comes up with just about any fact you want to know about the city.

The History of Detroit and Wayne County and Early Michigan, by Silas Farmer, can be dry reading at times, but it is a delightful look back at Detroit in the 19th century, before it became an auto manufacturing center. Published in the 1890, there are many woodcuts of old buildings that once graced the city's streets, and he paints a portrait of a small midwestern city that was even then becoming an industrial giant. The building of railroad cars was a large part of the city's economy. The book is available free online from Google Books.

Henry and Edsel: The Creation of the Ford Empire, by Richard Bak, takes a look at the start of the Ford Motor Co. Bak is also the author of *Detroit Across Three Centuries,* a history of the city.

Clara: Mrs. Henry Ford, by Ford R. Bryan, a cousin of Henry Ford, paints a delightful picture of Henry Ford's wife, a woman who was born on a farm near Detroit and ended up married to one of the most powerful industrialists of the time.

Brewed in Detroit: Breweries and Beers Since 1830, by Peter H. Blum, takes readers on a tour of all the breweries that have sold their products to thirsty Detroiters.

Detroit journalist Tim Kiska dishes up nostalgia in his *From Soupy to Nuts! A History of Detroit Television.*

LOCAL TERMS

Here are a few terms and expressions used by Detroiters that would be helpful on a trip to the Motor City.

Party store—In many areas of the country this means a store where you buy balloons and other party paraphernalia, but in Detroit it means a place that sells beer, wine and often liquor.

Coney Island—It's a hot dog served with chili sauce. It's also the generic term for any restaurant that serves them, and you'll find plenty of them scattered throughout southeastern Michigan. They're the region's version of a dinner.

The freeway—It's the most often heard term for the region's expressway system. Make sure to keep track of both the name of the freeway and its number. For example, most people call the John C. Lodge Freeway, simply "the Lodge," and probably don't know it's actually M 10. On the other hand, most people refer to the Edsel Ford Freeway as "94," and rarely use the name, "Ford." It's not logical, but that's what people do here.

Michigan left—It's making a left turn while driving, by making a right turn on a divided highway and the making a left through a lane through the median.

Pop—That's what people call soft drinks. You'll never hear the word *soda* from a native. If you really want to go native, try either Vernors, a local ginger ale that dates to the 1860s, or Faygo, a local soda pop made in Detroit.

UAW—United Auto Workers, a union that represents auto employees.

Index

A

D

E

G

H

N